The
PROSPECT
BEFORE US

"The time of destruction is ended...the era of reconstruction begins"

H. M. THE KING

Mr. Lecturer: "Maybe we'd better introduce ourselves."

The
PROSPECT
BEFORE US

BY JOHN DOS PASSOS

ILLUSTRATED BY MICKY STROBEL

1950

HOUGHTON MIFFLIN COMPANY · BOSTON

The Riverside Press Cambridge

BOOKS BY JOHN DOS PASSOS

ONE MAN'S INITIATION...THREE SOLDIERS...ROSINANTE TO
THE ROAD AGAIN...A PUSHCART AT THE CURB...STREETS OF NIGHT
MANHATTAN TRANSFER...ORIENT EXPRESS...THE 42ND PARALLEL
NINETEEN NINETEEN...THE BIG MONEY...IN ALL COUNTRIES
THREE PLAYS...U.S.A....JOURNEYS BETWEEN WARS
ADVENTURES OF A YOUNG MAN...THE GROUND WE STAND ON
NUMBER ONE...STATE OF THE NATION...TOUR OF DUTY
THE GRAND DESIGN...THE PROSPECT BEFORE US

Contents

The Preparation of a New Society

I

The Preparation

of a New Society

MAN'S INTELLIGENCE has always found it hard to keep up with the changes in the shape of society which his own efforts and conflicts bring about. Mental processes tend to lag behind events.

In more or less normal times when the institutions which mould men's lives change only gradually the traditional pattern of society forms an ethical cage that holds out a support for the weak and a firm frame of reference for the strong. Although the church-dominated New England town, for an example, trammelled in many ways the impatient spirit of adventure, it furnished a cosmogony which accounted acceptably for the alternations of happiness and misery, for the mischances of life and the quick swoop of death; and supplied its more restless and ambitious citizens with an ethical sliderule by which to sort out experience in the jumbled world outside.

In abnormal times like our own, when institutions are changing rapidly in several directions at once and the traditional framework of society has broken down, it becomes more and more difficult to measure any type of behavior against any other. New situations arise faster than the ethical norms, which the mental processes have to take for granted before they can function, can keep up with them. Reflexes become confused and people lose their power to choose between good and evil.

The old illustration of the man driving his dogteam northward all day over a drifting icefloe only to find himself further south that night than when he started out in the morning becomes apt in a dozen different senses. Men who have lost their conviction of what is good and what is bad find themselves without a sextant to check their position by. When they set out to explore the society they live in they are forced constantly to stop to try to discover whether the terrain from which they are making their observation really remains firm and stationary.

In a time of too rapid change everything has to be reinvented daily from its origins. We have at our disposal the storedup vocabulary of our civilization but our most acute observations are shortcircuited because we don't know our right hand from our left. We are in the position of a man with an elaborate camping kit who finds himself lost in the woods without his matches; to kindle a fire he has to resort to the stratagems of the caveman. We fall back through generations into the oldest terrors and confusions of the race. We are tormented by mirage and false appearances. The very words we have to use to describe what we see tantalizingly change their meanings. Slogans and phrases that only yesterday pointed steadily towards the lodestar of good today spin waveringly round the compass and tomorrow will have taken on meanings opposite from the meaning they started with. A moral judgment will turn inside out on you overnight.

Life has to go on nevertheless. The mind cannot support moral chaos for long. Men are under as strong a compulsion to invent an ethical setting for their behavior as spiders are to weave themselves webs. New cosmogonies are continually being rebuilt out of the ruins of past systems. Somehow, like the degenerate last Romans, who had forgotten the art of turning columns and had to use the débris of old temples to build Christian basilicas with, we have to improvise at least enough of an edifice out of the fallen dogmas of the past to furnish a platform from which to take an observation on the society we live in.

The creation of a world view is the work of a generation rather than of an individual, but we each of us, for better or for worse, add our brick to the edifice. A generation can't go much further than the average of the achievements of the men who comprise it, but every outstanding effort affects that average. Every one of us has to go as far forward as he can. Before a man can plot his course between the red buoys and the black he has to look around him and, having wiped all the deceiving ideologies off the slate, to try accurately to observe in what direction social currents are moving the society he lives in.

Start from your street or from the apartment house where you live; you'll notice that most of the men and women you know make their living by working in some capacity for corporate organizations. Whether the end of these concerns is to lend money or to sell bread or peanuts or to manufacture automobiles or to publish newspapers or to peddle humanitarian ideas their organization is remarkably similar. The corporation with its board of directors, its chain of command, its hierarchy of power is such a routine feature of our daily lives that it hardly ever occurs to us that its pattern has become only very recently the dominant social pattern of the life of a large part of the human race.

Wherever you find it the pattern is uniform. In the United States we call it Capitalism. If you go over to England you'll find people behaving in much the same way but calling it Socialism. In the Soviet Union and its satellite states you'll find a remarkably similar social structure going under the name of Dictatorship of the Proletariat, or by the oddest reversal of the meaning of terms, People's Democracy. Other factors account for the greater well-being that results from the pattern in some countries than in others. The same plant will yield differently in different soils. If an eighteenth century libertarian like Tom Paine were resurrected today he would find more similarities than differences in these industrial societies cloaked under their various ideological banners. People have been pointing out for years that the government of the Soviet Union, leaving aside the police power — the power to kill is of a very different order of magnitude from the power to fire — resembles more than anything else the government of a great American corporation. It makes you wonder whether the bogeyman we in America see in the menace of Socialism and that so many Europeans see in the menace of Capitalism doesn't lie somewhere in the structure of industrial society itself.

We have proof by experience that when you change from Capitalism to Socialism the hierarchies which administer industry or banks or railroads or chain laundries retain their basic structure. What happens is that under Socialism the men who reach places of power tend to do so through their political rather than their financial influence. Both systems offer to the critical student a web of bureaucratic intrigue and internal politics and an occasional example of a man finding himself in a job through plain ability. The fascinating thing to a dispassionate observer about the structure of life in the Soviet Union is that in their efforts to produce an unknown that we may let its ideologists call Socialism the Communist dictators have produced a brutal approximation of monopoly Capitalism, a system that has all the disadvantages of our own, with none of the palliatives which come to us from surviving competition and from the essential division between economic and political power which has so far made it possible for the humane traditions of the Western world to continue.

It seems obvious that if you want to find out what is happening to a society the thing to study is the behavior of the people in it and not what they say about their behavior, but most of the writing and arguing about social systems is about ideologies and not about behavior. The processes of thought are constantly being confused by a basic lag in the recognition of events. Groups of words that were once fairly descriptive of a given situation will survive for generations becoming more and more charged with righteous emotion as they become less and less descriptive of the situation involved. If, having tried to forget political slogans and ideological camouflage, you spend an afternoon talking with the men who work in one of the great stratified industrial enterprises either in this country or in England you'll notice two things. First you'll discover that the antithesis between Capitalism and Socialism is beside the point, that it doesn't affect the way in which the people who work the machines and sit at the directors' tables and run the teletypes and sweep out the offices actually behave. Second, you will be struck in either case, by the centralization of power and the isolation of the individual in his routine at an office desk, or in his job on the assembly line, or even at the more varied work of turret or lathe.

We mustn't forget that changing the name of our industrial system doesn't change the fact that the kind of man who has only learned to drive a tractor will go on driving a tractor and the kind of man who has only learned to sit at a desk and organize other men's work will go on doing it and the man who gets his pleasure from power to boss his fellow man will continue to find a way to boss his fellow man.

The knot which our society must untie, or at least partly untie, if it is not to sink into the stagnation of slavery, is the problem of controlling the power over men's lives of these stratified corporations, which, whether their top management calls itself Capitalist or Socialist, are so admirably adapted by the pull of centralization to the uses of despotism. Some way must be found in the United States to break the deadlock between the rival corporate systems of business and labor. Systems of dictatorship come into being in response to the need to administer societies which have become stalemated. If we are to have the kind of civilization our traditional aspirations aim at, machinery must be invented to control the power of the administrators not only in the public interest but in the interest of each private individual man. To survive, that machinery must be effective and efficient.

An inseparable part of this problem is the problem of communication between the isolated units which are the cogs in our society. An isolated man is an ignorant man. He has no frame of reference by which to test the selfserving propaganda (Advertising we call it in America or Public Relations or lately, God help us, Public Service) which is daily pumped in his ears by the political climbers who use corporations, labor unions, stratified organizations of any kind, as ladders to positions from which they may ride to glory on the backs of their fellows.

Even a hundred years ago in this country most of the operations of agriculture and industry were within the reach of the average man's radius of information. A Connecticut farmer living outside of Stamford, say, knew the operations of plowing and harvesting through the observation of his own nervous system. He knew how you kept store. He understood the business of buying and selling from personal experience on the marketplace. He knew how a bank worked: the banker kept a stack of goldpieces in a safe and lent them out to you at interest under proper security. A clipper ship was a complicated machine but he'd sailed a small sloop enough as a boy to understand what made it go through the water. Commerce was a matter of ships and buying and selling. The world outside was not too different from its microcosm in the farming community where he lived. Most of the events which occurred in it were comprehensible to a man of average intelligence. When the farmer went to town to listen to a politician tell him how to vote he could test the reliability of the orator's words against his own experience of practical life, against his fairly wide acquaintanceship with various types of men, farmers, mechanics, millers, merchants, the local judge and the doctor and the lawyer. For final arbiter he had his Bible, and the inner small still voice of traditional ethics.

Look at this man's grandson living in the same house. Like as not he works in an office and commutes into New York. He knows his family and his wife's family and a few neighbors and the men in the office who hold approximately similar rank in the hierarchy of the concern. When he was in school he used to know something about sports but now he follows them through the newspapers. He understands his car and his lawnmower but he can't mend the washing machine when it gets out of order. Ask him what the place of money is in our economy or how powerful the executive is in our government. He can't tell you and you can't tell him. All you can do is treat each other to the views of some favorite columnist.

His friends are in the same boat. He hobnobs with a few other men of similar experience and outlook in some club or lodge, and apart from that all he knows about the world is what he reads in the papers, hears over the radio or sees in the movies.

These agencies of selfserving propaganda from one group or another tease and inflame his mind with a succession of unrelated stimuli. These stimuli are rarely sustained enough to evoke the response of careful study and understanding and the resulting satisfaction which is implicit in the word understanding, so in the end they leave him frustrated. The mind of a frustrated man becomes a sink of fear, ignorance and hatred; his main response to the problems of community and national life, which demand cogitation and decision, is a stubborn apathy.

Apathy is one of the characteristic responses of any living organism when it is subjected to stimuli too intense or too complicated to cope with. The cure for apathy is comprehension. What happens when a problem has been made comprehensible is that it has been reduced to understandable component parts so that unfamiliar elements can be measured off by analogy against familiar elements which have already become usable terms in a man's own experience. The same man who stubbornly refuses to think out the problems of a presidential election will use his brains lucidly at a meeting of a union local or a parent-teacher association. The continuance of selfgoverning institutions now in such desperate decay will depend upon the invention of methods of communication by which the operations of the great macrocosms that rule our lives can be reduced to terms which each averagely intelligent man can understand — truly understand the way a good mechanic understands the working of an internal combustion engine — with the mental tools he is furnished by his own experience.

Selfgovernment demands real and not parroted information. If we are to govern ourselves we have to know how the machinery of our society works. We have to learn to measure the drift of change. As a society changes the men change who are its component parts. There has been too little exploration of industrial society in the terms of human behavior. One reason is that adherence to the Socialism-Capitalism antithesis (with Socialism equals good, Capitalism equals bad or vice versa) has kept investigators from seeing clearly the prospects that were opening out under their noses.

A sectarian approach to a study of society means a search for a bogey man. You don't need to understand why people behave as they do if you've already made up your mind who is to blame. If you are going to study an ant's nest you have to start out with a mind blank of preconceptions and prejudices about the behavior of social insects. Difficult as it is to be unprejudiced about ants it's a whole lot more difficult to be unprejudiced about people. The fact that it is difficult doesn't mean it is not possible. It has been done and can be done again. The intellectual tools with which to examine societies in the spirit of the search for knowledge rather than for party purposes are already in the language. In the parts of the world where free inquiry is still allowed by the police the investigation of society is easier to undertake than it was twenty-five years ago. In America at least the study of behavior, in the good old empirical tradition, has not run its course nor reached its highest fruition. We've just begun to take up the problem. An entire science lies ahead. In that science we may find the tools with which to build out of our runaway institutions a society which will be tolerably stable because it will offer participation to each individual man.

The people of the United States have been fortunate in many things. One of the things in which we have been most fortunate has been that so far, due perhaps to certain basic virtues in our traditional ways of doing things, we have managed to keep the crisis in western civilization, which has devastated the rest of the world and in which we are as much involved as anybody, more or less at arm's length. It is not entirely due to the benign insulation of two great oceans that we are still able to ponder trends and to make choices, and that the political and economic structure of our society has managed to keep on changing and evolving free from the heavy pressure of catastrophe which has been the rule in the rest of the world.

Our society is still fluid. The last word is still a long way from being said. We have cried calamity more than most but if you take a casual glance at the sufferings of the populations of this planet in this century of human misery, you will find that the Great Depression we made so much fuss about was by comparison a very mild malady indeed. We carried on so about it largely because the signal success of our institutions in furnishing a pretty decent life for the average and even for the less than average man had given him an exalted notion of his deserts. The United States, as it has been often said, has been a goose that laid golden eggs: it was not unnatural that the minute the golden eggs got a little scarce we should rush out to try to kill the goose.

In all the resultant lamentation there was far too little examination of how our people stood, not only in physical wellbeing but in moral wellbeing, in relation to the rest of the tribes of men. Capitalism is the cause of depressions, the idealistic college professors told their bright students in the Thirties; Capitalism must go said the bright young men and buttoned up their minds so tight that many of them have never taken another straight and independent look at our developing industrial society from that day to this.

There still is time to take a look. We have in the world many going concerns which are examples of completely and partially socialized economies to form a basis of comparison. It is devoutly to be hoped that the sharp young men of the present generation are nosing around the world and seeing for themselves how they work.

There is time, but not very much time. Like the British during the last war, we in the United States are already living on an island under siege. Happily it is a large island. The Communist dictatorship centered in the Kremlin is rapidly harnessing forces in the world which can completely destroy the very postulates upon which the sort of enquiry I am suggesting must be based. Our survival individually as men and women and collectively as a nation with hopes and purposes essential to all mankind depends — it cannot be said loud enough or often enough — upon our solving a few of the social and political problems of a corporate industrial society. To do that we've got to get it into our heads that these problems exist, that they are problems that will have to be solved by reason instead of by appeals to fear, envy and hatred (the Communist enemy can use that whole bag of tricks much better than we can) and that they have to be solved fast. Particularly we must get out of our heads the paralyzing Marxist doctrine of historical predestination that teaches that these problems will solve themselves if we wait long enough. If they are solved at all they will be solved by the patient daily efforts of people like the reader of these lines, the printer who sets them up, the bookseller who sells the books; everyone must participate in the building of our new society if it is to be strong enough to withstand the attacks of the lords of misrule.

About all a moderately observant man of letters with a certain amount of experience in a somewhat special sort of journalism can do to add his nickel's worth to these solutions is to set forth what he has seen and what in his opinion it means. He is hampered by his lack of rigorous training in the still rudimentary sciences of sociology and anthropology and perhaps too by a certain novelist's bent that sends him chasing off after traits of character and landscape, like a badly trained birddog who'll point at a chickadee as soon as a quail, when he ought to be keeping his nose to the trail of the argument. Well for what it's worth here goes . . .

(MR. LECTURER *appears on the platform carrying a long pointer. As the lights in the hall go dim the boy at the portable projector has shot a picture of the Tower of London upside down onto the screen. Highschool kids in the gallery of the hall titter and whistle. The lecturer looks about him apprehensively, then fixes his desperate gaze on the typewritten sheets of his prepared address. Looking down with nearsighted attention through steamy glasses, he starts hurriedly to read trying to drown out the epidemic of coughing that is sweeping the hall.)*

MR. LECTURER: Ladies and gentlemen, most Americans will, I think, agree that for us the most important of the socialist experiments . . .

A STOUT MAN IN A DRESS SUIT (*rushes out from the other side of the stage*): Excuse me, but I'm supposed to introduce you.

MR. LECTURER: Er . . . the audience seemed rather restless so . . . er . . . (*He takes off his glasses to wipe them.*)

STOUT MAN (*puffing*): Ladies and gentlemen, I humbly beg your comprehending indulgence . . . This is the sort of thing that never happens to the exclusive presentations of the Mesmer Agency and least of all at meetings of our unique Transcontinental Forum. Lights, please, lights . . . I thank you. Mr. Lecturer, you will I hope accept my profoundest apologies and the apologies of Mr. Mesmer himself . . . Circumstances entirely beyond my control . . . Well folks, I see there's no need for an introduction now, is there? Here we are all one big family . . . The man who . . . the gentleman you see before you, Mr. Lecturer, his friends like to call him — Mr. Lecturer is about to embark on a series of intimate chats highlighting his experiences with the great and near great in foreign lands . . . He has a fund of racy anecdotes. He will discuss trends. He will make predictions . . . He will answer questions from the audience and will lead an informal discussion in the cordial and tolerant spirit of the meeting of minds which has made our Transcontinental Forum one of the . . . (*As he turns from side to side to beam his broadjowled smile into every corner of the hall he catches sight of the picture dimly seen on the screen.*) Ah, what an entertaining novelty. An oldfashioned magic lantern slide . . . Ha ha ha. The young gentleman in the projection booth will please . . . (*The Tower of London vanishes.*) Thank you, son. But let me assure you that the pictures on the screen which will accompany Mr. Lecturer's discussion are of quite a different order. They are incomparable documentaries. They have never been shown before, at least never out of the firstrun houses; several reels have been flown in by air to furnish the latest piquant last minute unrehearsed realities of the fashionable whirl and the sordid slumlife of some of the world's great capitals . . . I thank you. (THE STOUT MAN IN THE DRESS SUIT *beams a last smile round the hall and backs off into the wings.*)

MR. LECTURER (*stuttering*): I'm afraid there's some misunderstanding . . . I have absolutely nothing to say about café society . . . Well I'd better begin all over again . . .

Ladies and gentlemen, most Americans will I think agree that for us the most important of the socialist experiments available for study at the present time is the British because our tradition of freedom under the law is a continuation of the great British tradition and because we are linked by so many ties to the people of those green islands.

The present situation in Great Britain, we must not forget, was not entirely the invention of the Labor Government. It came into being by a sort of morganatic marriage between the practices of the Tory régime of highly developed monopoly Capitalism and the doctrinaire social planning of the Labor Party. Many of its best features, such as the long overdue care for the children and for the neglected and underfed lowest third of the population, and some of its worst, came into being under the National Coalition Government of wartime.

VOICE FROM THE AUDIENCE: Do you mean to tell me that Socialism is just a continuation of Capitalism?

MR. LECTURER: That's just about what I'm trying to say.

VOICE FROM THE AUDIENCE: I thought it was the opposite of Capitalism.

ANOTHER VOICE: Socialism is Capitalism minus individual liberty.

MR. LECTURER (*firmly*): If you will please follow me we shall revisit Great Britain during the recent war, when the presentday socialist order was developing. (*The lights dim. The projector whirls.*)

FIRST LECTURE

Great Britain: Ordeal by Fire

CAPTION: *Beleaguered Island*

MR. LECTURER (*clears his throat and begins*):In Britain Nineteen Forty One had the most beautiful autumn weather of the war. Day after day the sky over London was clear and sunny. Nights of sharp cool moonlight brought no bombings. Late afternoons the streets had a holiday air under the silver barrage balloons that floated benignly overhead; when you saw them end on against bright patches of sky and cloud they had funny faces as if a child had tried to draw a cow or a moose. The Londoners were feeling themselves all over the way people do who have just crawled out unhurt from under a wrecked car, discovering with some surprise that they were alive. Walking around London was like reading the Hebrew prophets. Never before had I understood the significance of Jeremiah's curse, "And Babylon shall become heaps."

In the West End, as you see, the damage is scattered; you tell yourself that the accidents of war don't stack up to much more than the ordinary accidents of peace, but as you walk east down the Strand and past those two gutted churches still elegant in their ruin into Fleet Street you see ahead of you this view of St. Paul's standing up oddly alone on top of its hill, framed between scorched stone façades that have no buildings behind them.

The trip up Ludgate Hill is like visiting one of the ruined cities of antiquity. This is the region of what people are beginning to call the second fire of London. A whole tangled quarter of overbuilt lanes of the old city has already been obliterated. In places, as you see, you can't even find where the streets went. Stumbling over heaps, looking up at that grate high in a wall, or at a tangled liana of twisted steel machinery still dangling from some attic clothing shop that's lost its floor or at the white bowl of a piece of plumbing hanging from a ledge, you begin to feel a sort of remote archaeological interest. What kind of people were to have worn the burnt shoes piled in that pit? Why should this brick pile be littered with small tin trays? The visitor from another age begins to resent those husky young fellows with pickaxes and crowbars who are risking their necks to bring these remnants of a strange past crashing in dust to the ground. It is surprising how many trees there are and how green and leafy they grow. Nobody ever knew there were so many trees in the City.

Walking further east you come out quite suddenly on this long low building — the Bank of England — standing up firm and solid and complacent, and beyond it the group of the central offices of other great banks still sleek with marble facings and scrubbed steps that cluster round the Mansion House. There's a jerrybuilt improvised look about the new tube station in the triangle between. Even now people can't quite keep their voices steady when they name that station. That's the station where so many people were killed when a bomb broke through into the crowded subway.

Beyond the City the East End begins. The first thing I noticed there was that people looked better than the last

time I had been in London. I had never remembered seeing
people in the East End with color in their cheeks before.
The sidewalks were no longer crowded. Most of the stale
little shops were closed. There was neither smoke overhead
nor mud underfoot. Walking through the empty streets of
ruined slums here and there in a block of fallen houses a
vista would open up through an avenue of wreckage clear to
the dovegray Thames.

The lady from the Ministry who drove me down to visit
one of the oldest of the eastern boroughs was an anthro-
pologist from Cambridge. We kept getting on the subject of
the witchcult in the Middle Ages; whether there really were
witches or not kept getting mixed up with my dutiful questions about how the borough carried on its end of airraid
protection. We started in the town clerk's office. He was a
slowspoken quiet sandy man, a desk man all his life you
could see. Witches were nothing after what he'd been
through during the last year. He was all ready to go back to
sleeping in his office if the blitzes should start up again. Last
winter there had been months when he'd never got home.
He showed us his bed behind a screen and the alcohol stove
and kettle he used to make tea with. His pleasant yellow-
haired wife offered to have coffee for us when we should
come back from our tour. She didn't seem to feel that this
witch talk was quite proper. There was a cheerful domestic
bustle about the town hall, I am sure very different from the
air of dusty bureaucracy it must have had in the old days.
Although the only protection against bombs was a few sandbags in the windows you could feel that the town hall had
become in the minds of the citizens an acropolis for the
borough.

The basement had been fixed up for the central post of the
airraid protection service. There were clear largescale maps
on the walls on which the position of bombs, fires, squads
in action or equipment could be marked with pushpins at

any given moment. In the center of the long room were rows of telephones at rough board desks that were a direct link with the outposts and the fire brigades and the first aid and ambulance services. The town clerk explained the system with the confidence of a man who had helped build it up under fire. Every detail for him was full of unspoken terrors and satisfactions. Things had happened last winter to build up his selfconfidence; he felt now he was a man instead of a bureaucrat. Now they were all tidied up after a quiet summer, he kept explaining. "When the Jerries start up the blitz again we'll be ready," he said, rubbing his hands.

After a little more witch talk over a cup of coffee in the town clerk's office we went out into the chilly autumn sunlight and walked through gutted streets of what had been a region of small furniture factories and cabinetmakers' shops to a new building on a corner where was the office that rehoused people bombed out of their homes. There a volunteer socialworker sort of girl explained to us how the system worked and I found myself wandering with her through a warehouse where salvaged housefurnishings were huddled in forlorn groups. All the dilapidated relics of the poorer segment of Victorian society were there; brass beds, yellow oak bureaus, ornately carved walnut washstands. "You see," the girl said, "lots of people have no way of carting off their things so they just leave them behind. We clean them up to furnish new flats with . . . We even give them a few ornaments." She led me into a corner where I found myself walking in a sort of trance, stepping carefully through groups of painted glass oil lamps, pitcher and basin sets fancied up with Dutch girls and windmills in blue, plaster red men, framed tapestries of moonlight on the Grand Canal, plaster book ends with busts of Shakespeare, gilt and silver vases of that thin ectoplasmic glass which Christmas tree ornaments are made from. "Gruesome, aren't they?" said the girl. "But they mean so much, particularly to the old people."

Because the people don't like to move out of the districts they consider home, she explained that every effort was made to find places for bombed out families inside the same borough. One of the great surprises of the blitz period to the people of the West End was the discovery that the people of the East End liked it there and that it annoyed them to have those grim rows of hovels called slums. They were Englishmen. These were their homes. They were not at all interested in grandiose plans for building a garden city. When the shabby houses clattered down about their ears they could imagine nothing better to hope for than to get into other lodgings as much like the old ones as possible.

One of the most difficult things, explained the social-worker girl, about last winter's concentrated bombings was that so many families had no sooner been settled in new quarters than they were bombed out again. And again. I told her about a man I had met the evening before who had been bombed out of three flats in as many weeks. He worked at the British Museum and used to flatter himself in the old days that he had quite a taste for antiques. When his Chippendale went, he decided all he cared for was his piano. Whatever happened he'd keep his music up. So he took considerable pains to have it carted into his new lodging. The next time, the staircase of his house was blown away. but the piano wasn't even scratched. From the street when the dust cleared next morning he could see it still standing there in the isolated second story. It took him some time to collect a truck and some men with planks and ropes and pulleys who were to help him get the piano out through the front window. By the time he got to the house the piano was gone. Somebody had been there ahead of him. The guards hadn't seen a thing. He roared with unforced laughter when he told about it.

In spite of all you could do, she said shaking her head, people get accustomed to living in a suitcase, to sleeping in shelters where there was the cosy huddle of a crowd and no fresh air at all, and stopped worrying about their furniture, or their friends or anything but their own unwashed skins. All that summer in spite of the lull in the airraids the wire tiers of bunks in the tube stations were full of men, women and children who made a regular practice of sleeping there. As the bombings went on more and more abandoned furnishings piled up in the storage lofts of the rehousing offices. "Until we really don't know what to do with them," she wailed.

The next thing to see is the fire department. The big red engines and the brawny fellows shining the brass look much like a fire department at home, except that you find every chink of space in the enginehouse packed with these new small gray pumps. It is surprising to walk through the chief's office in back and to find it opens into a roomful of girls in becoming dark blue uniforms. These are the girls who work the emergency switchboards. They are remarkably good-looking, with that quiet energetic air you find yourself beginning to associate with people who do useful work during the blitzes. They are something new in our world's experience, these ordinary young women who have been in visible danger of death for days and weeks and months, and who have lived to see all the secure superstructure of their lives knocked to pieces before their eyes. It's hard to explain just why, except that they have that air of health about them, but you can't help feeling that all the civilians who lived through the bombing and burning last winter came out of it twice the people they were before. It is one of these pretty young girls in dark blue slacks (she was a hairdresser in the old days) who drives the fire chief's staffcar. Nobody has to be told that during an airraid the fire chief's car has to be driven into some pretty noisy spots.

The next thing on the program was the A.R.P. squad. They were drawn up with their truck on the brand new parking lot which the Jerries donated to the Town Hall by blasting away a block of adjoining houses. The Town Clerk said the borough had been trying to buy that block for years to clear for a public square and now he didn't imagine he'd have much more trouble with the owners.

These squads go to work the minute bombing starts in their area. They smother incendiaries with sandbags or try to scoop them up with a longhandled shovel into a bucket of water. There's usually a lot of tricky scampering about on roofs before they can get at them. If they can be reached in time they're not much trouble. They tell me of seeing a boy scout put an incendiary bomb out with a bag of Brussels sprouts. When a high explosive bomb explodes the old brick and rubble buildings are reduced instantly to heaps like the rubbish on the sites of cities ruined a thousand years ago. The mess is shot through with wooden splinters and strange amalgams of cloth and plaster so dense that, so the A.R.P. men says, the only way it can be moved is with the hands. Hundreds of people have been dug out of the ruins of their houses, and their lives saved, by men digging with just their hands. Of course whenever possible picks, crowbars and shovels are used.

They showed me with pride the great fifteen ton jack they carried in their truck. There was nothing like it they said for lifting fallen floors or beams. If any people were left alive in a ruined house it was usually because they were protected by a fallen floor that had to be lifted inch by inch to get them out.

These are the tools they use to hold off the attack of Hitler's most carefully perfected apparatus for destruction. Outside of their hands, the most important is the stirrup pump to wet down the blaze around the fresh incendiary, then there is the bucket to be passed from man to man; then the longhandled shovel, the sandbag, and the heavy jack. That is all. When I ask about shelters, everybody changes the subject.

In Stepney, further east along the waterfront, sitting another fine afternoon in the garden of a halfruined rectory beside the beautiful white marble skeleton of one of Queen Anne's parish churches, I was finally told the story of last winter's shelters. This Church of England priest had lived twenty years in the East End and never had a garden before. Proudly he showed me his cabbages and lettuce and string beans and a few puny onions. Before the blitz nobody would have imagined growing anything in the midst of this desert of masonry packed to the suffocation point with population. Now the padre's household had quite a rustic look. They had lived off this little patch of ground all summer. So many people had moved away. Since the blitz this part of the city had been quiet and fresh as a country village.

The problem of shelters, the padre is saying, was peculiarly difficult because the local administration to start with was in the hands of a crooked political machine based on floating groups of Irish Catholic longshoremen and sweated Jewish clothing workers and furniture workers from Eastern Europe. It was a population that lacked any sense of social responsibility. That was the first hurdle, the sort of situation that is common in the U.S. but rare in England. The second hurdle was the obtuse addiction to routine of the government at Whitehall. When the bombings began the efforts of authority to keep its end up in the old ways amounted to worse than nothing. Only one thing had been prepared: coffins. Everywhere there were plenty of coffins. The old Savoy Theatre on the Strand was stacked to the ceiling with papier-mâché coffins. The trouble was that not very many people were killed but that thousands were made homeless every night. People were terrified, hungry; they had no safe place to take their old people and their children. The result was that they crowded into a huge railroad warehouse building. Its cellars had been used as shelters during the tiny raids in World War I. This time thousands more were crowded in than the cellars could hold. They overflowed up into the upper floors

where foodstuffs were stored. Latrines were improvised behind cartons of margarine. People laid out their blankets on
the floor between streams of urine and filth. It had to be
smelt, says the padre, to be believed.

At least that place wasn't hit. For evacuation to the country the government ordered women and children and old
people to collect in a public school building. Somebody
blundered. The buses supposed to carry them out of town
to safety went to the wrong place. That night the inevitable
bomb tore them to pieces.

Meanwhile, as at Dunkirk, when the authorities failed,
individuals started taking things into their own hands. A
couple of newspaper men and a motion picture director
brought an old trailer down to be rigged up as a canteen.
They couldn't get hold of a car so they pushed it by hand.
Proudly they showed me its battered shell still standing outside the roofless church. "We can use it again, if we have
to," they said.

The padre, bombed out of one rectory after another,
usually managed to keep a kettle of soup on the fire for the
destitute. Latrines were dug, floorings rigged up in the
flooded cellars that had to be used as shelters. When he
wasn't working in the shelters he was in Whitehall, cajoling
and threatening the officials of the government. The West
End had its own problems; it kept forgetting that the East
End existed. At length it was the padre's threat to lead a
delegation of five hundred women to Whitehall (he'd done
it before during the rent strike) that really got action.

"When they come back," he says, getting to his feet and
swinging his long rustycolored cassock as he looks up into the
immense lavender sky of late afternoon, "we'll be ready for
them."

"I suppose your population is more scattered now."

"It's less by several hundreds of thousands. We'd better
walk you around."

Out of the little court with its single green tree in front
of the burned out church, we turn toward the river, walking
fast through the gathering dusk along empty cobblestone
streets where every window is shattered, every shop boarded
up, where shutters hang off their hinges and sprung doors
gape into the street. Occasionally from a corner saloon comes
a breath of beer and the grumble of a few sparse voices.
Sometimes the rotten masonry has cracked clear across the
face of a wall or a scab of rubble has dropped off showing
the crazy flooring of a room or a crumpled iron bedstead.
There is none of the careful work of cleaning up that had
been done in the West End. Heaps of broken glass and
splintered wood and plastery rubbish overflow the gutters.
Here and there a house has been knocked clean out of a row
like a tooth bashed out in a brawl.

We come out of the deep blue twilight of the street onto
a still canal with an iron bridge across it, and onto a row of
modern apartment houses with long balconies that have an
air of freshness and organized life about them. Some units
have been wiped away, but the remaining buildings look firm
and strong. Lights are beginning to come on behind oiled
paper windows.

Beyond is the warehouse section: "Here they really did a
job." As far as you can see down the river every dock
building and warehouse has been hit. These warehouses were
of a very different type of construction from the workers'
hovels. All the pride and power of empire went into the
great brick walls strengthened with blind arches of stone,
the buttressed elevators, the huge blank gable ends. In almost
every case they stood up against the high explosives. Only
the roofs gave way and the floors, where so much rich merchandise from all the corners of the world through so many
fat years of good business had been stored, caved and
burned.

"You ought to have seen the rats come out of them," says

the padre. "Nobody could have imagined there were so many rats on earth. You could see them scampering along the roads."

We are walking down a long straight street just back of the waterfront. Nothing moves through the dusk, not even a rat.

After a while we come to a little old house without a scratch; tucked in on the waterfront between great scorched shells of wharf buildings. It is a pub. My friends say it was a famous hangout for slummers in the old days. This was where the Westenders came down to look with prurient eyes on the rancid abundant life of the slums.

A roundfaced, roundarmed barmaid stands behind the bar. A cat sleeps curled in front of a small iron stove. Four very towheaded young men off a coastwise boat (they might be Norwegians) are drinking their bitter in silence round a table. We take ours out on the balcony that overhangs the bright leaden river, brighter in this evening light than the fast darkening sky. The tide is running in, swirling in great circular ripples. A gray camouflaged freighter is tied up at the dock opposite. A patrol boat noses downstream. Nothing else moves except the smudging smoke from the chimneys of a power plant.

Somebody points out that this stillness doesn't mean so much as it seems to mean; ships never stay tied up at a wharf longer than the time actually needed to unload . . . But the silence throbs in our ears. Even the gulls have moved away.

As we walk back towards the rectory, through streets dark blue and silent, with crumbled cornices like canyons in a desert, we come upon a big moving van unloading men, women, children, bundles, tables, chairs and beds onto the pavement in front of a windowless house. "Hop pickers," says the padre, "they've been doing it for generations in September. Every year they go back to the same farm in Kent when the hops are ripe. It's their annual outing . . . It

Egge, Klaus, 1906-
  [Concerto, piano & string orchestra, no. 2,
op. 21] Phonotape.
  Concerto no. 2 for piano and strings; sym-
phonic variations and fugue on a Norwegian folk
tune, op. 21. Fantasia i Halling [for] piano,
op. 12a. Norwegian Office of Cultural Relations
[and] Society of Norwegian Composers 63189-194.
Taped by David Hall, Rogers & Hammerstein Library
& Museum of the Performing Arts, New York.
    track 2:2, 3.
  Robert Riefling, piano; Strings of the
                    (Continued on next card)

saved a lot of lives last autumn — so many families were away in the hopfields. But can we get them to stay away once the customary season is over? Not a bit of it. Back they come, blitz or no blitz . . . real Londoners."

From the cushioned Rolls Royce on one of the Ministry of Information conducted tours I'd seen the hop pickers a few days before along the Channel coast doing their cooking in the evening in big pots over open fires outside of rows of windowless shacks that would hardly be considered fit for Mexicans in California — women with many layers of bright petticoats, sunburned children running and screaming, knottyfaced elderly men with soiled white handkerchiefs tied round their necks smoking their pipes in the doorways, all with that air of unexpressed satisfaction that belongs to people who are performing a timehonored rite. I'd been struck with something incredibly stolid about them, as they moved around with ungainly gestures through the bright tinted evening air, which the hops roasting in the conical brick oasts that rose among the trees filled with drifts of bitter sweetness.

There's an extraordinary power of resistance in that stolid addiction to routine, the resistance of tough seasoned oak. I felt it particularly when the M.O.I. guide took us to call on the mayor of Dover.

It is a beautiful pale blue morning. The harbor in its ring of stone quays, overlooked by motionless silent cranes, is a chalky emerald color. A northeast wind, that chilly fair-weather wind off the European coast, ruffles across it streaks of darker catspaws that break in little splashing scalloped waves on the shingle of the beach, where, in a gap in the web of barbed wire, some soldiers, very pink and white, are bathing. From the distance comes the sputter of a motor torpedo boat zigzagging nervously outside the breakwater. The only other sound is the complaint of the gulls overhead.

An incredibly peaceful day, but the fact that we know we are within range of the German guns on the French coast makes it hard not to talk in whispers.

We'd been walking around looking at the very slight damage shellfire had done among the handsome old eighteenth century seaside boardinghouses, built in a crescent to emphasize the crescent of the beach, when the subject of landmines came up.

"We 'ad a landmine 'ere. A proper one. They come down very gently on a parachute you know. It took the gas works. It was our worst blitz," said the local guide in a flat South of England voice.

We asked to see the damage. Viewing the damage was supposed to be the purpose of the tour to inflame us foreigners further if possible, against the infamous Squarehead. The Irish Senator, the Chilean journalist and I followed him away from the beach out on the main street and up a hill on the outskirts of the town. Several blocks round the gas works had been cleared off clean. He showed us how the top had blown off the gas tank like a lid without injuring the girderwork of the sides. Two rows of dwellings had gone down like card houses. By some freak the corner pub had been left standing, a gaunt yellow brick box with boarded up windows.

The Irish Senator clears his throat, and says that though he isn't a drinking man himself, all these ruins make his throat dry. The rest of us visiting firemen pipe up that indeed we need our bitter. "That'll be a good way of interviewing the mayor," says our guide. Then he tells us how, after the landmine, the original owner of the pub, a bit shaken up, it seemed, was in a hurry to leave town. Rather than let the place close, the mayor of Dover, out of cussedness or a shrewd eye for profit, bought it in his daughter's name, and finding himself with some spare time, as the town was in a military area, and many of his constituents had been forced to move inland, took to drawing the beer for his customers himself.

We talk to him, a large beefyfaced sandyhaired man in his sixties, as he stands in his white apron behind the bar. He and the Chilean hit it off at once on the subject of earthquakes in Valparaiso. He knows many towns in North and South America where he worked as foreman on construction projects for a British engineering firm. He helped build the Holland Tunnel in New York. He is proud of that. He came home to retire in the sleepy little seacoast town he'd been brought up in, and woke up one morning to find himself mayor of a section of the frontline trenches in World War II. "We feel remarkably safe here," he keeps insisting. "We 'ave magnificent shelters, those old passages in the chalk . . . it's 'ard for me to tell people to go away. Where'll I be safer than 'ere, they ask. We've even 'ad to open up a school . . . they will bring the kiddies back. Now in London they've 'ad it bad."

Of course this sort of thing can be carried pretty far. One Sunday evening in an Oxford college I found myself drinking port with the Fellows. We had marched in from the creamcolored panelled diningroom, where we had eaten under the level eye of solemn oilpainted dons out of the past, into a sittingroom. There we took our places on chairs grimly ranked in front of the fire according to the hierarchy of the place. After the wine and biscuits had been handed around by the youngest Fellow, the aged whitehaired Master started a monologue, which from the attitude of the others, I suspected had perhaps been heard not infrequently before, on the subject of bird life in the Channel Islands. The only interruption was an antiphonal digression on the decline of fox hunting and the evil ways of Scotch farmers, who would shoot foxes. During the whole time not a man said a word to indicate that he was aware that some strange Teutonic birds were nesting in the Channel Islands at that moment.

What can you do with people like that? No wonder Hitler chews the edges of his rugs when he thinks of them.

Before these weeks spent in England during the sunny autumnal idyll of the lull in the siege, I had never known that the moral formation of topdog and underdog Englishman was so similar. It's the sort of thing a foreigner can discover only at a time like this, when the structure of society has been laid open by events like a tenement when one wall has been peeled off by a bomb.

Undoubtedly this stolid refusal to be scared or hurried was the quality in Churchill, that erratic and brilliant topdog-by-definition, that appealed so immensely to the officeworkers and factoryworkers and farmworkers of England. The question in a visitor's mind was, of course, whether there was enough brains and stamina left among the other toffs to hold the fort until the under-English had time to learn the governmental knack. Nobody but Churchill seemed to embody the rocky base of English patriotism, this fellow feeling as islanders under siege which the toffs and underdogs shared. It was because they had this common denominator, because they could count, in all classes at a pinch, on a necessary minimum of national solidarity, that the British were still able to walk their shattered streets as free men and to eat three meals a day and to sip a glass of bitter in the ritual quiet of their pubs, and to entertain hopes for a better social order in the future. It is not only the Channel that saved England from the fate of France.

It has often been pointed out that the British like the Romans are essentially a ritualistic people. For the first time in my life I felt that this ritual had its uses, when I stood under the scaffolding in a lobby of the patchedup Parliament building, which for all the picturesque work of the German bombers, still looks to an American like an overgrown Canadian railroad station, and saw the Mace and the Speaker go by. The doffed hats, the silence, the awesome wigs, the set faces, the knee breeches and the antiquarian language . . . of course they were a bar to progress, but it had never occurred to me before that they were also a bar to retrogression. What was it but ritual that made Byzantium hold out so for many centuries against the hordes and the falsehoods of Islam?

A pretty good day in the Commons. Sitting there alone with one other lanky sprawling American in the visitor's gallery gives you a feeling of interloping in another age, like the Yankee in King Arthur's court. Questioners are heckling a certain Captain Margesson, then Secretary of State for War; his attitude and general manner are those of a doorman at an expensive hotel. Nobody unauthorized, you feel at once, is going to be let through into the parlors of high army policy. Other less impressive ministers follow him onto the carpet, and then the debate on the Buchmanites drives everything else off the floor. The question is whether these suave religionists are to be exempt from military duty.

An admirer of government by discussion can't help looking on the scene with mixed feelings. It is gratifying that at such a time such a subject as exempting anybody from military service should be discussed at all. On the other hand, it is appalling that so many pompous and elderly men on the back benches should talk so much vague nonsense at a time when the continued survival of every man jack of them, and of their wives and children, is desperately at stake. When Bevin gets to his feet to defend the government's position that the lay teachers should be treated like everybody else (unless they applied for special consideration as conscientious objectors) you feel right away a powerful cool foursquare mind attacking the problem in hand. No oratory, no literature. A certain amount of the sort of heavy kidding that goes on in trade union congresses. His language jars a little on your ears; you wonder whether the Board Schools hadn't intentionally deformed the language of generations of lower-class English, the way the Chinese used to deform their women's feet. But while Bevin is talking we are in the real world instead of the Tory land of Balmy. He plugs one crazy issue after another as deftly and expeditiously as a ratcatcher plugging up holes in a loft.

Looking into the faces on the back benches you remember that the ineradicable disease of this parliament is that the Commons was elected in November 1935 at the depth of Chamberlain's head-in-the-sand policy and represented the stodgiest of the conservative machines and the stodgiest of the labor bureaucracy. It was elected to be a house of dead-heads and remains a house of deadheads. Men of brains can pretty well be counted on the fingers of two hands. Hitler's bombers, by stirring up their time-honored background, and enforcing some tremendous transformations of locale, had caused a certain amount of activity in minds that had known nothing for years but thirdrate directors meetings, coupon clipping in safe-deposit vaults and perhaps a little grouse shooting in the fall. Britain was meeting the greatest danger in the island empire's history under a government very short on brains.

The American visitors, during the proceedings, are handsomely set up to drinks. The bar has escaped uninjured. The drinks are good, the company is good. There is none of the selfimportant bustle that puts the togaed statues to shame under the colonnades on Capital Hill. An air of frankness and relaxation. Nobody seems surprised to see a public figure, whose name some years ago was one of the hopes of liberal politics, teetering drunkenly at one end of the bar. Introductions are easy and friendly. Very little side. Still the best club in London.

Even in the House of Commons it was obvious that something new had happened in England. There had been no revolution, to be sure, not yet; top dog was still top dog; but the defense of England had brought about a great deal of stimulating interpenetration of classes. In shelters, in airraid protection work, in auxiliary fire services and in the Home Guard, men from all parts of Britain and from all social classes had learned to work together and to risk their necks together and to pick themselves up together after being knocked down by the blast of high explosives. Their fraternal spirit was something that would have to be counted on in the future.

MR. LECTURER (*taps on the floor with his pointer*): Meanwhile . . . if I can have the lights please . . . While the young man is changing his reels, I have in my notes a few more reminiscences of wartime London . . . (MR. LECTURER *takes a furtive drag out of his glass of water.*) Meanwhile the old order in its most antiquated form was still in command of most of the machinery of government and industry. How complacent the old order still could be was brought home to me by a gentleman who addressed the congress of P.E.N. clubs the first morning I was in London. This gentleman, who wore many letters after his name, said he was a diplomat. His speech should have been taken down on a stone tablet and sped to the British Museum. He expatiated largely on the fact that the inferior races did not understand cricket and would never play the game. He ended with a sort of toast to the spirit of liberty that still burned in Buenos Aires, New York and (I couldn't believe my ears) Barcelona. Half the delegates were anti-fascist exiles, many of them had been behind barbed wire in France or Germany and had escaped shooting by the breadth of a hair. Several had started their fight against Hitler in Spain. At the name of Barcelona, a shiver went through them. The only man who protested was H. G. Wells.

Like Shaw's wisecracks, the protests of H. G. Wells had
become as much part of the English scene as Lord's Cricket
Ground. The ruling class mind of England had been, for a
century at least, admirably adapted to cushion such protests,
and to absorb them, and the protester too, into the system.
But somehow Wells hadn't quite been absorbed. He had
been the schoolmaster of generation after generation of
young Englishmen with brains who were not quite wealthy
or not quite gentry enough to go through the mill of the
Public Schools. Out of the ruin of the world he grew up in
it had been his fate to live on into one of the fantastic futures
he imagined in his romances, as if Jeremiah had survived to
become a friend and dinner companion of the Babylonians,
and had seen his prophecies come true all the same.

That fall the main pleasures in going to a public function
in London, besides the Rowlandson oddity of people's forms,
and the Cruikshank exaggeration of their features, was seeing
Wells' spruce figure there. His immense talent, his inventiveness and keenness of mind, and the stream of imaginative
writing, some good and some shoddy, that had poured from
his pen ever since I for one first read a book, his perception
in the mechanical sciences and his moral fervor, had come
to embody a whole state of mind of masses of middling
people, who took for granted that there was still a chance
that industrial society would find some sort of reasonable life
for itself. As in those war years Churchill embodied England's past, it seemed to me that Wells, for better or for
worse, embodied her present.

The first time was one Saturday morning when arriving a
little late, I slipped into a seat at a meeting of the P.E.N.
clubs and found myself staring at a small gray dapper man
with a sharply trimmed mustache and a little veining of red
in his cheeks. There was something alert and at the same
time relaxed about him, a half bantam half penguin look,
as he sat there in the empty front row. Of course it was

H. G. Wells. His blue eyes had the bored film of a drowsy cat's. He sat on the edge of the discussion with a remotely interested air like a man loafing on the edge of a pool full of swimmers who has not yet been tempted to dive in. You could see that he was mischievously aware of his authority in this particular gathering. He showed a little of the special vanity of an elderly man who has been very much petted by women all his life, who is a little brittle and overbearing with other men, and somewhat more at ease with a female audience, of a man who knew he was a bit spoiled and intended to continue being a bit spoiled, who enjoyed cultivating in public his little private foibles. When some speaker made a polite reference in his direction with something about the presence of one of the world's most distinguished writers, he piped up sharply in a squeaky voice: "I'm not a writer, I'm a journalist."

It was years since I'd thought of Wells or read his books. Seeing him sitting there in the bright daylight of the meeting hall, that seemed like a tiny tent of order in the massive chaos of this half demolished London, brought sharply back a childhood memory of lying on the floor propped up against an upholstered chair in a room that smelt of mothballs up on the top floor of my mother's house, choking hot Washington summer nights, and reading stories by Wells from a pile of torn back numbers of the *Strand Magazine*. *When the Sleeper Wakes* one of them was called. I remembered the hot and cold chills the story gave me and how my eyes burned from breathless fast reading under the dim bulb of the dustyfringed standing lamp. *The War of the Worlds* had come out as a serial in some flat illustrated quarto that had come unbound so that I had trouble keeping the glazed pages in order. I remembered the usualness of the suburban people in it; the usualness and the standing up under disaster; that was what people were like in London now. How well he knew them. For years that Wellsian world had

formed the background of my dreams and of not a few
nightmares. Now I was living in it. Of course that was why
it seemed so natural to see Wells here. This mechanized
world in catastrophe we are living in now is the world Wells
invented in the gaslight and coalsmoke days of Queen Victoria.

I've forgotten what the discussion was about that morning.
It certainly wasn't about anything important but everything
that Wells said made very good sense indeed. As he got to
talking he forgot himself. You could see that he was still
more interested in what went on around him than in his
own personality. You began to feel he was the youngest man
in the hall. As the glaze of selfimportance slipped off him a
lizard alertness took its place. Suddenly you saw in him
only the cocky young Londoner who had made his way in
the world by the power of his brains.

The next time I saw him was at a meeting of the British
Association of Scientists . . . the dark brown, early Victorian
dignity of the theatre, the neatly trimmed gray beards, the
elderly attendants, the plain girls with glasses taking notes;
it was all so much like the London I used to read about as
a child that I didn't know whether I was seeing it or reading
it. As the seats were all filled a movie producer friend who
was filming the proceedings had smuggled me in among his
crew. We stood in the circular passage underneath the seats
looking out into the lecture theatre through a short tunnel.
I was looking over the cameraman's back into the rosy
horizontal afternoon light that streaked in through the tall
Georgian window behind the speaker's desks, and there, opposite, halfway up a flight of redcarpeted steps stood Wells,
penguinshaped, nimbly teetering, quietly observant, again
with that look of being on the edge of the proceedings, for
all the world like the man who tells the story in one of his
own scientific romances.

When he spoke he spoke very precisely in an amused half conceited half modest tone. He was broaching his favorite theory that the race of men was not adapting fast enough to the changing environment man's own inventiveness had brought about and was likely to go into the discard with the dinosaurs and the great reptiles. When he spoke he chose his words with a certain coquetry like a pretty woman sitting at her dressing table, choosing the jewelry to match her dress. Big stencilled words like Science he avoided with catlike care.

I saw him last at his own house in one of those magnificent blocks Beau Nash promoted round Regent's Park. He was alone in a high whitepanelled parlor. A little plaster had fallen in the corners but the room was still intact. There seemed to be no one else in the house. Like a cold gust from a cellar I felt the solitude of old age chill my spine. We sat down at a little table to eat a partridge and to wash it down with a bottle of Burgundy. As soon as Wells started talking the sense of age melted away. He became a young man again, just as he had at the P.E.N. meeting. He was full of questions about America. When he asked you something he listened to the answer. When he got interested in a subject a little sparkle of amusement came into his face like the bubbles sizzling up out of a glass of champagne. Naturally we talked about Stalin and the Russians, but he was at his best about the British ruling class. "When this is over," he kept saying, "they'll chuck us and go saddle themselves on you . . . You mustn't let that happen! You've got to make the future. There isn't going to be any future, it'll be the death of the dinosaurs all over again unless you Americans invent us a future . . . Maybe the Russians could do it if we could keep them on our side, but they are too . . . too . . . Moscovite. Maybe a world state could save us, but somebody has got to invent it . . . This if ever is the time for great political inventions. We Europeans are done. We've invented the present, and look at us. It's up to you to invent us a future."

When I left him I groped my way in the blackout along the palings of the Baker Street tube station, stumbling here and there over the broken marble and plaster that littered the sidewalks. Coming blinking into the electric light of the tunnel that led from the elevator down into the tube, I almost fell over a baby asleep in a crib. It was a plump pink healthylooking baby. Beside it a young man and a young woman were curled up together on a mattress with their arms around each other cosily asleep under a flowered quilt, under the glare of electric light, in the draft and the hissing whirr of the trains and the clatter of hurrying feet. I wished Wells had seen them. Was it adaptation or was it surrender, I should have liked to have asked him.

(When MR. LECTURER *stops talking there's silence in the hall.)*

MR. LECTURER: Any question? I was hoping there would be questions.

VOICE FROM THE AUDIENCE *(hesitantly)*: I don't see any Socialism there mister. It only looks to me like the war had unloosed a whole lot of free enterprise. Looks like the need for energetic action in wartime had kind of knocked the lid of class privilege and monopoly off the population.

MR. LECTURER: That's what I thought at the time young man. It wasn't until I went back six years later that I discovered that the English people had just changed lids. I take it that what we want is a society without any lid on it.

A WOMAN'S VOICE: Could it be that stolid addiction to routine?

MR. LECTURER: Possibly. Routine is like a turtle's shell; it's a protection against attack but it hampers movement.

OTHER VOICES: All right let's get on with the movie.

(MR. LECTURER *taps with his pointer.)*

CAPTION: The Working Class

AN AMERICAN feels more at home in Glasgow than he
does south of the Tyne. Faces, storewindows, signs, the style
of building, remind you of the Middle West or eastern
Canada. There are moments when you can imagine you're
in Montreal or Toronto. The porter who put your bag on
the sleeper in London when you started north touched his
hat with a deepseated sense of ritual. The Scot who dourly
did you the favor of taking it off had none. Now, in the
third autumn of World War II, in Scotland you notice still
another difference. There's more plateglass left in shop-
windows; there's less feeling of being under siege. You can
ride on a bus for miles without seeing any traces of bombing.
This is the industrial back country that's producing the tools
of war, not the front line.

What I wanted to see in Glasgow was what kind of people
were being produced by the war factories along with the
munitions. That was the question I tried to put to everybody I talked to: what kind of society is developing in
Britain as you fight the war? No easy question to answer.
One of the reasons why man has so little control over his
destiny is that it is so hard for any individual to gauge the
underlying drift of the society he is living in. Jolting along
on a bus over the oozy cobbles under the gray skies of this
castiron town I'd never seen before, I was thoroughly aware
as I looked at the closed faces around me and watched the
shabby groups slouching outside of bars or waiting for
streetcars (so like the people you'd see on the streets in
Toledo or in Bayonne, N.J.) that it was not a question I
could find any real answer to at all in a few day's trip. All I

could hope to do was to collect a few notions, infinitesimal straws, that might or might not give some inkling of the set of the wind.

My first exhibit I collected that morning right after stepping off the train. It was too early to make any calls, so after breakfast I started to roam about the streets. On Glasgow Green, famous center of a century's oratory and no little slugging and swatting in behalf of the working class, I found myself admiring the edifice you see on the screen. It is called the People's Palace. (*Laughter. Some applause from the back of the hall.*) . . . I know it seems out of date. Some of our favorite buildings will seem just as funny to your grandchildren . . . The back part is one of those great greenhouses with vaults and domes of glass and iron that were built in the middle of Queen Victoria's reign to satisfy the enthusiasm for tropical plants of an eager generation of lovers of natural history; the front part, that sooteaten mansard structure, is a municipal museum. The elderly guardian seems to want me to come in, so before I know what I am doing, I find myself in a dim hall studying with some dismay case after great glass case full of silver fruitdishes and punchbowls, sculptured soup tureens, huge silver set pieces, unwieldy cups built up out of groups of writhing figurines the relentless silversmith tortured into bases and handles: Sir Thomas Lipton's yachting trophies.

The walls of the rooms are covered with framed photographs of those endless yachts the sly yankees always were able to outsail, of Sir Thomas being piped over the side in company of windblown dignitaries, of Sir Thomas at sea and Sir Thomas on land and Sir Thomas grinning under a yachting cap. Then there are watercolors by members of the family, embossed parchments and testimonials, a sketch of the house where he was born; all the paraphernalia of one of the success stories of the last century: the Glasgow lad who made good. From grocery boy to merchant prince to yachtsman, swept on a flood of weak tea up into the world of sport and regattas and kings. That was Glasgow's golden legend for the nineteenth century.

Walking away from the People's Palace across the so fresh so often rained on Green you come out on a great carpet factory, which some architect giddy with Ruskin ornamented with a façade in colored tiles, a nightmarish parody of the Doge's palace in Venice. Well that is what they wanted. How much easier it is to plot the mind of the past than the mind of the present. Patently Lipton's life was what Glasgow wanted in Victorian days; what sort of thing was the city wanting today?

Later in the same day I ran across another exhibit, another Glasgow boy who'd made good, very much alive this one, a redheaded Irishman named Sir Patrick Dollan, who had made a great name for himself as a liberal Lord Provost. Instead of the older generation's thrift, and patient compounding of selfinterest, the canny adjustment of balances, and the wait for the gambler's lucky option on a shipload of goods, there had been quite different rungs in this man's ladder. Somewhere at the base were the uneasy hopes of betterment of working people caught in the industrial process like sheep in the boardedup passage that leads to the shambles. The driving force had been the reformer's urge, a touch of the revolutionists' belief that the golden age was at hand if only the Liptons of this world could be put down. He was a man with that knack for practical politics which seems to grow spontaneously out of the peat of green Eire, a warmheaded, coldhearted, explosive man, easily fired by any generous dream. He obviously had that cheerful aptitude for making a show of himself, for playing a somewhat comic part on the city's stage, that is so necessary to the politician's equipment. He was one of those men who never forget the kiddies' first names or what aches and pains the old people had last year, or how long a step the pallbearers should be taking when the grand old wardheeler was being carried to his grave, or how to look fatherly solemn standing bareheaded in the rain while the requiescat was being read over the victims of some industrial accident. You could see that his head was packed full of knowledge of the back alleys as well as the highroads of his city, that his reflexes were quick as a cat's to respond to the slightest stumbling move of that manyfooted, manyheaded blind striving beast the public. A lively example of the type of public man who rose to power in many places in the period of humanitarian adjustment between the two wars. Very much a figure for Glasgow's golden legend for the first third of this century.

But what new type of boss, I couldn't help asking myself, was being developed by the tough exigencies of this present time. The man beside me on the bus, who had been detailed by the local representative of the Ministry of Information to show me around, was a square quiet young man with rather colorless face and hair. He sat huddled in his raincoat not looking to the right or the left. Not much of a talker. Questions he answered in the fewest possible words. He told me he had started in life working in a sewing machine factory, going to night school meanwhile and putting himself through a work people's college. Now he was on the payroll of the Ministry of Information reporting workingclass matters. He had just come back from the Orkneys where he had made a survey of how laborers doing war work up there lived. He was a softspoken inconspicuous young man with a tough knot of notions under his skull my questions never quite managed to unravel. He believed, up to a certain point, in English ways of doing things, but he obviously was not shocked by the methods of the ally Stalin or the enemy Hitler. You felt that all capacity for righteous indignation had been exhausted at home long ago. To say this of a Scot is saying a great deal.

We were on our way down the long artery that links the

shipbuilding and factory towns that stretch to the westward along the Clyde. After leaving Glasgow we passed through one of those noman's land regions of ruined real estate values that are so much part of the landscape of our industrial cities and then came out on a bright new section of model apartment houses, the sort of project into which the Lord Provost and his friends had put the bulk of their energy and power of persuasion. They were comfortablelooking buildings well adapted to city life and represented what the period between wars accomplished in real social advance. Beyond them were freightyards, railroad tracks and then began the Clydeside towns proper.

My guide began to point out the work of the German bombers. Though they didn't seem to have scored many hits on the shipyards, they had done an extraordinary job of slum clearance in a band miles long and several blocks wide stretching parallel to the river. In spite of it my guide said that even on the worst days the number of men reporting for work in the yards never dropped below seventyfive percent of the total employed. It was obvious from the steaming and hammering that came from these yards as we were trundled past their gates that they were far from idle at that moment.

Near Clydebank we got off the bus on the very active and comparatively undamaged main street, and went to visit a new A.R.P. post that was being developed in the shoredup ruins of a blitzed school. The warden in charge was inordinately proud of his dressing station. He even had a real operating table. You could see he almost wished the Jerries would come back so that he could have a chance to try out his fine equipment.

Next we walked up the street to see the public dormitory for single men and the public diningroom that is so much of a necessity in the British industrial towns these days when men's families have had to move from thirty to a hundred miles away from the factory centers. In a country where even in peacetime only a few welltodo people had cars, getting workmen home even once a week taxed transportation. As a result many men were dependent for food and lodging on dirty dosshouses and inadequate eating joints that had to close up after a bombing because they couldn't get supplies. To fill this need a chain called the British Restaurants spread over the country (in spite of most desperate efforts on the part of the catering interests to stop them) furnishing meals at cost to all comers. It was one of these that my guide took me to see. It was set up in what had been a theatre and concert room connected with the Town Hall. A lot of stout freshfaced women were in a great bustle getting ready for the rush that would come when the shift that downed tools at five o'clock poured out of the shipyards. The tables were clean, the floor was swept, the soup smelt good. For ninepence you could get as good a meal here as anywhere in Britain.

As we stepped out in the raw drizzling afternoon again, my guide suggested that we might as well go to see his pigeons. He made the suggestion ever so shyly, but when I took him up on it, you could see that pigeons meant a great deal to him. He fancied carrier pigeons, he told me in his clipped unemphatic tones. He led me up a back street towards the suburb, where as he put it, again without any particular emphasis, his father's house used to be. It was a street of small comfortable dwellings of the type that are described in Britain as semidetached villas. They were fenced from the sidewalk by iron railings or little stone walls or hedges. They had gardens front and back. They would have been like any other suburban houses but they'd all been knocked down.

"Fortunately I only lost one pigeon from the bomb," my guide was saying. He pointed to an irregular pit full of rubbish. "This used to be Father's. . . . It was rather a mess before they cleaned it up."

An old man was puttering aimlessly with a spade round a little plum tree.

"This is my father," he introduced him vaguely and led the way out back through deep grass with quick steps to a shed.

He ushered me in cautiously, and then slipped in himself and closed the door tight behind him. In the dim light reflected off whitewashed walls the slender gray bluntbeaked birds looked out at us from nests and perches all around out of brightringed startled eyes. Suddenly my guide began to talk a blue streak about the great races his pigeons had flown in, from Brussels and Montpellier and Marseilles and Belgrade and Rome. His sentences that had been short and clipped all afternoon, became long and rhetorical. The pigeons rustled and fluttered on their perches. The worst blow of the war, as he felt it, you could easily see, had been the interruption of the pigeon tests. He thought of Europe as a map marked in red with the names of all the capitals his pigeons had been shipped to in their little crates. He'd never seen the Continent but his pigeons had. He told me their names and their numbers and their timing in the tests. I said I didn't know private individuals were allowed to handle passenger pigeons in wartime. "Registered fanciers can," he said proudly. Pigeons it was clear were the only thing in the world this man could call his own.

That night he took me to eat a haggis with some friends of his who lived in one of the modern apartments on the way into Glasgow. The man of the house was a foreman in the shipyard. He was a handsome grayhaired silent man. His wife did all the talking. She was a cheerful busty woman who did a lot of reading. Right away she started talking about books. She asked me about Bellamy's *Looking Backward* and about Debs and Big Bill Heyward and Emma Goldman. It was like a conversation at the Brevoort in the years before World War I. She liked American writing it was so real she said. She admired Dreiser. Upton Sinclair's novels she found too full of propaganda. She liked books, she said, that told her about things as they really were. There were two daughters in the house, lively welldressed young women who seemed a little impatient with all this talk. It seemed oldfashioned to them you could see. They hurried out to meet dates for the movies.

It wasn't long before we were on the subject of the Russians. Our hostess thought the Communists were pretty silly in England, but in Russia: that was different. It was only since Russia had gone in, she said, that British working people had really believed this was their war. I asked her whether working people didn't make a better living and have more human rights here in Glasgow than in Moscow but she wasn't interested in the question. It was the Russians who were holding out against Hitler; it was the Russians who had the workingclass state. She felt the government was sabotaging the Russian effort. The official upper crust in England had always wanted to help Hitler against Stalin. Could they be trusted to help Stalin even to save themselves? What about Churchill, I asked her, couldn't he be trusted? As far as he went, she thought Churchill was fine, she said; but there were too many things he didn't know about. Why in a debate in Parliament it had turned out he didn't know what a boardinghouse was. He didn't know that there were some people in this world who had to live in boardinghouses.

A few days later, in a tiny village of stone houses, looking out towards the north tip of Ireland and the Herbrides, I met the same state of mind again. I had been taken to tea at the house of a tall blackeyed beetlebrowed young man. His wife was pink and fresh as a hedgeside rose. He'd been a herring fisherman all his life. They both spoke a beautiful correct English with hardly a trace of a burr, the sort of ideally pure language I've heard occasionally among the older people in isolated places on the coast of Maine. The cottage was a tiny clapboard shack. They had a bigger stone house of the local picturesque type but they saved that to rent to summer visitors. The floor shone it was so clean. We sat on scrubbed cane chairs, and drank tea and ate hot scones and talked about the state of the world. Their information came from the radio and the occasional newspaper that drifted over from Campbelltown, but their opinions seemed to be their own.

At the word Russia, they really warmed up. They were not Communists, not in the least, but they felt that Russia was the workingclass state, that it was the Russians who were really going to destroy Hitler. As a herring fisherman the young man was interested in Russia because in the old days when England had had good relations with Russia, St. Petersburg had been one of the great markets for salt herring. The Russians used to eat a world of herring and that helped keep the market up. I put in that in helping Stalin destroy Hitler we were helping a lesser evil against a greater, but they weren't interested in the idea. They admitted that Stalin had wiped out every trace of personal liberty and destroyed the cooperative movement (I'd thought I could catch them on the subject of cooperatives) but still they said they trusted the Russians more than they trusted the treacherous Southerners who ruled the Empire. "For all that we fishermen," the young man said finally with a smile, "we fishermen can't complain of this war; we are getting a good price for fish."

Back in the south of England, when I had a talk with another young Scot, a metalworker, who a couple of weeks later at the shopstewards' convention at York, turned out to be one of the leaders of the shopsteward movement, it was the same story. I had gone out to meet him where he worked at an airplane-motor plant outside of London. It was the noon hour, so he took me around to the union local. There we met two other shopstewards who took us into one of their committee rooms and shut the door. We sat at a long table over mugs of bitter ale and the young man talked clearly and at length.

Like so many other metalworkers and engineers he was born in Glasgow. He was broadshouldered with light sandy hair, a dense white skin and widely spaced hard gray eyes. As he talked he emphasized points with a light tap of a chunky fist on the edge of the table, or by screwing up one eye in a confidential halfwink. Now and then he paused to let his friends, one a middleaged redfaced man, stoutish and quietvoiced, also a Scot, who had worked as a machinist all over the States; the other a skinny intenteyed Englishman with a scraggly mustache, explain something. They were all on fire with admiration for Russia. No, they weren't Communists but they felt that the British working class should take things into their own hands, the way the Russian working class had. You couldn't say that the Russian workers had the government in their hands now, could you? I asked them. If our admittedly faulty system of selfgovernment went overboard wouldn't you be installing another class of despots in office far more ruthless than the capitalists? They couldn't see the point. They were too busy with their class war against the present owners of industry to look forward that far. It seemed to me they admired the Russians not so much for what they had done as for what they had undone.

These were the men who represented the young fellows with neatly parted hair stuck down with brilliantine, and the trim girls (for these islands welldressed) I had seen at work in the bomber plants I had been allowed to visit. It was in these airplane factories that the brightest and most energetic of the new generation of workingclass Britishers were being prepared for the future. It was this younger element that the shopstewards were speaking for.

They explained that as shopstewards they were the direct representatives of the workers in the plant. They were elected by secret ballot and could be recalled by a vote of noconfidence. Originally they had been merely interested in the adjustment of grievances and minor details of working conditions in the shop, but since Dunkirk, and especially since Hitler's attack on Russia had brought it home to British workers that the Jerries were attacking them as well as the toffs who ran the Empire, their main interest, so they said, had been in increasing production. To increase production the efficiency of both management and labor had to be stepped up. They reeled off a string of cases in which workers in their own plant alone had increased production by technical suggestions. You could see they were aching to be running the plant themselves.

What had happened here, said the Scotsman who had been to America, was that to everybody's surprise they get on better with management than with the salaried officials of the trade union organizations.

The young man from Glasgow screwed up one eye with a dry laugh.

"They're fast growing into their desks like the other deadheads" he said. "They're part of the government now. They're too high and mighty to hear what a mere worker has to say."

The first thing, he started as if addressing a meeting, was to win the war. The boys at the benches had plenty of confidence in the boys in the R.A.F. The R.A.F. knew how to use the planes all right as fast as they were turned out. It was the men who'd grown into their desks at the War Office and the Admiralty and in the trade union offices they worried about. Why weren't they really helping the Russians? The Colonel Blimps had almost lost the war already and still they were as full of oldfashioned ideas as ever. There wasn't any great question for the present between capital and labor, the question was between efficiency and inefficiency. The workers had all the money they could use,

they weren't worried about food, one of the things that had
made them sorest was Churchill's speech last summer telling them they would have more food for Christmas. They
didn't need more food. Once they'd won the war, they'd get
more food for Christmas and they wouldn't run to Whitehall
begging for it either.

"That's wot worries us 'ere," the man who'd been to
America summed up in a soothing tone. He jerked his
thumb towards the young man from Glasgow. " 'E's the one
to make a noise about it."

The young man from Glasgow pulled himself back in his
chair and sat thoughtfully looking down at the table.

"What can you do about it?"

"Not so much . . . We can let 'em know we're alive . . .
But afterwards, they better watch out."

YOUNG MAN'S VOICE (*interrupting angrily*):It's natural that
the working class when it comes to power in a country should
sympathize with other countries where the working class is
in power.

MR. LECTURER: It may be natural but it would be more
intelligent if they tried to find out who is operating in the
name of the working class and to what ends. Workingclass
people in England ought to find out how the Russian régime
operates for their own kind of people at least. In my opinion
the Communist leaders in Russia exercise an autocratic
dictatorship for their own benefit in the name of the working
class the way Louis XIV exercised an autocratic dictatorship
in the name of God. I don't think the working people of
England want that any more than the rest of us.

A YOUNG WOMAN'S VOICE: In America we believe government ought to represent the people, not just the working
people or the business people or the farming people, but
all the people.

MR. LECTURER: Exactly. The minute you start governing

in the interest of one class of people that means that democratic institutions are going off the track. The enlivening thing about life in wartime Britain was that it gave an opportunity for people of all classes to show their mettle. To understand the change that came with the consolidation of the labor government you've got to have a little notion of what prepared the way for it. During the war it looked as if British society had received just the shaking up it needed to start out on a new career of enterprise and discovery. Middle-class people seemed more wide awake than they had been in a century . . . But let's get back to what I was actually seeing and hearing at that time . . . (MR. LECTURER *taps with his pointer.*)

CAPTION: *The Middle Class*

On the morning train down to Great Yarmouth from Norwich the compartment was full of ruddyfaced housewives in out of style hats on their way to take a look at the seashore houses the war had forced them out of. The train ran slowly across a flat region of black soil that turned in a sleek fat furrow behind plows pulled by big broad black horses past creamcolored cattle and windmills and canals that reflected the gray sky and the green shutters of the cabins of pugnosed barges. The ladies in the car talked mostly about furniture. Poor Mrs. Hopkinson had taken the trouble to get hers all packed up in a van, such hard work and her with a weak heart and they'd blitzed it on the way to the station. And then there was Mrs. Smithers who'd just got settled in the vicarage where everybody was so sure they'd be safe because it was so far from any target area and a bomb dropped on it that night. If it hadn't been that they'd all gone out in the country to see the grandchildren . . . Another lady had moved her belongings three separate times only to lose them in the end; and there was old Mrs. Swinnerton who would stay on in her flat right next to the naval barracks; she insisted she felt safer there.

As I got off the train I was pounced upon by an enormously tall and rawboned policeman.

"And what might you be doing in a protected area?" I hurriedly produced my passes and documents. "With a name like that," he said as he handed them back, "you'll have a hard time keeping out of custody."

I pointed out that the Ministry of Information had sent word about me to the local authorities, but he shook his head dolefully and started herding me along a broad dreary street of yards and warehouses towards the police station in the center of town. Along the hoardings, from which the paint had long since peeled, somebody had patiently chalked from time to time a wide victory V with the initials U.K., U.S.A., and U.S.S.R. arranged in an inverted pyramid inside. I saw the policeman looking at the letters with real satisfaction and thought how times had changed. As we walked I asked about bombings.

"Oh they're always overhead . . . Just two days ago they dropped a stick of bombs that didn't go off. There are five of 'em still in the town."

"Duds?" I asked.

He laughed hollowly. "The only bombs that wouldn't go off were the ones America sold us during the last war."

That kept me quiet. We walked along in silence for quite a way after that. Then he turned to me and asked in a confidential tone, "How's London?"

"London's fine," I said. "They smashed up the East End a good deal."

He didn't say anything for a minute. Then he said proudly, "Just wait till you see our damage."

We'd reached the center of town; a bridge across a puttycolored tidal river, a number of small boats tied up to the stone quays, a smell of tarred rope and weedy docks, some coming and going of men in navy blue, white gulls screaming overhead.

In the police station we found an agreeable plainclothes sergeant who collected stamps and admired Franklin D. Roosevelt. Instead of taking me into custody the sergeant went to work on the telephone to try to get me an admiralty pass to visit the local motor torpedo boat base, meanwhile broaching a theory that, as this little fishing port was one of the easternmost towns in England, the Germans were using it as a practice target for new bombing crews. It turned out the the Admiralty couldn't be budged. The Admiralty, the sergeant admitted sadly, hadn't much use for the Ministry of Information. Then he urged me to go look at the motor torpedo boats from the outside. "You can see them just as well through the palings," he said.

Things were rather at loose ends until I got hold of Mr. Davy. He is the local newsagent and represents the Ministry of Information in the town. Mr. Davy is a short wiry little man in his early fifties who in the last war was attached to the intelligence service in the Mespot. Recently he'd served several terms as alderman and was now an A.R.P. warden and knew everything and everybody on that coast. He walked with a remarkably springy gait.

Mr. Davy showed me the town. We started walking through straight very narrow old streets of fishermen's houses that, with their dark doorways and narrow windows, had that peculiar look of generations of poverty that fishermen's houses everywhere have. Then we came out suddenly on the broad streets and beersigns and boardedup restaurants, theatre posters and tinted plaster fronts of the hotels and boardinghouses of the beach resort. There we found a number of blocks roped off: the delayed action bombs. Policemen were detouring traffic and trying rather halfheartedly to discourage people on foot from walking through the danger area. Everybody was behaving with a surprising lack of drama. Here and there somebody in a hurry bustled right on through the lines without anything much being done to stop him. Passing the empty hotels of the ocean front, Mr. Davy and I found ourselves strolling in the pale autumn sunlight along a broad esplanade that ran parallel to the beach.

The tide was low. Slow yellow swells were breaking far out and spuming in across the shingle in shiny creamcolored sheets that swirled and splashed among dense spirals of barbed wire and poured over strange long halfburied metallic objects that Mr. Davy said were contact mines. Further up the beach, where in the old days trippers had lain inhaling the vacation ozone while their children built sand castles and rattled tin buckets and whacked at each other with their spades, there were concrete pillboxes concealed in peanut stands and, behind ornamental balustrades, all sorts of odd apparatus of dunpainted metal. The paleblue striped bathhouses and the stalls and booths where they used to sell candy or teas or fish and chips or chances on dolls with electriclight bulbs in their heads were still decorated with darkblue fancy scrollwork. On every wall were posters of one Mandeville, a magician who was to have put on his great illusion act in July 1939. The amusement piers and the glassed-in dancehall looked ready for a run of tourists, except that they were linked to the adjacent rollercoasters and the silent strangled merrygorounds by long tangling strands and snarls of barbed wire. The tourists that beach resort was ready for were more likely to come by sea than by land.

Antiaircraft guns sprouted briskly out of a pit in the middle of an elaborate set of flower beds. There was a summerhouse with benches where even on that raw wartime autumnal day a thin remnant of the old life went on. A few aged people neatly tucked in with blankets had been placed out in the sun in bathchairs. A nursemaid was watching a couple of tiny beadyeyed children. A shabby middleaged man lay sprawled on the balustrade reading *The Daily Express.*

A narrow path had been left through the barbed wire out onto the longest pier. On the way you had to cross some mysteriouslooking new cementwork. "There's 'undreds of tons of explosive 'idden 'ere. Rather a waste when you think of it," said Mr. Davy cheerfully. Out at the end of the pier we found a group of men with poles quietly fishing.

"It's the only way anybody can get any fresh fish 'ere," explained Mr. Davy. In front of us three obvious trawlers were smudging the misty horizon.

"Aren't they fishing?"

"They're not fishing for fish." A plane gave a protective halfcircle round a batch of small freighters at anchor off the mouth of the harbor.

"They're waiting for a convoy . . . Tomorrow's the day they usually take 'em down the coast . . . Now let's go to the library . . . Americans are always interested in a Carnegie library."

We struck off again through the densepacked streets of the old quarter. As we passed the shuttered windows of the buildings back of the waterfront we couldn't help noticing that behind drawn blinds and shuttered sun parlors hotels and boardinghouses were jammed with a new sort of young summer boarder in khaki or else in the bluegray of the R.A.F. After a certain number of detours for roped-off streets we came out suddenly on an area where the buildings had been razed to the ground. "Slum clearance," said Mr. Davy. "It 'ad to come." Across the cleared area we came on an ancient stone church tower standing lonely and intact.

Down a narrow ruined lane we found the library. The lower floor had been saved by the fire department but the water hadn't helped the books much. Amid the smell of damp bricks and wet ashes two elderly men were busy with the incredibly dreary work of salvage. Upstairs they'd gotten a temporary roof up over the wreckage of the reading room. There they were collecting the least damaged books and trying to dry them out. The fire engines had pumped salt water from the river the night of that particular blitz so that things were unusually hard to dry out. "As soon as I clean the mould off it starts growing again," one man complained as he rubbed vigorously with a rag at a volume out of a set of the novels of Marion Crawford. Standing forlornly about on the floor were cases of stuffed birds that had miraculously escaped, and in a corner was a pile of Saxon spearheads and flints and polished stone axes that had survived the burning of their showcase. The library attendant had been at work for weeks painfully sorting out the wreckage. I couldn't help thinking: Suppose we got some more bombs tonight.

We were about to leave when another elderly man in a wornout uniform came after us and said we must see the historical museum. He led us back through a gap in the library wall out and made us scramble down a pile of crumbling bricks into a sort of well among walls of scorched and calcined rubble off which the plaster had peeled.

"Here it is," he said. "People used to come from all over the world to see this little building, from America and everywhere. Very antique it was."

He gave a wave of a hand up towards some pointed stone arches still intact in the ruined wall above our heads. Then he insisted that we follow him further down the caving brick slope into the cellar. On the way we ducked under a door over which you could make out quite plainly the calcined form of a stuffed toucan on a perch. Beyond, against a wall of squared stones, parts of the skeleton of a whale were piled on an ancient wooden cart that somehow had escaped the burning. "Here they are . . . the dungeons." He pointed proudly at three small gratings. "The wood burned but the iron bars are still good. If I could get them open I could show you the ancient instruments of torture."

After that Mr. Davy took me to have some tea in a place upstairs over a bank on the main shopping street. "Only temporary quarters," he explained. "But this is the best place in the locality." While we drank our tea I sat looking out of the window at the remains of a department store. A pretty recent job, it must have been, because tiny wisps of blue smoke still rose from blackened timbers, and clusters of pipes and twisted iron shapes hung in festoons where the floors had been. In the back the steel uprights of the elevator shaft were curled into a spiral.

After tea we went to see the Town Clerk and the local newspaper editor, who explained the system for local news bulletins that had been worked out to keep the population informed of events in case they were cut off from the rest of England by a particularly bad blitz or by invasion. "Of course there oughtn't to be any population here," the editor said, "but they won't go away. They're coming back more than ever. I can tell by my newspaper subscriptions. What can you do? It's where they live."

"Now you must come and see where I live," said Mr. Davy. "The premises isn't quite what it was, but after all we were very, very lucky."

We took a bus to the adjoining borough that began on the other side of the river. On the way Mr. Davy showed me a new municipal swimming pool just back of a section of beach we hadn't seen before. The filtered salt water looked cold and clean, the color of washing blue in the late afternoon light. "That cost me my reelection," he said, ". . . as alderman . . . people 'ere are very conservative. They thought it was too costly. But they were just beginning to get to like it when war broke out."

When we reached Mr. Davy's premises it was apparent that they certainly weren't what they had once been. A bomb had exploded in the street outside his little stationery store and had blown Mr. Davy and handsome blonde Mrs. Davy and all their stock and their two fat little white dogs clear out through the back wall into the garden that sloped so prettily down to the river. They had picked themselves up from among the brick dust not very much the worse. The borough had rebuilt their chimney and stuffed up the gaps in the walls and they had laid out some board tables and opened for business again. The upstairs looked pretty well gone so I couldn't figure where they slept or how they got their meals. Their attitude towards the whole thing was that they'd been exceptionally lucky. When the war was over maybe they'd get some insurance.

We stood at the bottom of their garden and looked out at the sleekly flowing puttycolored tidal river. An M.T.B. on patrol charged past. We heard the engineroom bell as she slowed for the sharp turn between the two wooden bulkheads of the harbor's narrow mouth. Beside us two white ducks were making a cosy quiet gobbling noise over a pan of feed.

"Meanwhile," said Mrs. Davy with a contented smile, "we're carrying on!"

"What do you think of my ducks?" asked Mr. Davy. "I like to 'ave a bit of poultry for Christmas."

When I said goodnight, for my part footsore and dogtired, to Mr. Davy, he was just getting ready to walk around to the post to go on allnight duty as airraid warden.

"Aren't you tired?" I asked him before thanking him and saying goodbye.

"Oh no, I never get tired," he answered briskly. "Not in times like these. I 'ardly know why but I don't."

I went back to the hotel on the bus. There I found waiting a fine but small meal of firstrate roast mutton. When I turned in, not a sound could be heard in the dense foggy darkness. It wasn't until I climbed on the train to pull out of town next morning that I remembered the five delayed

action bombs . . . or were they duds? . . . The people of
Great Yarmouth had kept them so little in mind that I'd
forgotten them myself.

YOUNG WOMAN'S VOICE: Why it looks to me as if your Mr.
Davy was just the sort of man you needed if you wanted to
build a new society, a man with firm convictions who never
got tired.

AN ELDERLY WOMAN'S VOICE (*sighing*): Magnificent discipline. Over here your Mr. Davy would probably have
been playing the black market.

MR. LECTURER: That's one trouble with the British. They
are too well disciplined. That routine we were talking about.
People can be ruined by their virtues as well as their vices.
If we were a disciplined people we'd still have the Volstead
Act.

YOUNG MAN'S VOICE: Just what do you mean by those statements? You've got me on the ropes, mister.

MR. LECTURER: I admit it's risky to make crack judgments.
What's true once may not be true again. Human societies
will never lie still for you to dissect them. They are living
organisms that develop in various directions at once. You
keep coming on facts that don't fit into the argument, and
you have to digest them as best you can.

YOUNG MAN'S VOICE: I've got indigestion already.

MR. LECTURER: Right now I just want you to get the picture . . . If you don't mind we'll put off the discussion till a
little later . . .

CAPTION: *The Unchanging Britisher*

From the bright glare of the hotel lobby, stuffed with uniforms and blue tracings of cigarette smoke, you step into the
darkened revolving door that cuts out the chatter and the
glitter as it turns behind you, and pushes you out into the

wartime London night. For a minute you stand on the
doorstep dazzled by the blackness. Then the outlines of
roofs and chimneypots across the street begin to sharpen
against a sky that shows a light sprinkling of stars, and you
begin to make out the tiny blinking of red and green crosses
of traffic lights down the street and the moving oblongs of
pale glow cast on the paving ahead of them by buses and taxicabs. Starting to move along with the crowd, you begin to
notice how cigarettes all at once illuminate cheeks and chins
and lips, how a struck match will shine bright in the eyes of
a man and a girl, draw their profiles, model their faces; or
how a lighter, moved around from mouth to mouth among
a group of people talking in a doorway will emphasize long
comic shadowy noses or witchlike upcurved points or chins,
or hollow out cheeks and eyesockets or prettily carve an ear
or the tilt of a neat jaw to top the slenderly moulded column
of a neck. You find yourself looking inquisitively into every
barely seen face that passes. The soles of your feet warily
measure curbs; out of a corner of an eye you check on the
corners of buildings. As you get used to the dark you find
yourself enjoying the cosy privacy of the crowd. Your nerves
and senses are gradually keying up to a brittle anxious interest in every dark shape that looms. Your hearing seems
to get sharper. Above the shuffle of feet and the rumble of
sparse traffic you begin to distinguish voices, accents,
brogues.

You find yourself slackening your pace to listen to a very
young soldier and his girl who have just slipped out into
the streets from the darkened door of the picture theatre
where they have been seeing the movie about the bombing
of Chungking. Their speech has the near-Cockney twang of
the London suburbs. Their mouths are very close as they
talk. They can't get over the fact that right across on the
other side of the world there's bombing too, only there it's
Chinamen that are being blown to bits. Finally the man

hits on a phrase that seems to satisfy him. He says it over
and over again: It's the gay twentieth century.

Sometimes only a muffled sound of voices behind a chink
of light announces a pub, or sometimes the name is spelt
out in faint red letters in an embrasure. You push on the
swinging doors and shoulder your way through the heavy
curtains beyond and find yourself among red faces in the
not unfriendly reek of beer and tobacco. This time it's
Canadians, huskylooking lads with a Winnipeg burr to their
speech. It's like being in Chicago. They are arguing and
grousing about the lull in the war in the West. They want
to fight. They want to get their hands on the Jerries. Their
talk makes a loud growling sound as they sway against the
bar.

In the next compartment things are very quiet. A number
of local Londoners are inhaling their beer out of mugs;
elderly men in derbies, with meaty faces that have something of Hogarth's exaggeration about them. Their faces
have character but not a trace of expression. They take
their beer in short pulls the same way they smoke their pipes.
Only occasionally there's a ghost of a wink or a pursing of
the lips to smother a smile as somebody passes a remark out
of the corner of a mouth in the direction of the barmaid who
has red knuckles and big red elbows and a look of having
been stuffed with difficulty into her black crepe dress with
little inserts of light material down the front. Above a
bosom that would easily heave, her neck and cheeks curve
whitely. Under her frizzy black permanent she shows a pair
of steady black eyes that keep the customers in their places.
Moving on you find yourself in the next segment of the pub
facing a snack bar where busy eaters of all sexes and uniforms are demolishing cold tongue and meat loaf and left-
over fried fish and salmon salad. Having just managed to
come in on the end of the salmon and to get hold of the
last plate of sliced bread and margarine, you carry it off to

a small glasstopped table where you fall into conversation with a middleaged Canadian who has strayed away from the rest. His speech is embellished by a rich Irish brogue. As a co-inhabitant of our western continent he offers you a slice off some real butter he carries in his pocket, in a ball wrapped in waxed paper. It turns out that he has a plan for World War II. He was a sergeant and then an officer in a Canadian regiment in World War I, by God he must have learned something about fighting. All this stuff about sending armies to the Near East, munitions to Vladivostok to help the Russians was rubbish. Sure the Russians must be helped, but why go all that way? Why not land some troops in Brittany? He'd been to everybody with his plan, but they wouldn't listen to a Canadian. He'd been bashing his head against a stone wall for four months. "You know how the English are if you try to talk about something that matters . . . they look at you as if you had made a bad smell." He was almost crying with vexation.

You remember you have an engagement in Hampstead and get up to go. As he shakes hands he begs you not to forget the plan; if you run into anybody influential you must talk it up to them. Maybe they'll listen to an American citizen. Canadians are just British subjects, second class. You leave him staring gloomily over a double Scotch at the paperwrapped ball of Irish butter on the table in front of him.

From the top of the bus you can't see the people any more, only a succession of buildings with blind windows. Suddenly you are seeing stars through a building. The building's a burnt out shell. Beyond rise shapes of ruined walls, guttered arches, jutting hunks of masonry. Then again, long stretches of boardedup windows.

Meanwhile a sort of music hall turn has begun in the dark on top of the bus. Everybody's taking part in high good humor. Nobody misses their cues. Everybody laughs happily at the cracks.

It began with a thick beery Cockney voice that shouted out from the back that the haristocracy was rotten and 'ad to be swept away it 'ad, before Hingland could be sived. A definitely Oxford voice took him up: "What are you doing that's so important?"

"My man, where did you get your educytion?" came back the beery voice in a high and mighty tone that made everybody laugh.

"In Whitechapel," cracked the Oxford voice very unconvincingly.

The drunken voice evidently felt it had the crowd with it. It took up a rich university drawl. "My people . . . er . . . sent me . . . to Oxfaad, but the authorities there . . . er . . . sent me down . . . So they sent me . . . er . . . to Cambridge where I parsed on my farther's degrees . . . I've been trying to parse them ever since, so I follow the employment of navvy . . . laborer I believe you'd say."

The beery voice was out of breath.

The passengers were slapping their sides. The bus stopped. "What stytion is it guvnor?" asked the navvy in his normal tone.

"The police station," cracked a wit that had so far not been heard from. That gave the navvy the chance for his big scene.

"Very good my friend, couldn't be better . . . Not 'arf . . . That's what I pay the bobbies for, to look arfter me . . . With the rates and that . . . They're paid to look arfter me." That went biggest of all. The bus started up again with everybody chuckling in their seats. The navvy tried to keep it up with dark hints about various members of the aristocracy who had "gone to Germany" as he put it. His voice dropped to a mumble about all he'd been through at one time or another. Meanwhile a discussion had broken out about how many glasses of beer he'd had. Estimates varied from sixteen to sixty. He'd pricked up his ears at that. The word beer gave

him a chance to get back in the center of the stage. "Beer,"
he shouted hoarsely, "all the bleedin' rotten haristocrats myd
their money brewin' beer."

"So that you can drink it," came back somebody. That
time the laugh was on the navvy. He didn't take it in very
good part and went off in tragic tones. "You cahnt shut me
up. . . . I'll say my say till I die (As he said them the words
all rhymed). That's wot I'm 'ere for, to say my say till I die."

"I say," says the man next to you in a low voice, "that
last phrase was strangely reminiscent of Winston. I always
felt Churchill had a classless voice . . . I'll say my say till I
die . . . " The bus has come to a stop. As you are climbing
down the man shouts after you cheerily, "Well, that's England for you."

YOUNG MAN'S VOICE (*as the lights go on in the hall*): In a
time of emergency every society has to be run socialisticly
because that's the most efficient way to do it. No room for
fat cats or fat profits . . . That means there's much more give
and take, class lines disappear, everybody's happier all
around . . . Why isn't that what we want? It seems to me,
mister, that you've proved exactly the opposite of what you
set out to prove.

MR. LECTURER (*sits down at his desk to wipe his glasses*):
Maybe we'd better introduce ourselves.

YOUNG MAN (*hopping to his feet*): Sure, my name is Jones,
Eddy Jones. I'm educational director for a retail workers'
union, a labor skate in other words.

THE ELDERLY LADY (*bobs and smiles*): Miss Smithers, a
retired schoolteacher.

THE YOUNG WOMAN (*half rising and bowing to the right
and to the left*): Mrs. Ethel Edwards and the mother of twins,
a career woman, divorced . . . It's for the boys' sakes. I want
a society that doesn't have to have a war every twenty years
to keep out of bankruptcy.

A MIDDLEAGED MAN (*gets up*): I haven't said anything yet but I'm planning to. I'm a manufacturer, retired, forcibly retired by Mr. Jones and his friends because I refused to let other people tell me how to run my own business. My name is Fred Rufus.

MISS SMITHERS: Don't you think we'd better listen and stop doing all the talking?

MR. LECTURER (*speaks up all of a sudden*): Quite the contrary ma'am. Discussion from the floor is just what we want . . . But before we say goodnight I should like to ask Mr. Jones what he meant by his statement a moment ago . . . I'm not trying to prove anything . . . not yet.

EDDY JONES: I can tell by your tone of voice you're on the capitalist side . . . They wouldn't let you appear on this program if you weren't.

MR. LECTURER: My dear young man, there just isn't time this evening to explain to you how wrong you are. That doesn't mean I'm on the socialist side either. (*He pulls out his watch and gives a low groan when he looks at it.*) Some of us have suburban trains to catch . . .

(MR. LECTURER *makes a lame little bow. A few people applaud but most of them are too busy reaching for their hats and coats. Ramming his notes into his briefcase* MR. LECTURER *hurries out.*)

SECOND LECTURE

Great Britain: Ordeal By Government

MR. LECTURER (*comes out on the stage briskly. His manner is more confident than it was before. He even dares look around the audience searching for familiar faces. He smiles and nods in various directions*): Six years have passed . . . since last week. (*He pauses for a laugh. There's no response but a feeble giggle from a little girl in the gallery.*) Britain and the United States after showing themselves by their conduct of the war far from the decadent democracies their enemies liked to call them, have been trapped by their ally the Great Stalin into a peace, as disastrous for the victors as it is disastrous for the miserable peoples of Eastern Europe who were turned over by the millions to the imperial purposes of a Kremlin régime which honored neither faith nor charity nor pity, nor practiced any of the humane palliatives which alone make life in society tolerable for man.

Apart from the disaster of the peace, for the United States World War II turned out a prosperous war, the sort of war the Napoleonic Wars had been for England in the early nineteenth century, but for Great Britain it meant calamity. The coming of peace was the reckoning. The empire was lost. Fortyeight million people geared by habit and tradition to the processing and the consumption of the tribute of that vast system of dependencies on which the sun never set had to be found a livelihood. The tories who represented the empire ruling class had learned very little during the turmoil of the war. They had nothing to suggest. It was inevitable that the Labor Party, which had a firm organization based on the bureaucracy of the trade unions, should come to power. Theirs was the only plan. Their plan was inspired by the humanitarian socialism of the late nineteenth century, a body of precepts which had grown up during the long afternoon of Victoria's reign when society was permeated by a sense of wellbeing which emboldened even thoughtful men to build every social theory on the dogma of the inevitability of progress. Never did wellintentioned people put their plans for human betterment into effect under more difficult circumstances. (*This time he's found the buzzer on the corner of the table. He smiles as the lights dim obediently. There's a cosy buzzing from the projector.*)

CAPTION: *The Gradual Revolution*

At London Airport we walk off the plane into the middle of an endless warm midsummer afternoon. After the motors' long vibration the dense air is startlingly quiet. In the distance the shadows are soft under the softgreen trees. A few rooks fly lazily, far away. Everything has a distant holiday air. Outside the terminal building the welltilled flowerbeds are on fire with snapdragons sprouting spikes of red and lemonyellow and garnet and maroon much taller and finer than we could grow them at home. They smell of honey. "Yes they are fine sir," admits the uniformed man at the gate with a pleased and deprecatory smile. "It's the fine summer weather."

We drive sleepily into London along broad thoroughfares where to eyes fresh from New York the traffic seems sparse and Sunday-like. On the greensward of Hyde Park under great trees that seem to bulge with the weight of their watery green, men and women sprawl barearmed. As far as you can see motionless groups of recumbent figures spread over the glaucous grass.

The great houses on Park Lane where the wealthy and fashionable flourished in Edwardian days stare out with blank windows. Their owners have moved away for longer than the holidays. At first glance the Dorchester Hotel has the old look of quiet ostentation and expense, but except for a sprinkling of anxiousfaced sleek East Indians and their childlike women in silk tanagra costumes, the people in the lobby look shabby and frayed. Gone are the uniforms and the swagger of wartime. Gone are the wellheeled gentry with their look of having just come in from the huntingfield or the paddock with assurance in the very knot of their Ascot ties that their sight drafts would be honored by the banker. Gone are the horsefaced gentlewomen in tiaras. Instead you see officials with sallow countenances blank from sitting out too many conferences, or the shark and remora shapes of fly-by-night financial operators who skim a rich living off calamity, the buzzard features of the scavengers of sick currencies.

Out in the streets again we look down from a bus on gray uncrowded streets of tidied ruin. London is no longer the mart and nerve center of the luxuries and miseries of an empire, no longer the tense magnificent fortress where every airraid warden stood like Horatius at the bridge. The glint of power has gone off the windows of Bond Street. Through the unwashed panes of Piccadilly clubs here and there the mustached face of an elderly Indian colonel stares out at emptiness. The theatres round Leicester Square have taken on a dim provincial air. In the bookshops there's nothing to be had. "England's dead, quite dead, quite," the young man in the bookshop on Charing Cross Road whispers in my ear in fluty Oxonian tones. "We're the lost island of the Atlantic, sunk in everlasting ennui, the Scandinavian ennui."

Down in the City past Victoria smug on Temple Bar and the gutted Temple and the roofless churches of the Strand, there's a smell of burning left in the air from the great fire. Giant fireweed grows out of the heaps of broken stone among the bared foundations of the ancient hilltown round miraculously intact St. Paul's. Fireweed is new in Britain. In America we are used to its magenta stalks sprouting up out of the charred loam wherever a forest fire has passed. In Wales they say it now grows round abandoned mines and people call it Miners' Blood. In midsummer London the air is thick with the small silky seeds of fireweed drifting through disfigured streets.

In Westminster the red steel framework of the new House of Commons is almost complete. From the moment you step into the lobby you can feel the rigid structure of the Labor Party machine firmly in control of the stationary engines of bureaucratic government. The Labor election was a revolution but a very partial one. A few representatives of business and of the ancient castes and privileges were pushed off one end of the bench of the national coalition and a few trade union officials and agitating intellectuals climbed on the other end, and the workingman was in the saddle by proxy. The government benches are full of people who know better what's good for the workingman than the workingman does himself. The Commons still meet in the Lords' Chamber. In spite of a certain amount of argument in the accustomed style of the great debating club, as measure after measure comes up to curtail the already frail liberties of the individual Briton, the machine moves smoothly. After one of Bevin's canny foursquare statements in rebuttal has dug the ground out from under the gentle remonstrances of the Opposition, the guillotine falls and the bell rings for a division, calling the members from their whale steak and their Pym's Number One in their pleasant diningroom by the Thames, and Labor representatives of all groups troop obediently through the proper door. When the tellers come up the aisle bowing in unison three times like frog footmen to the Speaker the vote is always Labor by a hundred and fifty votes or more.

At the corner of Hyde Park beside the Marble Arch under the immense lavender twilight of eleven o'clock on an English summer's night the popular debating academy, which has somewhat the relation to Parliament that the curb market in New York used to have to the Stock Exchange, still fills the heavy London air with oratory. There the Commies and the dissident Socialists have their pulpits. A skinny evangelist leads his group in singing:

> *Abide with me, fast falls the eventide,*
> *The darkness deepens . . .*

"Question time hasn't arrived yet," barks a Socialist shaking off the Communist hecklers. At a reading desk marked *Poetry* an illfed youngish student with a soft hat pulled down over his tortoiseshell glasses is reciting *The Hound of Heaven* and reciting it damned well. A tired little fat man climbs on a stool to defend private enterprise. The adherents of private enterprise have already joined the forlorn minorities. Patiently he explains to a hostile crowd that socialism is leading them to starvation, slavery and ruin.

"Not so farst, it's our government," roars a barebreasted navvy.

"The best government England's ever 'ad," echoes a hollowcheeked man in a peaked cap.

"I'm better off than I've ever been in my life," says a stocky fellow with a mat of blond hair like shredded wheat.

Beside me a young man in a frayed jacket shiny with grime and grease starts to blow his top. "Ave a 'eart," he shouts. "Ah've seen the starvin' kiddies run barefoot down the streets to beg a bit of bread. Ah've seen too much of that,

Ah 'ave. That's 'ow I grew up. Now there's the school lunch and five bob a week for every child." He turns to me and grins confidently. "Under a Labor government it's delight to get married."

FRED RUFUS (*from the audience*): Well a dollar a week wouldn't be much help in this country, but I suppose prices are lower over there.

MRS. EDWARDS: Why shouldn't the state support the children? It takes them off to the battlefield as fast as they get to be eighteen.

FRED RUFUS: That statement shows up the delusion of the welfare state. What the state gives you never catches up with what it takes away.

MR. LECTURER (*interrupting*): Now ladies and gentlemen I'm going to beg your indulgence for a few moments to get a little perspective on today's socialist England . . . I'm going to show some pictures of the eighteenth century England two of the libertarian founders of our government visited on their travels. The amusing thing is that they were shocked just as I was shocked a hundred and sixty years later by the lack of interest they found among English people in the struggle for personal liberty. They had dedicated their lives to liberty and they were full of reverence for English traditions of liberty. It shocked them that the English didn't seem interested. (*He presses his buzzer and an eighteenth century London doorway appears on the screen.*)

CAPTION: *An Eighteenth Century Sunday*

One day we find ourselves walking round Golden Square looking for the house where Thomas Jefferson had his lodgings during his stay in London in the spring of 1786.

Number 14 has disappeared but number 11 has a beautiful Adam doorway that must have been standing freshpainted and fashionable at the time. While we are looking at the delicately carved mouldings under the scaling green paint of the door a comfortablelooking middleaged woman opens it and obligingly invites us in to see the oval drawingroom which she explains is now a lawoffice. "A bomb fell in the back of the house but it didn't explode," she says briskly. "It makes you appreciate lovely things all the more, doesn't it, to know they are so fragile?"

At the corner as we turn away we catch sight of a pushcart full of Italian peaches moving along swiftly propelled by a sweating young man in a torn shirt. As the pushcart proceeds another man weighs out the peaches and sells them to people tagging along after, elbowing their way through the noontide crowd that packs the narrow pavement. Both men keep looking nervously over their shoulders as they go.

"Why won't they stop?" you ask.

"They're barrow boys, they carn't stop."

Then you notice that a tall cop in a tall blue helmet is sauntering along after them.

"But what's illegal about selling peaches?"

"Barrow boys 'aven't no license to set up a stall but there's no law against trundlin' a barrow through the streets," your informant considerately explains. "It's a cyse of regulytions," he adds in a tone of finality.

When Jefferson lived on Golden Square, most likely in a similar house as fastidiously decorated in the fashionable Pompeian style as the house we have just seen, he was Ambassador to France. He had crossed the Channel to talk over matters with his dear friend John Adams, who was our Ambassador to England. After months of tedious and fruitless conversations with the Portuguese Ambassador about a scheme they had to get the European nations to unite against the Barbary pirates, and a thorough snubbing at the Court of

St. James, the two Americans agreed to take a little restful jaunt round the country; so, early on the morning of the second of April Jefferson drove around to Grosvenor Square to pick up Adams and they set out amid the jingle of harness and the cracking of the postillion's whip. They drove over the cobbled streets of new elegant Mayfair and out through the rutted roads of Hyde Park and the rural lanes of Kensington and Hammersmith. Their first stop was to be at Chiswick where the showplace was the Earl of Burlington's famous reproduction of a Palladian villa. It was the passion for architecture and landscape gardening which Jefferson shared with the ruling gentry of England that impelled him to the trip. He carried Whately's recently printed *Modern Gardening* in his hand as a guide and undoubtedly read passages from it out loud to John Adams, who was going along more for the ride and for a sight of spring after the mud and soot of a city winter and for the pleasure of political and philosophical discussion with his Virginia friend.

As they jounced along in their rattling hired chaise, they tried with keen transatlantic eyes to penetrate every detail of the green countryside that was like home to them and yet not like home. On a fine summer Sunday a hundred and sixtyone years later we are following on their trail in a minute English automobile.

When Jefferson and Adams took their tour England was reaching the peak of empire as a seafaring and mercantile nation. The manufactories that were to dominate the next century were just beginning. The loss of the Thirteen Colonies was being made up for amply and fast by the wealth pumped out of the East India trade and profits on Jamaican sugar and rum and on the exchange of goods on the Board of Trade's own terms that was fast coming back to life between England and the American ports. Although the merchants and bankers were growing more powerful year by year, the great landed families of the Whig aristocracy still controlled preferment and place sufficiently to siphon a continuous stream of guineas out of government into their own strong-boxes. They spent it on their mansions and their parks and gardens. Brought up from boyhood on the literature of Imperial Rome and Periclean Greece the ruling English moved in a pomp of personal power and dignity that seems unbelievably Olympian to any massmoulded man of today. In every corner of England, in the great parks and hunting forests and farming estates they inherited from the feudal lords of the past, they were building themselves palaces in the imperial style they learned from Palladio's version of the work of the Roman architect Vitruvius, and these palaces they were surrounding with parks landscaped by the square mile according to the taste for the natural set on the continent by Claude Lorrain, Poussin and the painters of the late Renaissance. Their heads full of the Augustan verse their teachers at Eton and Charterhouse had made them learn by heart, and of Cicero's reconstruction in stately rhetoric of the senatorial republic, they governed the rustics and burghers of England by the right of birth and wealth; and imagined a background for themselves of Roman colonnades overlooking royal vistas where, between mighty oaks, the red deer ran shaking their clumsy antlered heads; and of grand lawns sweeping to the sedgy edges of lakes, where the gleam of a white swan or the reflection of a stucco temple accented the blurred sap greens of the island countryside. For all their treading down of the men and women whose humble work helped to produce their glory, their aristocratic pride in power was helping stamp on the mind of the English-speaking peoples a conviction of the potential majesty of man.

In those days the noble lords were so proud of the estates they had put so much thought and planning and money into that they were more than willing to have them shown to the less privileged traveller. Jefferson and Adams carried no letters of introduction. As upstart Americans they were barely recognized as gentlemen by English society.

At Chiswick it cost them four and six paid out to the Duke of Devonshire's servants to see the park. A century and a half later you can see what is left of it free. It is a public park now. The iron gates and palings that were such a feature of the English countryside were all broken up for scrap during the war, so landowners couldn't keep out trespassers if they wanted to.

After the racket of the crowding green busses and the lorries and the tall elephantlike trams of the thoroughfares out of London, Chiswick village looks quiet and yellowed and faded as an etching in the window of a secondhand store. Behind dooryards full of great fragrant roses a row of eighteenth century houses sinks into greenery and forgetfulness on low alluvial ground facing the puttycolored Thames. In a loop of the river a couple of barges, built of dark varnished wood, lie stranded on gleaming mud banks fringed with loosestrife and reeds. At the far end of the mall an old stone church sleeps in the green graveyard where Hogarth and Whistler are buried. Searching for Hogarth's summer cottage we find a tottering frame shell within the highly dilapidated confines of a brewery. It must be shut down because there is no smell of brewing.

"If you're looking for the pictures," says a busconductor who's waiting at the corner, speaking without any inflection of reproach in his voice, "they've been sent to America. Nothing left 'ere."

A grove of magnificent evergreens still shelters Chiswick House. The original design was distorted by additions soon after Jefferson saw the place and caught from it part of the notion that finally developed into his second plan for Monticello, but the pedimented core of the building, cracked and battered and boarded up as it is, still has beautiful balance and proportion. Temporary wooden fences cut at random across alleys of yew and box, down which you can still catch a glimpse of a carefully composed view of a balustraded bridge reflected in a green stream.

There's a litter of broken campchairs on the trampled lawn. A considerate child has rouged the cheeks of one of the Frenchified Regency sphinxes that guard the approach to the house. In the basement there's a squalidlooking municipal lunchroom marked Refreshments and the stench of public toilets. When we ask the caretaker to let us look inside, he says without looking up, "It's agynst the regulytions."

"Gave servants at Twickenham, Pope's garden 2/-" Jefferson next entered in his accountbook. Today an elderly nun with steelrimmed glasses shows us around gladly and gratis. She explains that the place is a Catholic school. She loves to show the garden and the grotto, she says and she seems to mean it. She shows the shells and the lumps of lava embedded in the plaster wall. "He was a great poet and people sent him things," she says.

In the grotto one statue was of St. James. "The pilgrim shell, that meant something to him." The other, some people said, was Dante's friend Beatrice but the sister thinks it was his sadness. She is Irish.

"Now don't be frightened now," she titters as she runs ahead through the tunnel under the road. We come up blinking in the garden. "Two sisters and an old gardener that's all we have to do the work," she says breathlessly indicating cabbages and sprouts and kale and lettuce and potatoes in flower with a wave of her hand. Beyond are berrybushes and appletrees. "During the war and now in the austerity we have to rely on our vegetables. We wouldn't eat without the garden," she says.

The lower walls of the house, which was rebuilt in Victorian days in a sort of Swiss châlet style, are still as they were in Pope's time. There are still traces of the sloping paved landing you see in the old engravings of the place. The green river in the sunny morning is full of shells and punts. A packed fat cheerful looking excursion boat passes headed upstream.

When we drive into Hampton Court the river is even more crowded. The excursion boat is just pulling in. The green bank opposite is strewn with swimmers. In the gardens people walk quietly. In the long rectangular pond that opens out from Wren's garlanded façade a man in shorts stands up to his knees in water, fishing. Children play quietly along the edge and point out the fluffy gray cygnets. Tonguetied courting couples sit on the benches and stare and stare down the long avenues.

The English have few pleasures now. With quiet passion they enjoy their countryside and the parks and gardens out of the royal and aristocratic past, the flowers so abundantly blooming, the meadows bounded by the soft trees of the island landscape, the play of the sun on their lean and sallow carcasses.

After Hampton Court we strike out into the country. We pass cyclists in shoals, whole families out for the day with babies and pet dogs strapped into the baskets on the handlebars. Men and women sit out in the sun on benches and doorsteps in front of the pubs drinking their thin ale with expressionless faces. In this rich Thames valley the trees are magnificent. You could stop for an hour to study the spread of the small-leaved English oaks, the majesty of the beeches.

At Esher Place where Whately had admired a grove of trees Jefferson paid out six shillings. We find the park turned into a modern residential development in the American style. The windows of the gray seventeenth century hall are full of the peaked faces of little girls. While we are admiring the balance of a doorway in the wing a flustered woman comes out to ask us what we want. She looks at us with a cold suspicious eye. Have we permission to visit the orphan asylum? No thanks; already we are on our way.

At Payn's Hill which Whately mentions as an example of a magnificent park, the servants got seven shillings out of Jefferson and Adams. We find the estate still intact but there are signs on the gateposts: *Auction sale this day of antique furniture and furnishings.* The glass is broken in the greenhouses. The fountains are dry. The gardens are overgrown with weeds. Nobody has cut the dead limbs out of the great trees or filled up the slit trenches an antiaircraft battery left there during the war, but from the terrace of the vacant Regency house you can trace the design according to which the trees were planted to emphasize the steepness of hills, or to outline a little valley, here screening, there opening a vista through to the reflection in a mahogany pool of the old stone arches where the road crosses the stream.

At Wotton-under-Wood, which John Adams described as great and elegant though neglected, we ask a man living in a wing of the great house whether he can let us walk in the park. He passes the buck by sending us to find the postmaster. The postmaster, a Mr. Phipps, is even more careful not to commit himself. "If you meet the bailiff," he says, "maybe he'll take you up for trespassing but I don't imagine he will. You may tell him you've seen me and that I couldn't give you any authority but that I didn't think you'd be doing any harm."

You have the feeling that nobody has walked in that park in a hundred years. Wild ducks fly up from Wotton water. Loudvoiced doves coo in the elms of the avenue. Frogs croak in the little temples that frame the clearing up the hill towards the shuttered mansion. Magpies squawk indignantly. Clouds of black squashy flies whine about our heads. 'Great and elegant though neglected.'

We follow Jefferson and Adams through lanes that wind between hawthorn hedges, among hillsides misted with palest green blue of ripening oats. Occasionally after passing a sign *danger* we drive for a mile or two through ranks of corrugated huts full of ammunition that hasn't been moved since the last German plane was shot down over Britain.

We turn into the main road at a village built of small squared stones. We pass airstrips and great dumps of war machinery under camouflaged canvas covers. We pass fire stations with red buckets and longhandled paddles to beat out the flames from incendiary bombs, a used-car lot, and an old lady speeding along in a motorized wheel chair, imperturbable as Britannia in a streaming veil, and we are in Oxford. Jefferson and Adams visited the colleges there but had nothing to report about them.

"Edgehill and Worcester," wrote John Adams, "were curious and interesting to us as scenes where freemen had fought for their rights. The people in the neighborhood appeared so ignorant and careless at Worcester that I was provoked and asked, 'And do Englishmen so soon forget the ground where liberty was fought for? Tell your neighbors and your children that this is holy ground.'" . . . Through sheets of rain we look out over the battlefield of Edgehill from the small castle on top of the sharp steep wooded rise that gives the place its name. On the sloping meadows where Cromwell's psalmsinging footsoldiers beat back the Royalist charge are scattered the small boxlike buildings of a munitions factory left over from the latest war. In the cottage garden below us a gangling boy is tying up with string the climbing nasturtiums the rain is beating down. It is raining too hard to try to talk to him.

Further on at Worcester, to be sure, the beadle in the

cathedral seems to remember that battle. "It was outside those walls. The cathedral towered above it," he says in tones of ecclesiastical pomp.

Looking after the cars in the parkinglot outside the cathedral we find a tall broadshouldered bony man with a west country accent. As soon as he notices that we are Americans he starts off as if in answer to John Adams' question. Liberty is lost in England, he says. Here he is out of the army after fortyfive years' service . . . Gib, Malta, the Punjab, Singapore, he'd seen them all, every blarsted place on earth and now that he is out with a bit of a pension and a bit of money saved up he and the old woman might have started a bit of a business and spent an agreeable old age but it was no go. What did they get? Regulations. There was no liberty in a land ruined with regulations. Rights? What rights did an Englishman have if he couldn't start up a bit of a business to better himself by? He and his old woman didn't even have a roof over their heads they could call their own. "It's a ruined country I've come 'ome to . . . Their regulations'll 'ave us all in our graves before our time."

Driving back to town through the long evening we talk with the young man who is driving the car about Robin Hood and about the Howard Pyle world of our childhood, the yeomanry and the beef-fed men-at-arms of Chaucer's day with their longbows and their crossbows; and of the knights and their ladies we'd seen lying in their stone robes on the early tombs in Worcester Cathedral; and of the muttoneating eighteenth century England of haughty rich and sodden poor both jostled by the rising middle class; and of the suburban England of Victoria's reign when all traditions and snobberies seemed embalmed in an endless imperial afternoon; and of Wells and the socialist aspiration towards a better world for all, which had grown out of the nonconformist conscience and the Commonwealth and the glorious Revolution.

Suddenly the young man driving the car changes the subject hard: "It's not the austerity," he says. "We could put up with anything if we felt we were getting anywhere. But they (he meant the government, everybody speaks of the government as 'they') can't seem to start anything, all *they* can do is keep anybody else from starting anything. A young fellow gets out of the services. He's sick of being ordered around. He wants to do something on his own. Now you can't even get married because you can't get a flat or a house. The small businesses that pulled through the war are having a hard time making a go of it. There are plenty of jobs but there's no future to them. The expense and the regulations make it impossible to start anything new on your own, unless you're a spiv and toady around and keep your notes in your pocket. There's no opportunity for a young man. If you try to go to the colonies you're blocked. Every passage to South Africa is taken for eighteen months. If all you want to do is loaf it doesn't matter but if you want to make your way in the world a little, every direction you turn it's a blank wall . . . I used to be so proud of being British, but now I don't know."

We've passed Windsor. The castle's gray battlements still hover above the trees behind us. We are driving slowly, stopping and starting in a double rank of cars, the Sunday afternoon traffic jam, gradually making our way across a green meadow littered with resting cyclists and parties sitting on the grass eating picnic suppers on the sunny side of parked cars. The Thames is dense with punts and canoes. Bathers are still stretching pale arms in the last ruddy sunlight. What is this place? I ask the driver. He thinks for a moment and answers: "Runnymede."

MISS SMITHERS (*in great excitement*): Runnymede was the little island in the Thames where the barons made King John sign Magna Carta.

MR. LECTURER: Exactly.

FRED RUFUS: Today where would you say the battlefields were where free men fought for their rights?

EDDY JONES: I'd say on the picket line in any major strike.

FRED RUFUS: In our time we've done more fighting than thinking about freedom.

MRS. EDWARDS: When we bowled over the Kaiser we thought we were fighting for freedom. We thought the same thing when we slapped down Hitler, and Hirohito and Mussolini. After each war for freedom there seems to be less of it left in the world than there was before . . .

EDDY JONES: War isn't the way to do it. In the modern world the fight for freedom takes on economic forms. Trade unions fight for the rights of the workingman, cooperatives for the consumer. We live in an age of corporate struggle.

FRED RUFUS: How much liberty do you think Jefferson and Adams would have found in the modern world?

EDDY JONES: Damn little, but their theories applied only to an agrarian society. Today Marx and Lenin's theories apply.

MR. LECTURER: That is exactly what I am prepared to deny. In my opinion the political discoveries upon which the government of the United States and its constitution were founded apply to men living under any economic system. The struggle for power is more fundamental than any organization of it. Jefferson and Adams and their friends went back to the fundamentals of human behavior. The only way to protect the liberties of the governed is to limit the power of the governors. The great weakness of Marx is that he didn't understand political behavior . . . If you allow me a small digression.

EDDY JONES: (*throws up his hands*): What, another!

(*A titter runs through the audience.*)

MR. LECTURER: This is up your alley, Mr. Jones. The part

of the Marxian theory which I consider still valid is the part that deals with automatic class behavior . . . Now I want to show the development of the new ruling class.

CAPTION: *They Guide Their Boys Past the Pithead*

We lost our way several times driving out from Birmingham in search of the regional office of the National Coal Board so that when at last we found a pair of stately gates and entered a winding drive among one of those royally planned plantations of great trees we never got tired of admiring we were already late. I couldn't help slowing down passing signs on the lawns that spelled out in fresh black and white paint: Trespassers will be prosecuted. We slowly rounded a curve and came out on the breathtaking façade of Hinley Hall which up to the time the coal board bought it for fortyfive thousand pounds was the very princely seat of the Earls of Dudley. By the time we reached the entrance of the offices it was already twelve and the last officeworker was hurrying out his briefcase in his hand. An American car resplendently new was sweeping the last officials lunchward from the door. Walking back disappointed to our car I noticed that the windows in the main wing of the hall were blackened gaps. Inside was that calcined emptiness of ruin you get so accustomed to seeing in British cities that you end by hardly noticing it.

"What a hell of a thing for the Germans to bomb an isolated building like that," I said to the man who had shown us the way.

"It wasn't the Germans," he answered, a look of cynical glee overspreading his face. "It was the coal board. It just burned last Easter. Illdisposed people will say that they were burning so much coke in the heating system that the flues couldn't stand it. Anyway it burned. It was one of the handsomest eighteenth century interiors in England."

Back in Birmingham I met a man who had been a spokesman for the coal owners. He too had a briefcase. Although nationalization had won he was still fighting the battle against it. "What we mustn't forget," he said coaxingly as he pulled out a dense sheaf of figures, "is that productivity per man has been going down steadily since 1942. That's due to several factors. Now the miners won't put their backs into it because there's nothing to do with the extra money . . . When the women drive them into the pits it'll be because they need the money to buy food for their children . . . But now there's no penalty on slack work and no prize for effort . . . If a man works an extra day the government takes half of his paypacket for taxes and his mates call him a blackleg for his pains."

"How do they like not being allowed to change their employment? Isn't that a little like slavery?"

"A miner doesn't want any other life. He wants to work in the mines but he's been so mollycoddled by these socialist reformers he's just like a crybaby . . . all he can think of is how sorry he is for himself. Mind you I'm not talking against the miners. They're as fine a body of men as there is in Britain. But the truth is that like everybody else the miner'll only work when he has to . . ."

One of the leaders of the miners in the North, a broad-shouldered man with bright eyes and bat ears, like Ernest Bevin of the new race of thickset foursquare shorties who have come out of the working class to govern England, in a moment of candor, told me very much the same thing. He added in explanation that in his region at least there hadn't been a strike in ten years "to take the bad out of the men." After a strike managers and miners used to settle down to work. They'd all be out of pocket and they'd have to. "Of course," he added soothingly resuming his platform manner, "now that they understand the crisis they're really going to dig coal. I have every faith in the men."

We picked our friend up at the miners' hall in an ancient town in the North. He was a little slenderer and taller than the general run of miners, a grayeyed man with a thoughtful look about him. He was dressed in the ordinary clothes of an officeworker but from his sallow skin and the coaldust under his broken nails you could tell that he wasn't long out of the pit. First he told us the names of the leaders whose four statues stood in the sunlight against the shrubbery in the spacious courtyard in front of the building. Pointing out the turnings to take as we drove out from the huddled mediaeval hilltown dominated by the great towers of its Norman cathedral and the leafy battlements of its castle our friend, who was thoroughly up on the history of the place, talked of the border raids of the middle ages and the political position of the bishopric of Durham. "When anybody wants anything historical," he said smiling, "they come to me."

We left the cosy ancient houses of the town and entered a region of scarred hills and tipples and conical dumps. We drove through several colliery villages. They seemed to average a little better than ours, much better than our worst, not quite so good as our best, but on the whole as places to live the British colliery villages would show up favorably I think beside our miners' towns round Pittsburgh.

Beside a row of gray identical dwellings we stopped opposite the yellowbrick pithead baths. Our friend took us to see the wives of some cronies with whom we had scraps of conversation about wages and rations and the reason why so many men were absent from the pits . . . holidays . . . football . . . after war stagnation. A man working on the face made around eight pounds ten shillings a week and a surface worker about half of that, beside his coal and his house. The food for a family cost between two and three pounds, said the women. The men were shy about talking I could see. After all my friend was a sort of public relations man for the union and they waited for him to speak for them. In the recreation hall, built in the days of the owners, a stocky old man did break out about Bevin's boys as he called them. He said they had been a flat failure. What did he think of sending a man to jail because he wouldn't work in the mines? "You can force a man into a pit," he said with a laugh, "but you can't make him work."

"This recreation hall and the pit," said my friend, "is where the miner spends his life. Here," he pointed to the billiard room, "is where he comes in as a lad and learns to play a bit of billiards, and here," he pointed into the other room where old men sat smoking round tables, "he chats away his old age."

I asked if there had been any change in management and methods since nationalization. "No," he said, "the same men sit in the office at the pithead . . . The only difference is the National Coal Board has taken the place of the owners. Of course there'll be changes. There are great plans . . . The man you talked to this morning now, he wants the engineers to find a way to increase our workings under the sea. We've only nicked the edges of the great field under the North Sea. But that will need a new system of work, new shafts. Much of our coal is four or five thousand feet deep. It's not only how much you can take off the face it's how much you can get up the shaft. The owners said it would cost three hundred million pounds to reorganize the coal fields. Our coal board hasn't published its figures yet . . . He's a man of brains you talked to this morning. He's not often here any more. I'm afraid he's going beyond us . . . on up." He cast up his eyes as if watching a balloon rise.

Next he took us to see a widow who had lost her husband and a son in a mining accident. Another son had lost an eye and a third had had his foot crushed. She was a red-headed woman who sat with heavy eyes on the edge of a bed in a close shuttered room. She echoed our friend's encomiums on how much the union had done for her in the droning tone of a formal dirge. Miners everywhere are great for emotional oratory. Leaving her we drove silent and with shaky lips over a green bald hill into the next village. That was where our friend lived himself. He asked us to stay to tea.

His house is typical of the better miners' houses we have been seeing. There is a little parlor in front and a kitchen-diningroom with a great range heated by an open coal fire that occupies one whole wall in back, and sleepingrooms upstairs. He owns his house. Before the war there was quite a movement among miners to own their own houses, he tells us, through building and loan societies, but now nothing new is being built. Of course the government now owned the colliery houses. A man who owned his own house received a small rent allowance on top of his pay.

In the diningroom we surprised his wife helping an old woman to wash some kitchen things in a dishpan on the table. She hurries the pan out of sight. She is a remarkably handsome dignified woman with light auburn hair. We speak of the good looks and the air of breeding of these North country miners' wives and daughters; and our friend, obviously pleased, tells us a story of a great Scotch lord who took refuge among the miners at the time of the last Stuart rising in the mid-eighteenth century and who, as he had never been able to get his attainder repealed, settled there and became a miner. His descendants are miners to this day. And maybe he wasn't the only one.

While we wait for the kettle to boil he shows us the family photographs. He comes of a long line of fighting miners and union leaders. His father and grandfather were in the labor movement. An uncle was a liberal M.P. There are shelves

along one wall of the parlor packed with a really firstrate
library of books on the miners' hundred year struggle, first
for a decent living and then for unionization and political
power. It's obvious that he reads his books, reads them
with discernment and intelligence. He talks a little too
fluently, as miners are apt to, but well. When I tell him I'd
been wanting to meet a young man who really wanted to go
into mining, he reminds me of the bright young redhead
with glasses he had introduced me to earlier in the afternoon. That one has just received a scholarship to study
mining engineering. But that isn't going to work with pick
and shovel, is it? He shows us pictures of his own sons. One
boy was a flyer and was lost with a bomber over Germany.
The other was going to college. "Yes," he says a little sadly.
"We can't help it. The father guides the sons past the pithead."

When we sat down to table they tell us rather bashfully
that next week they are going to receive the freedom of a
city in the south of England as representatives of the miners
— the first time in history that a workingman has received
this honor, just because he was a workingman. "That's
usually reserved for ambassadors and earls," he says. "Of
course it's not us that's being honored. It's the miners."

We ate their tea with them. They didn't seem to have any
more to eat than any of the other people of various classes
and conditions up and down the country who had so hospitably shared their meagre supplies with us. It was a pleasure spending the afternoon with them. Both the man and
his wife gave you an impression of steadiness and competence
and quiet dignity you find so often in England once you get
away from the weedy intellectuals with their forced university accents. After tea the wife brought out a long package wrapped in brown paper. It contained a truncheon with
the arms and crown of George IV on it that our friend's

greatgrandfather had wrenched out of the fist of a constable and brought home during the Chartist riots in the early nineteenth century. "It's been a long fight," he said, laying the truncheon before us reverently, "but now we miners feel we've attained freedom at last."

EDDY JONES: That's what I was saying. The Edgehills of today are fought by the labor unions. The sitdown strikes in Akron and Detroit were your modern Edgehill and Worcester.

FRED RUFUS: Does anybody remember how Cromwell's régime ended up?

MISS SMITHERS: As a hereditary dictatorship followed by a restoration of the Stuarts.

MR. LECTURER: Well, the Commonwealth failed for a number of reasons. Dictatorship was one of them. In talking to that nice family of coalminers I got the feeling that I was talking to members of a new ruling class. The labor government offers great opportunity to the limited élite of the working class and the trade unions, but the danger to the future of Britain lies in the fact that it doesn't offer freedom and opportunity to a large enough segment of the whole population. We may see it go the way of the Commonwealth.

MISS SMITHERS: *(in an accusing shriek)*: How can you say the Commonwealth failed? How about Roger Williams?

MR. LECTURER: I think we can say that while the Commonwealth failed in England it succeeded in America. The New England town and even in a sense the organization of the Virginia counties by the gentry and yeomanry were offshoots of the same political current. The labor revolution in England may have succeeded in the same sense. Whatever happens there the lot of the man who works with his hands probably won't ever again be worse than the lot of the man who works with his head. The question is whether any man's life will be worth living in the kind of society we seem to be headed for. After all Britain like the United States is traditionally a middleclass country. The middleclass majority of the population is caught in a dead end. Let's see what they had to say about it in the Midlands.

CAPTION: *Nine Shillings in the Pound*

The Manchester street was black as a railroad tunnel. Over head the slanting sunlight gave a little glisten to sooty walls and cut out as with scissors the scorched window openings of great office and warehouse buildings left hollow shells by the bombing. The number I was looking for turned out to be on one of the intact buildings, a small brick building carbonized and cavernous as an old fireplace. The ground floor was taken up by a dark ironbound entry for merchandise into which two elderly men with tallowy arms and a scraggle of sandy mustache over yellow teeth were heaving a big packing case. Beneath them gritty stone steps led down to a glass basement door where traces remained of gilt lettering: Import-Export . . . Office and the firm's name.

Inside I had a glimpse of a low room lined with ledgers full of old men on ancient high stools against tall desks squinting at papers in the dim light. Reluctantly I was admitted and ushered down a long corridor into an office stuffed with the yellowed cardboard folders of a hundred years' transactions where a broad elephantlike man, with small sheep's eyes twinkling out from behind a huge warty nose, dominated a littered desk. In the buttonhole of his checked suit he wore a red carnation.

A couple of tall blond men danced attendance. While he sorted a pile of letters and telegrams that rose to his chin he carried on with them a conversation in a genial roaring tone that was punctuated by the sudden savage sorties of a cornered warthog. "Look out," he trumpeted when I was pointed out to him as something to do with the American press. "There's a Yank in the house . . . Well you can tell 'em one thing over there. You'll never get it back." The pile of papers rustled in front of him as he bellowed out a laugh . . . "The loan, of course, you'll never get it back. Exports? Where's any exports?"

As he parried my questions the embattled old elephant carried on a conversation with the other men about a race meeting he was going to preside over that afternoon. Meanwhile he read through his letters and telegrams half aloud.

"A Yank in the house," he'd snort and glare at me grinning with a sort of genial hostility. Then he would go back to his communications from Karachi and Cape Town and Rio and Montevideo . . . "No can't get that in New York better try B.A. . . . No go . . . Give us 'arf a chance we're only 'ooman." Now and then he'd whisper directions to a grizzled clerk who was reverently holding out a basket to receive the letters as he conned them over.

Then he'd remember the American press and wave a thick forefinger and roar, "So you think you've got us down, do you? We're not out of the runnin' yet . . . give us 'arf a chance. Export business? There isn't any export business. There isn't anythin' to export. The boogers won't work . . . They want to ruin the middle clarss . . . I'm middle clarss. The middle clarss is the backbone of England . . . 'Ow's the export business? I don't know . . ." The small shrewd eyes twinkled humorously on either side of the great red angry proboscis. "If I knew I wouldn't tell you."

A shaking jellylaugh surged up through the big bellied frame. Not wanting to be responsible for a case of apoplexy or to keep him from his race meeting the representative of

the American press said good day and retired down the
cluttered corridor. Muffled by the files and antique ledgers
the trumpeting of the cornered middle class followed after.
"You won't get your money back."

In Birmingham Mr. X and Mr. Y a pair of big bulging
sandyhaired blue-eyed potatofaced partners who produced
kitchen utensils in a cramped shop on a back street were
more cordial. They sat opposite each other at a table in the
window of a tiny office that shook with the vibration of the
electric motor that ran the machines in the shop behind.
They were working class themselves they explained, they'd
started life as toolmakers and twentytwo years ago had gone
into business for themselves.

"Suppose you were young fellows coming out of the service now. Could you do the same thing?"

"I'll let my colleague answer that," said Mr. X.

"Couldn't be done," Mr. Y said emphatically. "You'd be
licked before you started by the regulations and where would
you get the capital when taxes take all your savings? It
would cost five times what it did prewar. And 'ow could you
get the materials when the quotas are based on what a firm
used in 1938?"

During the war — his face and his colleague's lit up when
they told about it as if they were talking of the good old
days — they made snaps and catches for ammunition boxes.
They only lost three days when they couldn't get in the plant
because the street was roped off for a time bomb. They
always paid over the union rate. No it wasn't a union shop,
no need to be, they had no trouble with unions. The trouble
was different. "The boogers won't work . . . No use givin'
'em the sack. The workers 'ave the whip hand an' if a man
walks out at a quarter to twelve it's no use givin' him the
sack because the next one'll be just as bad. They'll be no

good till we get ten percent unemployment . . . In the big
companies the shopstewards pick out the men to be sacked
. . . a bloody bunch of commissars they's gettin' to be . . .
Workers 'ave got to realize that there's somethin' in life
other than the paypacket."

"One trouble," took up the other partner in a deep
rattling voice, "is the income tax. A man won't want to
make more'n five quid a week for fear of the nine shillin's
in the pound . . . " But they could handle labor, they both
agreed . . . they knew the men the men knew them; they
were labor themselves, . . . if it weren't for the regulations.
Every single object they used in manufacturing had to be
licensed by the Board of Trade. They had to have three
times the clerical staff to take care of letters back and forth.
It ran into money. They could only get twenty percent of
the steel they needed at that.

"Now some of our products 'ave to be packed in cardboard boxes," interrupted Mr. X.

"We 'ave to tell 'em three months a'ead 'ow many boxes
we need for the next quarter," shouted Mr. Y, "but we can't
tell 'ow many articles we can finish so we 'ave to order more
than we need an' the boxes 'ave to be stored an' that runs
into money for ware'ousin' . . . Some of our articles use little
wooden 'andles. Instead of ringin' up the firm wot makes
'em we 'ave to write to London for a license an' they don't
know wot we're talkin' about an' 'arf the time me colleague
or I 'ave to take the train an' go down there an' wot do we
find in the Board of Trade? Just a mere slip of a gal, a
young gal about twentyfive. She tells you wot you can 'ave
and what you carn't."

The noon whistle blew. The motor stopped. We found
ourselves yelling at each other in the silence that followed.
"Now if you'd walked through the shop ten minutes ago you
wouldn't 'ave seen a man at his bench," said Mr. Y.

"An' then they send men around to exhort you to produce for export. We want to produce but they won't let us": Mr. X put in his word. "We used to send 'arf our product to Denmark. Why can't we swap it with the Danes for their butter an' cheese? We'd be willin' to swap for butter . . ."

Talk about food had made everybody hungry. It was lunch time. We walked out together through the silent deserted shop.

"There's a saying in business today," a ruddy young man with a cheerful competent manner who was a squadron commander in the R.A.F. and is now manager of a plant that manufactures leather goods takes up the story, "that it's not what you know it's who you know . . . It helps if your suppliers know you and have had long dealings with your firm because then they give you preference over somebody else when you get your permit . . . I'm trying to think of an example . . . We use rayon linings in our product. Here's what you have to do to get a yard of rayon. First you have to find a firm that has some to supply and that's willing to supply it to you. Second you've got to get your accountants to certify the yardage you used for the last quarter. There are four quarterly allocations and if you guess wrong what you'll need for the next quarter it's your hard luck. Third you send your export orders to the Board of Trade so that they can see you're not getting more than you're entitled to for those particular orders. Then if they haven't forgotten about you by that time they issue you a license to send to your supplier and he sends you the rayon if he hasn't let somebody else have it first. Then if you haven't lost your mind you go to work . . . " He lit a cigarette and looked up at the ceiling. "For seven months we've been corresponding with the Board of Trade over fiftyseven yards of silk and we don't know yet whether we can have it or not. All our output goes to America and is paid for in dollars . . . Maybe you're thinking that the troubles of one little firm turning out a fairly unimportant item aren't important but multiply these cases by thousands and you'll understand how British industry is being strangled."

"No," the sales manager is saying at this big new plant — white and airy and well lit in the American style — of a famous firm in the potteries, "I can't say that we have much to complain about in the controls . . . During the war our industry had to be telescoped — that meant that the small independents had to close — and as our plant was modern and highly efficient we were possibly somewhat favored. A rather good manufacturers' committee has been formed for the industry. That committee deals with the Board of Trade. As the only thing we import is a small amount of flint we have very little trouble. The independents don't bother us with their pricecutting. They are most of them out of business. The productivity of our labor has gone up, due again partly to increased plant efficiency. We were very lucky that the new plant was completed just before the war. We had planned a housing development for our employees, a new village, but we've had to be content with the few houses built before the war broke out . . . Wages are double and treble what they were prewar. The trade as a whole works by agreement. There hasn't been a strike in living memory. There's a very active works committee of employees and management . . . We can produce up to the limit of the fuel we are allotted . . . Perhaps I should say that we do notice a reluctance among our employees to run up their paypackets too high . . . After the three pound a week limit they have to pay an income tax of nine shillings in the pound you know, and that seems to worry working people more than it does, shall we say, whitecollar people who are used to having the taxcollector strip them to the bone. That's probably why our married women aren't coming back into industry."

"Furniture factory," an old man sitting in a doorway across from the cathedral in Worcester echoes my question impatiently. "There isn't any. I've gone out of business." He raises a cupped hand to his ear to hear my question. "I used to produce some very nice reproductions but under present conditions it's only the big shops with plenty of strings in London that can do business. For me to try to make furniture in my little shop would mean ruin. I find it more profitable to pick up a few antiques here and there and sell them to the London dealers. English furniture. *They* don't care for English furniture. *They'd* rather have rubbish made out of matchwood by the Czechs and the Finns than proper English furniture made by Englishmen."

In the little town in Staffordshire where the first iron bridge in England was built over the green gorge of the upper Severn we find, having stopped to ask the way in another antiqueshop, a young man and his wife who are waiting to emigrate to Canada. "Don't think we don't love our country," he is saying. "We're both out of the services; but we can't make a go of it here . . . It's only the big monopoly companies with friends at Whitehall who can survive taxes and regulations . . . During the war I was in the airforce. Then we had at least the excitement of battle and the feeling of being wanted, but now middle class people like us are a drug on the market . . . We are just trying to survive until we can get on the boat to Canada."

All of a scorching afternoon we have driven through the Black Country over a nomansland of high seared ridges and abandoned mine craters. The sootfilled air gives a rosy

glare to the unusually cloudless sky. We are passing farms.
Thatched roofs and hedges and stone walls are filmed over
with coaldust. The soot has blackened the fleece on the
sheep. Farmers getting in the harvest have the grimed look
of miners. The bodies of little boys swimming froglike in
old quarries look oddly pink and white in the black water.

Gradually the great Midland city closes in on us with
endless rows of identical twostory houses in stone and blackened stucco. Not a tree. Here you don't even see the carefully tilled dooryards full of prime flowers and vegetables
which are the last vestige of the crowded Briton's heritage in
his green and fertile island. Sooty housewalls rise sheer
from the black pavements. Only round the City Hall, after
driving for miles through a wilderness of stone and brick,
pitted and beaten down by war bombings, do you find an
oasis: a few trees and pots of geraniums and petunias in
green tubs to refresh the eyes of the aldermen.

It is a relief to find that we can get a room in a large and
wellknown hotel, and baths, and even towels, which the
management doles out suspiciously because in this time of
great scarcity of goods guests have taken to smuggling them
out in their baggage. It is too late for tea, that most desirable
of meals because you can have bread and margarine with it,
but the tall longtailed waiter in the lounge manages, with
the air of a magician producing something very special out
of a hat, to set out a couple of tiny drinks of Scotch. A local
newspaperman, a frail young man with a crinkle in his hair
and an almost inaudible way of talking, has stepped in for a
drink and, reassured by the elegance of the waiter and the
presence of the Scotch, I ask him to stay for dinner.

For a traveller in England meals in hotels gradually become a major ordeal. There do survive a few rural inns
where the host and his wife still have some standards and as
the result of really heroic struggles manage to put on a
skimpy but decent meal, but in the city hotels that are run

by great anonymous chains the waiters are perfectly willing to serve up food that is actually rotting on the plate. In fact you can't help forming the theory that the class war victors are giving themselves the crowning triumph of poisoning the last remnants of the dethroned bourgeoisie. If the miserable consumer protests about quantity or quality, the diningroom staff, with all the moral majesty of austerity to back them up, treats him like Oliver Twist when he asked for more. Only the pretense remains, the long tails on the black coats, the alien petulance of the half obsequious half insolent headwaiters, the multiplicity of knives and forks, the menus disguised in silly maître d'hôtel French. Truly the English are a people who care more for ritual than substance.

Tonight things seem a little more promising. There are pink lights and soft carpets and the unusual pleasure of napkins and the music of an orchestra. Around tables ornamented with wineglasses people are sitting in their best clothes with that expectant look of being out on the town for the evening. The soup turns out to be the same brown bituminous fluid to which we have become only too accustomed but, being very hungry on account of having missed lunch as well as tea we are able to put it down. Meanwhile we lean forward over the table to catch our young friend's blurred selfdeprecatory phrases as he most unobtrusively talks.

"We're not getting production because they haven't got a brain in their heads," he keeps repeating. "They haven't got a brain in their heads. Who? The working class. It's their government. In every speech they play up to them. Blame it all on spivs and drones or the profit motive, but how can you get them to work when they haven't got a brain in their heads? The politicians told them that socialism meant paradise and now they are quietly waiting for paradise. Their families are large. A family can do pretty well on five or six rations. They can pool them and get a joint once a week . . . At home there's only Mother and I and it would be hard if I didn't take most of my meals out. Then there's five shillings a week for each child and the prospect of a pension . . . A man doesn't have to work for his children, the state'll take care of them . . . If they do work there's the nine shillings in the pound tax. The only money a man can make that isn't taxed is gambling money. If he works an extra day he loses almost half of it but if he wins on the races or in a football pool he can keep it all. It's a system for penalizing production. When the government begins to tax gambling money and to get after the four hundred thousand girls that are employed by football pools we'll know they're serious. Austerity is for the people who want to do some productive work in the world. The loafers in the unions are doing better than ever. There are plenty of working people who'd like to give honest time for their money but they can't. They are frustrated by the rest of 'em who don't think of anything but football and football pools and a little beer in the evenings. They got everything they want and they can't see that we're all going on the rocks because they haven't got a brain in their heads."

Listening to him I had been cutting nervously into a piece of chicken that lay on my plate under a mantle of dark brown gravy which strangely resembled the soup we'd just swallowed. My attention was attracted by something that stirred uneasily under the gravy. With the tip of my knife I uncovered a maggot that was still quite alive and twitching. So that the others wouldn't see it I killed it and tucked it back under the quivering mass. Ceremoniously, with expressionless face the waiter removed my plate.

"I'm a conservative," our friend was saying modestly as if confessing to a painful but not infectious disease, but I don't want to emigrate. After all there's something in being an Englishman." For the first time his voice was clear with

conviction. "It's frustrating not to be able to marry because
you can't get a house . . . They are to be had but they cost
four or five thousand pounds which is more than I can afford
on my salary . . . It's frustrating to feel there's no future in
your job, but I'll stick it out. I wouldn't even want to move
away to London. The Midlands is my home . . . and there's
something . . . you can't explain . . . in the feeling of being
an Englishman."

MRS. EDWARDS: I can't believe they'd intentionally serve
up maggots in a firstclass hotel.

FRED RUFUS: Putting the bourgeoisie in their places, just
as he said. A nice little example of class war.

EDDY JONES: Well your friend in Manchester was sticking
it out. That proves he expected things to get better.

MR. LECTURER: It may have been lack of energy . . . One of
the grim facts we have discovered in the last few decades is
that people can adapt to almost anything. I suppose it's one
of the causes of the long survival of the human race. Men
can adapt to conditions that would kill off most of the animal
kingdom.

EDDY JONES: If things get too bad they revolt.

MR. LECTURER: Not necessarily. It looks as if one of the
discoveries of the Communist and Fascist tyrannies has been
that the number of people in any society with enough energy
and imagination to revolt is strictly limited. By killing them
off as they appear the rulers can reduce the multitude to
numb acceptance of any régime, of any ideas however monstrous.

MISS SMITHERS: Surely they aren't killing off the Opposition
in England.

MR. LECTURER: Of course not, but they are killing off the
chances of middleclass people for useful and active careers.
The only career open is government. That is a great shame
because the difficulties that lie ahead if we are to succeed in

adapting corporate industry to the uses of a good society are so great that we need to harness the energy and brains of all sectors of the population. In England the upper class has made a quicker adjustment. A sizeable section of the old ruling class has joined the new. I don't say that is a bad thing. It may be a very good thing. You will soon see on the screen a gentleman who is a very good example of that very process.

CAPTION: *The Future of Food*

On a warm summer afternoon we are waiting in the park for the Minister of Food. Word has just gone through the crowd that he will be late. People nod and whisper to one another that he has been detained in London by a cabinet meeting over the crisis. Heads shake. People scatter through the green hillside gardens of Aston Hall that crop out so unexpectedly in this slagscored wilderness of mine tipples and industrial plants, where rows and rows of twostory houses spread like a brick rash over the corroded country-side. Talking in low voices they stroll sedately in the sweltering late sunlight. Occasionally somebody glances up uneasily at the mounting clouds on the horizon. If the Minister doesn't come soon that rain will get here before him. More than half the crowd is made up of workingclass people, the rest come from the worn remnants of the middle class, with a surprisingly large sprinkling of countrymen off the farms who stand out from the townspeople, because they look so much taller and sturdier and better fed. Roaming among the quiet throngs we are on the lookout for members of the

Housewives' League who we had been told were planning a demonstration. The police at the gate had made them furl their banners but they were said to have hecklers lying in wait for the Minister. There are plenty of tiredeyed women who are certainly housewives, but their attitude is hardly truculent. While they wait they sit patiently on the grass reading papers or playing with their children and their dogs or else study, in the formal garden round the mansion, the brilliant beds of snapdragons and roses of a size and color that speak well for the skill of the city of Birmingham's municipal gardeners, or look questioningly up at the lichened statues out of Bulfinch's Mythology set against curved clipped hedges, or stare with a sort of impersonal curiosity into the long windows of the great hall where officials of some kind are holding a reception round a long table with a white cloth and refreshments, for other officials.

"Ask him about the pineapples . . . Why did they spend so much on pineapples?" a tall stooping grayhaired woman says to a chunky redfaced woman in an aggressive black hat.

"Ask him why they spend so much money buying nasty tinned things and artificial cheeses in America."

"Ask him what's in the national fat that makes it bubble so."

"Ask him why our children don't want to play any more."

At last a movement starts back toward a grassy open space where the microphones are set up on a modest wooden scaffold. From the platform a little plump politico, smooth as a plum, is hard at work laying on the class flattery to prepare the audience for the Minister. He beams with pleasure at beholding this gathering of the sturdy workingclass voters of Aston Park. He is confident that the intelligent workers of Aston Park whose mighty efforts in mine and foundry and factory and shop are helping Britain surmount the crisis will give their own Minister a friendly reception. He congratulates the intelligent voters of Aston Park . . . The crowd's attention has begun to waver. They are looking towards a long black limousine nosing its way slowly into the park. A tall man with a hooked nose and high cheekbones is walking with long strides from the car towards the platform. He is taller by a head than most of the men in the crowd.

The Minister of Food is a very competent political speaker. He hastens to put his opponents in the wrong by saying that the conservatives are the only people in England who are taking satisfaction over the government's difficulties and that they are the people who in their greed for privileges and profits would take advantage of the nation's misery if the working class should falter for a moment in their support of Labor. He spells out a sheet of statistics, with which he seems somewhat unfamiliar, to prove that many food items are more plentiful and cheaper than people imagine. "That's not meat," a voice cries. The Minister laughs genially with the crowd. Except when he speaks of the capitalist opposition he keeps strictly to the we're all good fellows together tone.

When he brings up the Cabinet's plans to meet the crisis his words sound oddly patronizing to American ears. The government is going to cut down on petrol for private cars and on travel allowances abroad. That won't affect the people of Aston Park, now will it? The inference is that as they can't have cars and trips to Europe they'll be mighty glad to hear that nobody else can. He outlines the government's scheme to grow groundnuts for oil in Africa. Perhaps the name is unfamiliar to the audience: peanuts or monkeynuts, some people call them. He refers scornfully to the ruckus illdisposed persons raised when he bought those tangerines last year. There's more than a memory of Lady Bountiful distributing gift baskets to the tenantry when he asks, "We were very glad to have those nice tangerines at Christmas time, now weren't we?"

The Minister is far from sparing in his use of the pronoun I.

The crowd is not enthusiastic but it's certainly not hostile. There's some spontaneous laughter and applause. He brings out a last lollipop. Vegetables have grown so plentiful he's going to allow anybody who wants to sell them, even without a greengrocer's license.

"Why can't we get any vegetables then?" mutters an elderly woman behind us.

"Why's so much corn spoiling in the barn? That's what I want to know," shouts a tall countryman behind us.

"What about the black market?"

It's question time. The crowd has spread widely up and down the hill. There are no microphones for the hecklers so all we hear are the Minister's answers very deftly class-angled in his even voice of a parliamentary debater.

"What are our real prospects for the future?" a woman's voice quavers. The clouds in the south have become a gray blur. With a rush the rain comes sweeping in a silvery curtain across the park. The Minister and a few embattled hecklers stand their ground but most of the crowd streams down the hill towards the double row of trolleycars waiting on the street below.

On our way to see where England's vegetables are grown we cross the green Avon at Evesham and enter a rich plain full of small truck gardens. Wherever there's a rise in the ground orchards have been planted. Cherries and plumtrees are weighed down with fruit. Here and there in the corner of an orchard wall you see an encampment of gypsies come to pick the fruit, dirty yellow babies and dusty women in full skirts sitting among brightcolored litter beside green and blue caravans and tethered scarred horses that show every rib. We turn into the warehouse of a farmers' cooperative.

Out through the window of the manager's office you can

see stubby middleaged men in suspenders hoeing between the rows of narrow strips of cabbage and cauliflower. "It's all rented land," says the manager. "Between here and the hedge there are six or seven different occupancies. A market gardener only rents what he thinks he can manage . . . Yes we have good crops. It's good land and well tilled. Since taxes are so high a man'll spend more on fertilizers than he used to. Mostly they buy and sell through the cooperative. A man with five acres'll turn over seven hundred and fifty pounds a year. That's slightly more than he'd make as a farm laborer working for hire but of course he works harder for himself."

Talking we stroll through the airy warehouse admiring the net bags of peas and stringbeans, the piles of gleaming cauliflowers, the green mountains of marrows. "It's too bad," the manager is saying in the tired voice of one weary of the subject, "that this is all surplus. In London cauliflowers are a shilling and here we are giving them away. They are plowing under their cabbage. One trouble was that this year we had some bright weather after a late spring and all the sowings were made at once, so everything ripened at once."

"Isn't that the sort of thing a planned economy was supposed to avoid? Hasn't the government any plans to get this stuff to people who need it?"

He doesn't answer my question. He merely shakes his head.

"We'll move our soft fruit," he says dreamily. "We'll do well with our plums."

Down on the densely green banks of the Severn below its confluence with the Avon we visit a dairy cooperative. There are ranks and ranks of brown and white Ayrshire cows with long slender horns. The manager is a tall studiouslooking man with dark eyes behind his glasses. He was brought up for the textile business, he says, but when he got out of the army he decided he'd better go into agriculture. "Agriculture in England has a future," he says. His voice is firm and emphatic.

Talking about lays and grasses we walk across the rich meadows that stretch to the river between hedges. The problem for the British dairy industry when the war began was to find a substitute for imported oilcake, he is saying. Down here in the Severn valley they had to feed from Christmas to April. They went in for high-protein grasses. Off a hundred acres of mowing land and pasture they got three cuttings which amounted to three hundred tons of dried grass a year. That meant the grass had to be artificially dried. Of course the dryer was expensive, labor and fuel. We walk past the bullpens and the calfpens in the ancient stone barnyards and look up into the lofts full of fragrant quickdried grass that still was green and come out into a huge shed where a gasoline engine throbs. Strawhaired young men stripped to the waist are forking freshcut grass onto a conveyor that carries it up into the dryer. The blower roars. The place is hot and full of a baked grassy smell. The young men work hard and silently sweat.

"They are P.O.W.'s," says the manager. "I don't know what we'd do without them. We could attract English labor to the farms if we were allowed to put up the housing for them. These are housed in camps by the government."

"Are they paid?"

"I believe they do get a little pocket money now," he mumbles. "But we pay the government regular wages for them." He stumbles over his words. It is obvious he doesn't want to dwell on the topic.

"Isn't that slavery?" I want to ask him, but already he is leading the way towards the whitewashed house where they cool and bottle the milk.

"We're not bothered much by controls and rations and that sort of thing," the manager continues his explanation.

"Agriculture is one industry that is improving in England. It's only the labor problem. When they send home the Germans maybe they'll let us have some displaced persons . . . "

We got a different picture from the next farm we visited, not a cooperative this time. We arrived at noon and after lunch we walked around the garden and looked out over the great tract of ripening wheat beyond the hawthorn hedge in back. "At least," I was saying, "agriculture doesn't suffer from controls."

"Who told you that?" the tall man asked sharply.

Then he told me a story. Before the war one of the showplaces of Wiltshire was a dairy farm that had a famous herd of Friesian cattle. The owner was reputed to be one of the best breeders in England. Now, under wartime regulations — and the tall man pointed out that since the Labor Party had put through Parliament what he called the dictatorship bill, these regulations would continue in effect indefinitely — the Ministry of Agriculture was empowered to take any farm from a tenant or owner who didn't comply with orders as to the growing of necessary food crops. No appeal to the courts was allowed. The Ministry's orders were carried out by local Agricultural Committees. Well, this breeder of dairy cattle was ordered to plant so much of his land in grain and potatoes that he couldn't grow enough forage to feed his herd through the winter and was forced to sell the greater part of it. Then the local committee came down on him for not producing enough milk and forced him to sell out altogether. One of the mysterious features of the case was that when the farm was sold it came into the hands of the man who was Minister of Agriculture at the time. A modern Naboth's vineyard. The Labor Government couldn't be blamed for this incident, which happened before Labor took power, but the fact that it could happen at all was a danger sign. There had been no appeal possible from the decision

of the local board. The owner's only recourse was to sue the
chairman of the local board for libel for saying that the farm
had been improperly cultivated. The owner had won his suit,
but that didn't get him back his farm, or his herd of Friesian
cattle. "Perhaps agriculture hasn't suffered so much," said
the tall man quietly, "but agriculturalists have."

"The lowland Scotch are the great farmers," people told
us all over England, so we stopped at Cockburnspath on the
road north to Edinburgh to make a call on a man who grew
small grains for seed. Hospitably he asked us to tea. By the
time we had finished tea the rain had stopped. We stepped
out into the freshwashed afternoon and looked down the line
of low stone farmbuildings that shone brown as chocolate
against the emerald hedges and the misty bluegreen fields of
oats that rolled down towards the ferny headland beyond the
road where cropping sheep moved against the leaden stretch
of the North Sea. Our host was a grizzled blue-eyed man
with a fresh tanned skin. He had broad shoulders and a light
footfall and he laughed a great deal, talking back over his
shoulder, as he led the way around his farmyards.

No, he was saying merrily, the controls didn't bother him
too much. Of course he had trouble getting parts for his
machinery. And nails. My word what a lot of forms you
had to fill out to get nails. You had to remember what you'd
done with the last ones . . . His land happened to be some of
the best grain producing land in Britain and the wheat and
oats he produced went for seed that sold on the open market.
No he didn't have very much trouble with labor because the
farm had good cottages. The farm buildings were old, some
of them were hundreds of years old, but they were good.
People were coming back to farm labor a little.

As he talks we follow him through barns of brick and
squared brownstone set in squares to form a series of cobbled
courts. "It's dung that's kept Britain's agriculture alive
through all these centuries," he is saying. "If you keep your

cattle in courts in the winter you get plenty of dung. These lands are as productive as they ever were though they have been continuously cultivated since the days of Robert Bruce or earlier. For all we know the Romans grew corn here and the Picts and the Scots before them ... It's a pity now it's too wet to take you around the farm. Up over the hill where those trees are is the prettiest bit of pastureland and then beyond are the fells where my sheep are ... We were lucky, we lost very few in the storms due to the unsparing labors of our shepherd. Others weren't so lucky. One third of the hillsheep of England perished and fifty thousand head of cattle and it was lucky men's lives weren't lost."

We have made the circuit of the farm buildings and come out into a long shed redolent with the rich bready fragrance of stored wheat. A loft ran the full length of it.

"As Americans," he says showing his neat white teeth in a smile, "you'll be interested in our threshing machine. It was built in Glasgow more than seventy years ago. The fact that it's old doesn't mean it won't work. If you're raising wheat for seed you have to be sure it's properly winnowed and sorted and cleaned so I know it's a splendid thresher ... " We walk up wooden stairs past the great iron flywheels into the loft ... "You see we thresh our grain in the barn in the winter that's why we have to have plenty of space here ... This is where the belt goes," he says, affectionately patting the flywheel's smooth circumference. "I thought it would be a surprise to an American. You Americans think everything has to be new or it won't work," he adds laughing in a friendly teasing way.

His voice grows serious: "In those days men who loved their work put a fine finish on things. They made machinery and barns and houses that lasted ... How shall we get back a man's pleasure in a piece of work well done? Nothing'll be any good until we get that back. Now people only work for the paypacket and they find it won't buy anything ... money buys less every day ... You're working for leisure ...

leisure they tell you over the B.B.C. . . . What's the good of leisure except to have time to do the things you don't have a chance to do when you're working? And now they're going to set up a ministry to teach people how to enjoy their leisure . . . Teach them how to enjoy their work I say."

When we get back to the freshsmelling farmhouse and are about to take our leave our host and his wife come forward smiling and say we must stay to supper . . . "Just a slice of our own bacon and an egg. We're not so short we can't do that," they heartily insist.

This was the third egg we'd had since we landed in Britain. I was too hungry to refuse. As we eat our supper we talk about the scarcity that is closing down like a vice slowly and inexorably tightened. "We're too crowded in Britain," our host is saying. "It's no good being too crowded. Twenty millions of us ought to go to the colonies. If we had twenty million less people on this tight little island we could bring up our agriculture to feed everybody and we could produce more manufactured goods than we do now and be prosperous again. It's no good being too crowded. We're just getting in each other's way . . . If I was a younger man I'd go to America or Canada myself. Maybe I would now," he leans across the table laughing, "if I didn't have such a good farm."

VOICE FROM THE GALLERY: At last you've gotten around to something optimistic. It looks to me as if farming and farmers in Great Britain were pretty darn flourishing.

MR. LECTURER: One reason is that they have been highly subsidized because food is at a premium.

VOICE FROM THE GALLERY: My name's Jake Jeffries. I'm an Iowa farmer. I didn't like the way they worked the prisoners of war or the way they didn't worry about the spoiling of those vegetables that people a few miles away needed to eat. That's just the sort of callousness we used to complain of in capitalism. Just like you said. We used to think Socialism and a planned society would cure all that. At least under Capitalism if a concern gets too darned inefficient it fails and something else takes its place. When you abolish profit as a yardstick of the efficiency of an organization you are hard put to it to find another.

MR. LECTURER: The Russians have put in a lot of work on that problem that deserves study, but I don't think they've found any answer except forced labor. The bankruptcy court seems a more humane way of treating business failures than a jail sentence or a shot in the back of the neck.

MISS SMITHERS: But the British are a humane and civilized people. They'll find other ways.

MR. LECTURER: Maybe. But already you begin to notice a certain callousness toward the human material. I've noticed it among social workers in this country. They are out to do good but they expect their clients to be mighty humble and submissive. In our society only the very poor and unfortunate suffer from the ministrations of social workers. Now in England the whole country is under the thumb of a government where the social worker psychology is very strong.

FRED RUFUS: I've always understood one of the blessings of liberty was that within certain limits every man could go to hell in his own way. That's one of the meanings of the phrase in the Declaration of Independence about the pursuit of happiness . . . That's the opposite of the Welfare State.

MRS. EDWARDS: How can anybody be opposed to welfare? (*Shushes drown out her voice.*)

MR. LECTURER: (*putting his hand to his forehead*): Lord, I met some social workers in Britain who froze the marrow in my bones . . .

CAPTION: They'll Learn to Like It

"What you mustn't forget," said one dry little East End spinster as we walked around the scaffolding of a new apartment house being built in the Stepney slums the Germans levelled so successfully during their bombings, "what you mustn't forget is that the dockers who are going to live here have never been so well off before. During the twenty years before the war they lived most of their lives on the dole. That meant twentyseven shillings and thrippence for a family. Now they make five pounds, ten . . . Of course these flats were planned before the war."

"Didn't you say some families were reluctant to go into them?"

She looked me in the face with a sharp condescending smile. "They still don't like giving up their small independent houses where the man had a bit of a garden to putter about in evenings . . . But this will be landscaped . . . We are arranging communal workshops for carpentry . . . They'll learn to like it."

In the bar of a little hotel in one of Arnold Bennett's Five Towns I met another young idealist. He'd been to Oxford.

"If I would bring about Socialism," he kept saying cheerfully over a glass of bitter, "I'd be willing to see the English people live on potatoes for five years." He had been to Oxford but not for long. He happened to be an American he told me with the tone of letting me in on a disgraceful secret. He'd picked up all the worst Oxonian mannerisms, the frizzy lovelocks round the forehead, the overenunciated speech, the quirks and smiles, the little mouths. He had spent the war working in England. Now he lived in a government hostel and lectured to the workers on Political Philosophy, he explained over a second mug of weak brown ale. And they paid him for it. Adult education. I asked him if he didn't sometimes want to go home.

"Oh America stands only for the blackest reaction," he shrieked. "I hate reaction . . . I'm the kind of fellow," he rolled his eyes skyward, "whom the Communists line up against a wall and shoot . . . but I think the future lies with the Soviet Union . . . I'd let them shoot me if they felt they had to . . . That way I'd feel I was dying for the future."

In contrast with this young Lochinvar, there was something rather bracing about the state of mind of the sunburned young man in a bathing suit who rented rowboats on the beautiful green river at Cambridge. He said he'd heard Churchill the night before over the wireless and it had worried him. Winnie had said the Conservatives ought to stay home and fight, but this boy was all ready to emigrate. He had an uncle in Canada. "It's all so boring," he insisted as he handed me the oars. "After seven years in the navy I thought I'd come home and go to work with my father building rowboats . . . I love building boats . . . In normal times I'd have inherited a nice little business but now we can't get materials and he doesn't see when he can ever start his business up again. He can keep these in repair but that's all. Nonessential . . . And if I hang around too long they'll direct me into the mines. After the navy that would be too much. After the navy I don't ever want to be directed in my life again. Somebody ought to fight. They've got us down," he said, pushing a boat into the water off the end of the float. He crouched and held the boat by the thwart as we stepped in.

As I settled myself on the seat he whispered in my ear: "We ought to rise and clean them out, but of course we won't. After the war and everything it's such an awful bore." He pushed our boat deftly by the stern out in the stream. "Have a nice row," he added politely.

EDDY JONES: That young man was a dirty fascist.

VOICE FROM THE GALLERY: And I shouldn't wonder if the lecturer wasn't one too if you'll excuse my saying so.

MISS SMITHERS: A man's got a right to freedom of opinion in this country.

MR. LECTURER: Freedom of opinion usually means freedom

to hold opinions that don't differ too much from the opinions of the majority. Any new opinion has to expect to be received with brickbats. But while we are on the subject, let's talk a little about opinions . . .

Opinions, ladies and gentlemen, are rarely the result of a logical process of thought. Some of the most intelligent people I've known admit that they had their opinions of the world impressed on their minds like decalcomanias by contact with the minds of their fellows sometimes during the impressionable college years. The bending of the twig in childhood is something much more basic. Opinions dwell on the surface of the mind. The development of men's ideas after adolescence tends to be a culling out of those parts of their experience which confirm the original impressions and the discarding of those that conflict. The man whose opinions come from actual experience and observation is very rare indeed.

In the years when I was growing up most Americans had standard political notions which were pretty well encompassed by Brisbane's editorials and by Lorimer's editing of the *Saturday Evening Post*. That was a prejudice the minority had to combat when they pointed out certain flaws in the body politic. The views of that minority were diverse and astringent, stemming from Henry George and Veblen and Marx and from reading the Bible and Blackstone and Coke and the *Federalist Papers* and from that inherited body of old saws and sayings known as common sense.

Today entrenched prejudice is all on the other side. It is as if the fads and theories of the Greenwich Village rebels who used to gather and drink and gabble in the basement of the Brevoort in the innocent days of World War I had become the coinage in which unthinking and stereotyped judgments on events were dealt out. The heresies of thirty years ago are dogmas now. This state of mind strikes you particularly when you talk to newspaper reporters or literary critics, or editorial writers or almost any professional moulder of public opinion. Most of the younger men and women who work for the newspapers were trained in schools of journalism instead of in that harsh school of realities that surrounded the oldfashioned printing press. Even if the policies of their newspapers are rankest Republican the stereotypes that rise in their minds are those which were cut out by the old time radicals in Greenwich Village. The general drift of social thinking is toward approval of administrative government and apathy towards individual effort. The nonconformist conscience seems to be extinct in the right-thinkers of today. It is not the selfstyled liberals who have protested the crimes against mankind that have been committed in the name of the American People since the fighting ended in World War II.

If you try to explain that socialism as it works in Great Britain, say, is not necessarily all of it a force for progress, you are likely to meet a rubber stamp condemnation. "But I thought you were a liberal," people will say almost tearfully, "and now you have turned reactionary."

MRS. EDWARDS: But isn't that true? How can an idea be progressive one year and conservative ten years later?

MR. LECTURER: Society changes. The same phrase appears in different contexts. An example in our history is the way the growing stock companies used the personal liberty clauses in the Constitution to assure to themselves almost unlimited freedom from social control. The labor unions today are going through a somewhat similar process in relation to the community. The extreme example at the moment is the perversion of the word democracy by the Communist dictatorships.

EDDY JONES: Then why doesn't the minority speak up? I'm a Socialist but if there's something wrong about Socialism I'm willing to be shown.

MR. LECTURER: That's what I'm talking about. We've got

to invent a new minority. The minority views which are essential to the working of selfgoverning institutions are today a dim welter of negations. The timid dissent to this or that socialistic scheme which the Republicans in this country and the Conservatives in England emit during political campaigns is fairly representative of them. When you try to get people to see that the problem of liberty is the catalyst that resolves the class war ideologies, you meet the same wall of incomprehension you used to meet years ago when you used to argue the right of working people to form unions and to strike for improved working conditions or to try to explain that we ought to show a sympathetic interest in the social experiments that were going on in the Soviet Union. Then it was the Capitalist slogans that were holding the fort. Today the stencils of Socialism are charged with a virtuous aura in the public mind. Public ownership, planned economy, controls and even the dreaded word Socialism itself have grown heavy with virtue, while profits, free enterprise, investment and dividends have taken on an evil context that needs to be explained away. In all the long public argument about rationing and the O.P.A. at the end of World War II the least common denominator opinion always seemed to be that government controls were desirable in themselves and the operations of the free market undesirable.

This comes partly from a reasonable change of attitude brought about by the success of some of the socialistic measures of Franklin Roosevelt's New Deal, but mostly it results from the unthinking acceptance of the vocabulary of "liberal" propaganda which spread out in ripples from New Deal Washington, becoming vaguer and more confused and more destructive of clear thinking as the ideas that engendered it lost their vitality at the source. Thus it comes to pass that the phraseology that had some meaning in the nineteen-twenties has now in midcentury become a definite hindrance to understanding events.

Back in the twenties those of us who were willing to be called Socialists had some perfectly definite things in mind that we thought the taking of the ownership of industry out of the hands of the finance capitalists and the vesting of it in the community as a whole would bring. We thought it would bring into economic life the sort of selfgovernment from the ground up that we have to an all too feeble degree in our political life. We thought public service could be substituted for money profit as the driving motive of human behavior. We thought that the ascendancy of an antimilitarist class in the socialist economies would replace war and the threat of war by peaceful cooperation in international affairs. Then, too, we were carried away by the blind enthusiasm of a new dispensation at hand that was sweeping the masses of the western world, by that fervent belief that revolution would install utopia which is still the basis of the propaganda of the Communists in Europe.

MISS SMITHERS: If we lose faith in progress what can we believe in?

MR. LECTURER: We can believe in the barely attainable ideals of freedom . . . The revolutions have happened and régimes and empires have crashed in the mud, but the old problem of how to control man's domination by man remains unsolved. Socialist governments (with the exception of the British, perhaps) turn out to be more militaryminded than capitalist governments. Immense armaments have become the flywheel of modern governmental economy. The scramble for political and bureaucratic power has taken the place of the scramble for money power, but the question of the control of all power in the public interest has been left to one side. Enough socialised systems and institutions have been going concerns over a long enough period of time for us to begin to get some idea of how they are working out. It's a most curious comment on the blindness which dogmatically held beliefs induce that in all the avalanches of print for and against free enterprise there's so little comparative examination of capitalist and socialist organizations to try to discover how they work out for the men and women directly involved.

As citizens of a selfgoverning community we have continually to be asking ourselves what is it we want from our institutions. Do we want them to serve us or do we want to serve them?

EDDY JONES: That's what Socialism means. Institutions that will serve the people.

MR. LECTURER: From the point of view of the wellbeing of men and women the important thing to discover about institutions is not how they can be labelled under the Capitalist-Socialist dichotomy but how they work. Some sorts of organization stimulate individual initiative and some sorts fasten on society the dead hand of bureaucratic routine or the suckers of sterile vested interests.

EDDY JONES: You can't tell me people in this country as a mass aren't better off than they've ever been before.

MR. LECTURER: The rosy side of the picture so far as this country is concerned is that, although we have formulated no new philosophies, we have shown signs of beginning to learn that the road must be kept open for experiment and growth. We have begun to learn that no society is stronger than its weakest members. By our habit of government we are committed to trying to keep a rough balance between the demands of different sections of the population expressed by pressure groups. We haven't solved the problem of protecting every man's freedom from domination by other men but we have made a little bit of a beginning.

VOICE FROM THE GALLERY: Then what's all the crêpe-hanging about?

MR. LECTURER: We haven't done well enough. The fact that a society is prosperous doesn't necessarily mean that its foundations are sound.

MISS SMITHERS: Excuse me. I used to teach ancient history. The Carthaginians were at their most prosperous when the Romans overthrew them. Athens was at the peak of greatness when the city's whole future was ruined by the failure of the Sicilian expedition. May I suggest that the gentleman read Thucydides?

MR. LECTURER: We have lost the sense of urgency that gave vigor to the political ideas of the founding fathers. They knew it was root hog or die.

FRED RUFUS: The question is whether the American system has been able to secrete enough adrenalin . . . In my opinion an active and critical minority is the adrenalin in the body politic.

MISS SMITHERS: Why in the moment of victory did we lose faith in ourselves?

MR. LECTURER: Because of our failure to formulate anew our philosophy of government in the face of a changed society the Communists were able to defeat us again and again in the daily struggle for men's minds. It was this lack of profound convictions about the importance of human liberty on the part of Franklin Roosevelt and his advisers that cost us the fruits of our wartime victory to the point that the things Americans hold most dear remain in greater peril today than they were on the afternoon of Pearl Harbor. You and I, my friends, are partly responsible for the ruin of the Baltic republics and the terror in Warsaw and Prague and for the expropriation of the peasantry in the Balkans. (*Laughter in the hall.*)

MR. LECTURER: It may sound far fetched but it happens to be true. The responsibility for our failure to win a peace, which is the typical example of our failure to understand the world we live in, lies not only in a small group of political leaders in Washington, but in the whole body of thinking Americans whose thinking has just not caught up with the times. We have forgotten that our sort of selfgoverning community can only survive by opening up constantly new avenues for men's ingenuity and enterprise and by expanding instead of contracting the areas open to the exercise of individual liberties. We have forgotten that liberty like peace was indivisible.

EDDY JONES: You can't tell me that the average working man in England hasn't got more liberty than he had under the Conservatives. What good's liberty anyway to a jobless man who can't buy food for his family?

MR. LECTURER: The men and women of the Labor Government in Britain are far more scrupulous about protecting the liberties of the constituents than Roosevelt's New Dealers ever were, but in spite of their good intentions the drift of British socialism is towards servitude to the state. The British Laborites are the first to deplore this fact and to reassure you with pious hopes that the "direction of labor" will be only a passing phase, but in listening to these pious hopes I couldn't help remembering similar assurances by equally humane and wellintentioned Russian Communists in the early days of the revolution: Military communism would only be a passing phase, they told you, which would disappear as soon as reactionary opposition was crushed. Thirty years have gone by and military communism has conquered a third of the population of the globe and it is more military and more tyrannical than ever. A man has a right to ask the British Labor Party whether thirty years from now direction of labor won't be the cornerstone of a system of exploitation of the productive workers by a ruling class entrenched in government.

If there is one thing that mankind should have learned from the experience of the last four decades it is that it is never safe to do evil that good may come of it. The good gets lost and the evil goes on.

MRS. EDWARDS: Would the Conservatives have done any better?

MR. LECTURER: We have to admit that the present situation

of the people of Great Britain would be difficult enough if a choir of archangels, superhuman in brains and in selfabnegation, had assumed the government. The island's economy was built up as the processing and financing center of an empire which has irrevocably gone. The ruling class which had controlled that economy through its ownership of the land and its grip on centralized finance and industry and on government itself had become overweeningly rich and powerful. In their wealth and selfsatisfaction the owners of Britain forgot to keep their industries tooled up to date or to protect the standard of living of their working people. When the Labor Government came in after the war it inherited a concern that actually had long been bankrupt.

Government control of virtually the entire economy had already been instituted during the war. About all the Labor Government did was to continue and to amplify the wartime apparatus of bureaucratic management. The living standards of the working people who were their chief constituents had improved during the war. The Labor Government has continued that improvement, particularly for the lowest paid third. As there wasn't enough to go around anyway, this was done at the expense of the middle class which traditionally has been Britain's nursery of brains and initiative. Everybody except the lowest paid third of the population was reduced by high taxes to a bare subsistence level of existence. The people of the lowest third were raised to that level. Automatically incentive for effort and innovation disappeared. A man was better off if he soldiered along in the shop and spent his Saturdays betting on the races than if he worked himself sick trying to rise in the world, because the more his income rose the more taxation would take his earnings away from him and the more he'd feel the dead weight of the bureaucratic tangle hampering his every move.

What has happened up to now is that socialism has accomplished very little more than to freeze the bankrupt capitalist economy at its point of collapse. Its bureaucratic machinery has put up the bars against the sort of revolutionary initiative and thoroughgoing reorganization of industry through which the British people might escape from their dilemma. Subsidies from the American government have concealed this situation without improving it in any fundamental way.

Man does not live by bread alone the Socialists will tell you. The answer is that he lives too much for his own good by the exercise of power over other men. British capitalism certainly gave people whose only social gift was the knack of accumulating money too much power, but the trouble with British socialism is that it gives too much power to people whose only knack is getting themselves elected to offices in trade unions. Neither financial skill nor political skill have much to do with skill in industrial production.

England has a new ruling class. Added to such remnants of the old ruling class as have remained in office through their holding of administrative jobs in government and industry and the civil service is an infusion of new blood from the trade union leadership leavened by an occasional intellectual who has talked or written his way into office. Now the main training of trade union officials has been in sabotaging production in order to wring concessions from the managers for the workers and neither idealistic intellectuals nor civil service employees have any training in the needs of industry. The result is that at the very moment when the British people need to bend every energy to discovering and exploiting new methods for manufacturing food and clothing and housing and export goods, they find themselves in the hands of a ruling class which is not only hampered by tradition and training from doing anything effective to stimulate production but is so blinded by the utopian illusions of the word "socialism" that it can't even face the problem.

MRS. EDWARDS: Well, if the government can't help them why can't they help themselves?

MR. LECTURER: The British people in my opinion represent

just about the highest development of Western civilized man. In all classes you find a higher level of education than we have reached in America. The level of individual skill and craftsmanship in most trades is higher than ours. They haven't our techniques for mass production, but they are certainly capable of learning them and even of improving on them. In the professionally trained part of the population, though there may be some flagging of creative spirit, there's still a great reservoir of first rate scientific and mathematical brains. The British people proved themselves to be still a great people by the dignity and discipline with which they fought off the German air attacks during the war. These highly trained, highly disciplined and civilized people can't help themselves because the all-pervading state has made individual action impossible.

British apologists will tell you that they are quite free, quite. But we don't need to believe them. When a man can't change his job without permission from someone sitting at an office desk, when he can't perform any of the normal operations of buying and selling necessary to carrying on a productive enterprise without license from the government, when he can't appeal to the courts from administrative decisions, when he can be sentenced to jail for refusing to work in the mines, he's not a free man but a slave.

The Britisher still has his secret ballot in parliamentary and municipal elections. He's free because he can vote, he'll tell you. Unfortunately it's doubtful how far the vote alone without economic and personal liberty of action can protect a nation against the exercise of arbitrary power by government. The experience in the United States has several times been just the opposite.

This brings us squarely up against the dilemma of our time. Under the cover of communist and socialist illusions, just at the moment when our technology is opening up the certainty of really widespread wellbeing in material things, the masses of mankind are being plunged back into a regime of servitude such as has not existed in the west for thousands of years. We can't entirely blame on war damage a situation which has resulted from the strangling of production by the socialized economies that accompanied the war. So far the socialized economies have opened up no new aspects of self-government, no broader reaches of liberty for the individual. Quite the opposite. In the Soviet Union particularly failure to solve the problems of production at home has thrown Russian communism into a habit of aggression upon the rest of the world. In Great Britain we can still hope that the failure of the socialized economy to provide its people with a decent life at home will produce a new explosion of migration and colonization which will transmit to the future world of the West the valuable heritages of English culture. What we don't want to forget is that we won't have any Western world fit for a free man to live in unless we keep the avenues open for the growth of the individual.

DERISIVE VOICES FROM THE GALLERY: How are we going to do that? You tell us, mister.

MR. LECTURER: The first thing is to ask ourselves what kind of society we want to live in.

EDDY JONES: Nonsense. You can't control social forces. Marx . . .

(THE JANITOR *has been standing yawning in the back of the hall.*) Time's come to close this place up. The rental expires at eleven-thirty. (*Already people are snatching up their wraps and filing out, arguing in little groups as they go.*)

Principles
of Power

II

THIRD LECTURE

Campaign for the Americas

MR. LECTURER: (*appears on the platform with a briefcase under his arm. He looks down into the hall and notices a great many empty seats.*) Well (*he says with forced cheerfulness*), at least there'll be room for everybody. I'd like to suggest that you bunch up in the first few rows so that the discussion can be carried on more informally. (*He squints down through his glasses into the rows of faces in front of him.*) I'm glad to see some familiar faces. How do you do, Miss Smithers. Mrs. Edwards, I hope your cold is better . . . Mr. Jeffries, I'm glad you haven't gone back to Iowa yet. (*He clears his throat.*) I was wa-aiting for the latecomers, (*he stammers. There's a titter from two girls in the gallery . . .*) I guess I'd better begin . . .

The subject today is political power. The examples are taken from a trip to South America in the fall of 1948. I'm afraid my hearers will again have to be very patient. When you try to study the social process from the life all sorts of facts and fancies get into the picture that confuse and sometimes run counter to your original argument. In human societies, as I said before, several trends are usually found developing in different directions at the same time. In South America the tide still sets strong in favor of dictatorship but you can find hopeful countercurrents. The prestige of the United States is at a very low ebb, and with it the prestige of selfgovernment in general . . . It's really lower than it should be because some of the methods of dealing with peoples and societies alien to our own which the American government worked out during the war were in a quiet way quite new inventions. The base was laid by the extraordinarily altruistic work of the Rockefeller Foundation. The Special Public Health Services set up in Brazil and other countries managed by the skillful use of American funds to create a practical pattern of cooperation between our technical knowledge and the aspirations of native doctors for their country's betterment, from which everybody benefitted. To say that this sort of organization is a cure for dictatorship is like saying that earth dams in gullies are a cure for floods on the Mississippi, but enough earth dams in enough gullies could have quite an effect on the situation . . . The creation of a society of free and selfgoverning men is more a matter of many small factors than one of grandiose political pronouncements. Before I ask the young man at the projector to take us to Brazil you'll have to allow me to review the history of the use of the machinery of power in the modern world.

When the Russian revolution exploded in the fall of 1917 World War I had settled down to a stalemate along the trenches in northern France. The stubborn resistance the French and British were putting up to the equally stubborn German invasion was bleeding Europe to death. In the armies a feeling of rebellion against the senselessness of the butchery was rising to a hysterical pitch. In the same year two separate flickers of hope appeared on the eastern and western horizons. In Washington Woodrow Wilson announced his Fourteen Points and in Petrograd Lenin and Trotzky fired the hungry and disorganized Russian mobs with the belief that communism would bring them peace, land and food. No one who was on the Continent at that time can ever forget the surge of crazy confidence in the future that swept the peoples of Europe when Armistice Day came and the fighting stopped. At last civilization would come into its own.

The people's trust in the American way faded as Wilson let himself be trapped into the stale councils of the old men of Versailles, but from Russia came leadership and action. While in Paris they haggled about oil and superannuated boundaries, Lenin let Finland and the Baltic countries form their own governments, let the conscript soldiers go home, distributed land to the peasants and encouraged in the soviets or workers' councils what seemed then to be a new organ for selfgovernment. For a moment it looked as if the working class under Marxist leadership would succeed in renovating Europe.

It was not to be so easy. The old ruling interests of the world banded together for the protection not of their people's liberties, but of their own sources of income, and the Russian civil war ruined the hopes of the free development of a new social system. The Communist Party hardened into a military caste. The soviets and trades unions in the Soviet Union, instead of developing into organs of selfgovernment, developed into machines run by a tightly organized and dogmatic Marxist minority for the domination and exploitation of the masses. The symbolic act which accompanied Lenin's throwing overboard of the humanitarian baggage of Western socialism was his moving of the capital from European Petrograd to Asiatic Moscow.

The civil war had become a struggle for order, any kind of order. The only order the Russians knew was despotism.

From the Czarist autocracy the Communist government inherited the secret police. Political liberty had hardly a breathing spell before it was stamped out again, first in the unorganized mass of the people and then, under Stalin, as a result of his struggle for power against Trotzky, within the Communist Party itself.

By the early thirties the social organization of the Soviet Union had come to resemble much more the slave-run autocracy of the Ottoman Turks than it did any of the European blueprints for a socialist utopia. This backsliding into methods of dominion that had been discredited among civilized men for hundreds of years was accompanied by the building up of one of the most extraordinary propaganda façades in history. A constitution was promulgated on the Western model. The entire vocabulary of Western selfgovernment was borrowed and applied to the machinery of despotism. It was from the success of Soviet propaganda in calling evil things by good names that Hitler learned the lesson which he stated so clearly in *Mein Kampf*, that if a lie is repeated with enough conviction it becomes more effective than the truth.

With the massacre of the European-trained Bolsheviks Stalin cleared out of the Kremlin the last traces of Western humanitarianism, but by sheer weight of power his régime managed to retain its grip over the aspirations of a large part of the European working class. The Communist Party, appealing through its basic utopian dogma to the emotions of confused and tortured people, everywhere backed and kept in line by the authority of the secret police, managed to create one of the most efficient machines for the domination and exploitation of mankind the world has ever seen. Though it seems likely from what we hear dimly through the screen of lies that hems in the frontiers of the Soviet Union that in the center the illusion has lost its power, in the periphery Communism's utopian dreams still dominate many men's hopes. As the ideals which animated its inception have withered away, the Party's technique for using everything vile and weak in human nature for the ends of power has improved and developed. Ruined nations fall easy prey to its closely disciplined organization.

We even find Frenchmen and Americans and Canadians who otherwise lead sane and normal lives willing to turn their backs on all the traditions they were brought up in and to give their allegiance to the Communist Party to the point of treason to their own people. The success of the aggressions by the Soviet state rests very largely on the Kremlin's command over adherents and sympathizers in the outside world. These deluded men and women have watched the Soviet Union develop into a force for pillage and conquest such as has hardly been seen since the holy wars of the primitive Mohammedans or the raids on civilization of the Ottoman Turks, but their faith in the Kremlin's idealistic aims has never faltered.

If what we wanted from socialism was the growth of self-government and an increase in individual liberty and a wider distribution of goods among the masses of men it's pretty obvious by now that the Soviet Union is not the place to look for any of these benefits. Not even the Communists claim such achievements; what they tell their adherents is that the present miseries will be atoned for by the régime of justice and bliss that will be established once communism has completed its conquest of the world.

EDDY JONES: There's no unemployment in the Soviet Union, I understand.

FRED RUFUS: Neither, to quote an old saw, is there unemployment in the State Penitentiary . . .

MR. LECTURER: It is one of history's miserable ironies that the only real social invention of the Russian Marxists, who set out to build a perfect society, has been this technique for the destruction of the liberties which we in the West consider the backbone of civilization. Out of the combination of the conspiratorial skills which they inherited from the old rev-olutionists' underground war against the Czar, and capitalist methods of gaining control of corporations and joint stock companies by financial leverage worked out in the West by the financial empire builders of the Morgan-Rockefeller-Carnegie era, the Communists have developed a mechanism which has proved very nearly unbeatable.

The reason this mechanism has been so successful is that no selfgoverning institutions, whether financial or govern-mental, have been able during the last hundred years to keep up with the growth to gianthood of industrial society. The same helpless apathy in matters of selfgovernment has made the investors in American corporations and the voters who were supposed to control political institutions the vic-tims of any minority disciplined enough and ruthless enough to keep to one aim and one aim only: the seizure of the levers of power. The populations of nations industrially advanced and industrially backward have been as helpless against the technique of disciplined infiltrations as Mocte-zuma's armies, with their feather helmets and their stone axes, were helpless against the steel-armed horsemen of Cortez.

Fortunately for the surviving segments of Western civiliza-tion too quick success is almost as dangerous to the life of political institutions as failure. When a method is too easy anybody can learn it. Hitler and Mussolini took over the techniques of the Communist Party and used them for very different purposes. In Yugoslavia, Tito's dictatorship has developed a dissident national communism which has man-aged to stand up for a while at least against the Kremlin. In Argentina the Perons have developed their own version of party government. We may expect that in Asia eventually all sorts of intermediate dictatorships will sprout into being to cushion the impact of the great organization for world conquest which centers in Moscow. Writing of a similar period during the early Middle Ages historians are hard put to it to decide whether it was the bloody discord among the successors of the Khalif or the fighting ability of Charles Martel's Franks that saved Christian Europe from being overwhelmed by Mohammedanism. Discord among the despots, Marxist, Marxist-Nationalist and Nationalist-Marxist, may save the Western World once again.

During 1948 when, in Western Europe at least, the Communist tide seemed to be receding, South America offered a field for the study of the competition between government by dictation and government by consent. The ruin of Spain by the civil war and Franco's resultant dictatorship, at the moment when the peoples of the Peninsula were about to step into their rightful position as one of the civilizing forces in Europe, cast the South American countries adrift without metropolitan leadership.

Since the collapse of their monarchies, neither Spain nor Portugal, nor their greater extensions overseas, have been able to work out really satisfactory political institutions. Time and again various communities have tried to set up parliamentary governments on the British, French or American model, but nearly always these governments have been paralyzed or overthrown by an innate drift towards personal domination by some strong man, whether a military bandit or a civilian leader, and his gang of devoted adherents. Some of these despotisms have been absolute and brutal and others have been tempered by the individualism of the Spanish tradition and by the mild habit of tolerant decentralization which has characterized Portuguese dominion the world over.

The countries of the Peninsula and of South America have hovered for a century and a half on the edges of modern industrial society without quite being part of it. Various traditions out of their Christian and even their Mohammedan and Roman past have lingered on to make them a borderland region where the industrial revolution which produced modern England and the modern United States never quite took hold. Their industrial backwardness has made them subject to exploitation by foreign merchants and investors and their own capitalist development has tended to take grotesque and erratic forms. Hence they offer us an opportunity to study the growth of the techniques for the domination of man by man in a slightly different environment from our own.

The years since World War II came to a close have been a difficult period for all South America. The demands of North American production stimulated the growth of agglomerated cities and dislocated the simple village economy by which the people outside of the European style capitals lived. Except in the region of the river Plate the mass of the population has always been poor, but under the pressure of wartime production of raw materials and the lure of easy money many of these exchanged the dignified and bearable poverty of the primitive village community for the much more painful poverty of the industrial slum. The paralysis of world trade which has resulted from the lack of any interchangeable international currency has left the economies of all the South American countries dangling in a kind of nomansland between inflation and deflation.

The result for the masses and for a large part of the middle class has been poverty and more poverty, following a dangerous taste of comparative wellbeing during the war. Desperate men searching for a way out will listen to any counsels that seem to offer a livelihood and to flatter their sense of personal and national dignity. In their search for leadership the Spanish and Portuguese-speaking peoples tend to oscillate between North America and Eastern Europe. They have a thinly diffused knowledge of the realities of the wellbeing of the average man in North America, but the Russian propaganda machine has the immediate advantage in the intoxication of class and national antagonisms.

To a professional Communist, meditating over Marxist-Leninist-Stalinist texts in the quiet of the Lenin Institute in Moscow, South America must seem the promised land for conquest. All the classical elements are present for a revolutionary situation on the Russian model, exploited labor which after a fleeting taste of comparative prosperity has been pushed back into starvation again, inflated living costs, a greedy and oligarchical class of rulers who think of very little except enriching themselves, and a snarledup economy teetering on the edge of collapse. Since the United States is the last really powerful center for free institutions in the world, the capture of South America must seem an essential part of the Kremlin's world strategy of encirclement. As the years drag on, sizeable Communist parties appear and disappear, Communist leaders arise with great prestige like Luis Carlos Prestes in Brazil; agitators travel virtually unhindered from country to country; in Havana right on the doorstep of the United States the Communist Party reaches great power and cohesion; but somehow the revolutionary moment does not come.

The uprising at Bogotá during the Pan-American conference in the spring of 1948 is an example of the advantages and disadvantages of the situation in South America from the point of view of a Communist organizer. We don't know yet exactly how large a part the Communists, foreign and Colombian played in the preliminary propaganda which set the stage for this strange explosion of mob violence. But we do know that, although the uprising helped discredit the United States and our longterm policy of cooperation among American nations, the Communists gained little immediate political advantage. It is even likely that they lost prestige almost as much as the United States and the continental policy against which the move was directed. They are still, as the most casual reading of the daily papers will show you, a power to be dealt with.

Bogotá in an extreme degree offers an example of the transformation which South American capitals have undergone in recent years. Only a couple of decades ago Bogotá was a tileroofed colonial city so isolated in the mountains you could only reach it on muleback. During the period of wartime expansion the city enormously increased in size. Most of the new inhabitants came in from the halfwild life of the ranches and forests. Undoubtedly the wageworkers were paid higher wages and had higher living standards in the conventional sense of the term than they had ever enjoyed before, but city life in itself, for which nothing in their training or experience had prepared them, was a profound strain. Talking to people in Bogotá about the outbreak a few months after it had happened, I kept being reminded of what I had read of the equally strange outbreaks of mob hysteria such as the Lord George Gordon Riots that took place in London in the eighteenth century. There, too, you had a mass of people recently uprooted from a primitive country society, with its rigid frame of conventions and traditions, packed into city slums and set to unaccustomed tasks, crowded and confused by strange stimuli until the tension reached the breaking point.

In each case the spark that set it off was incommensurable with the magnitude of the explosion. In Bogotá the working class had been stirred up by antiforeign propaganda from various sources. Galván, whose mysterious murder lit the fuse, was, everyone admits, a great popular hero. Months later old women were still piling flowers on the spot where he was shot down. But none of these things account for the hysterical conduct of the mob. If there had been a political plan it was immediately forgotten in the madness of looting and burning. Whatever Communist *cadre* tried to take over direction once the mob had captured the streets was as helpless as the Colombian police. The populace fell to pillaging liquor stores and arms stores. People went clean out of their minds in a delirium of drunkenness and shooting and burning. Many of the dead died of alcoholic poisoning or by shooting it out among themselves. Even before the troops arrived the convulsion was subsiding like a spent hurricane.

The Colombian administration was certainly to blame for not having taken greater precautions but it had the justification that Colombia had for years been one of the most stable and most constitutionally governed of South American republics and that a revolt in Bogotá was about as little to be expected as a revolt in Washington, D.C.

The thing that it is important to remember is that, outside of Montevideo and Buenos Aires, the same malnutrition, the same misery and disease, the same frustrations and strains that produced the crazy April days in Bogotá exist in every large city in Latin America. The Communists have undoubtedly studied their successes and failures in Bogotá very carefully. In these situations, where their aim is to destroy the fabric of existing civilization at whatever cost, they have an easy advantage over the proponents of government by consent who have the difficult task of saving and improving existing institutions. If we are to win in the contest it is up to us to study more carefully and more dispassionately than they do the social situations we have to deal with.

In spite of our besetting national ignorance, we are not entirely helpless in our contest with the Communist minority in South America. We have already established through the work of the Rockefeller Foundation and the State Department's Institute of Inter-American Affairs some particularly successful methods of helping South Americans help themselves in matters of health and sanitation which deserve a great deal more attention than they are getting from Congress and from the American people as a whole. An example of the best sort of thing that North Americans can do in the southern continent, or in the rest of the world, for that matter, can be found in these Special Public Health services, set up to fight malaria and yellow fever and other tropical plagues in Brazil.

(The buzzer sounds and the lights in the hall go out. On the screen appears a map of Brazil. A toy plane shoots north from Rio to Vitoria near the mouth of the Rio Doce.)

CAPTION: *Opening a Road to the Mines*

WHEN I REACHED VITORIA in the State of Espirito Santo they had hardly driven me in from the airfield before everybody was forcibly bunched up for a photograph on the terrace of a clubhouse built on the ruins of the fort which used to guard the harbor's narrow mouth. Outside of the doctors and sanitary engineers I had come to meet, there were a local newspaper editor, some smiling bystanders, and a couple of Americans who worked for the railroad that wound up the Rio Doce to the great Itabira iron mines. It was Sunday and the sun was bright and the bay was blue and the men wore shining white suits. Inside the clubhouse young people were dancing the samba. While the photographer was crouching and peering one of the Brazilians was pointing out some old prostrate cannon rusting on the ledge below the clubhouse terrace. In the seventeenth century, he was saying, the Dutch had tried to take Vitoria and the defenders had stretched cables from this fort to the granite shore opposite and had sunk a Dutch warship and saved the city for Brazil. It was in this war against the Dutch that Brazilian nationality first came into being. His chest puffed out as he turned to beam at the camera.

The sun was hot and the breeze off the sea was cool. After the shutter clicked, we stood a moment looking out over the dancing blue waves of the harbor hemmed in by hills, at the redtiled roofs of the brick and stucco town and the small freighters tied up to the wharves and the yellow bulk of the oredocks opposite. There were gulls. A few dark manofwar birds skimmed overhead.

Was this the mouth of the Rio Doce? I asked. Good Lord no, the mouth of the Rio Doce was miles away to the north. Vitoria was the port for the Rio Doce railroad down from the mines which had to climb out of the valley over a mountain range to get to it. The Rio Doce emptied into a shallow delta and had no decent harbor at its mouth. Everybody began to explain at once that the historical impediment to development in Southern and Central Brazil had been the fact that you always had to climb a mountain range to get into the interior. The iron ore deposits up in the center of the State of Minas Gerais had been known and worked since the beginning of Brazil, but it was only now that largescale shipment was in sight. In the early days hostile Indians blocked the use of the waterlevel route up the Rio Doce into the mining country. Then it had been malaria . . . "But the main impediment is bureaucracy," one of the engineers interrupts as we climb into the car to go into town to lunch . . . "Brazilian bureaucracy."

Brazilian bureaucracy, someone starts explaining from the back seat, is a little special because of the inborn ignorance and horror of productive work of the literate Brazilian. The sort of people who were brought up to become public servants had no practical knowledge of any of the processes of production. The old habit of wearing a long fingernail on the little finger had been the symbol of the educated class that had never done any work and never intended to do any. So the Brazilian bureaucrats' notions of production were purely theoretical. This was true more or less of all Latin countries, but the gulf between the illiterate

barefoot producer and the man at the office desk was wider
in Brazil. In the States we suffered from bureaucracy too,
but the man at the desk had maybe worked as a section hand
on the railroad summers when he was in school, or at least
he went home and stoked his own furnace and mowed his
own lawn. In Brazil you came out of school belonging to a
different race from the man who hoed your garden.

By this time we have arrived at the already shabby
modernstyle building where the Special Public Health Services, known to everybody as SESP, has central offices for the
Rio Doce region.

Going up in the elevator Dr. Penido, the remarkably
youthful looking Brazilian who heads the Rio Doce service,
is telling sadly in his low rather singsong tones about the
building. It was built as a hospital. A modern hospital was
very much needed in Vitoria, but the money ran out and all
that had come of it had been a small private clinic on the
lower floor and the rest was rented out for offices. That was
the sort of thing his service was determined to avoid. SESP
never entered into a project unless the funds were on hand
not only to complete it but to maintain it. Did I know the
history of SESP? I nodded. I had spent some time in the
main office in Rio where I had found the same low tones, the
same frankness and modesty, talking to Dr. Candou, its
Brazilian chief, and Dr. Campbell, who represents the State
Department's Institute of Interamerican Affairs.

Although Brazil had a public health service way back in
the fifties of the last century, before the United States indeed, it had fallen into bureaucratic lethargy. The Rockefeller Foundation, during its worldwide war against yellow
fever in the twenties and in the all out battle fought against
the Gambia mosquito in northeast Brazil in the thirties,
had trained most of the effective public health men
in the country. Then in 1942 Major General George C.
Dunham, the author of a famous textbook on public health,

had been sent down from Washington to set up a health program for Latin America. He had had experience in the Philippines in inducing local governing bodies to come in on public health programs and was convinced that a health organization to be effective had to be based on the cooperation of the people themselves. That was the genesis of the SESP idea. Most of the Brazilian staff had their practical experience in the field under Dr. Soper's Rockefeller organization and their training at public health centers in the States.

Now the first problem in the Rio Doce, Dr. Penido is telling me as we stand looking at one of the maps of the railroad and the valley tacked up on the wall with its little glass-headed pins in various colors indicating the various services, is malaria. That was on its way to solution when SESP came in. Now with DDT it is fairly simple . . . "We try to round out the picture. What we have tried to do is to produce an island of public health in each place we work. First we built privies for the people. You see we start from zero in this country. Then we gave them pure water . . . "

Monty is looking at his watch. Monty Montanari is a lanky young American engineer with a long North-Italian nose, a graduate of the Seabees in the Aleutians and on Guam, whose special business is building water systems. "We'd better go eat," he says, "because I ordered the linecar for three o'clock. We'll let him drink the water when we get up in the valley."

After one of those ample lunches Brazilian hospitality provides, which start with salad and cold cuts and go on through steak and rice dishes and chicken and, if you're not careful, lamb and pork, and fried eggs besides, we drive across the iron bridge — Vitoria turned out to be built on the flank of a steep rocky island — to the railroad station on the mainland.

The linecar hasn't arrived yet, so we roam around looking

at the old woodburning locomotives with their belltopped
stacks, like the locomotives in prints by Currier and Ives,
that are shunting cars in the freight yard, and at the great
piles of wood along the tracks, and wonder how many man-
hours of work it takes to cut all that wood up in the hills
and to bring it down by oxcart or on the backs of burros or
of men to the railroad. At a church along the shore a ringing
of bells has started. The steamboats at the docks across the
harbor are blowing their whistles. Down the middle of the
stream in the sparkling sunlight comes a long string of
launches and rowboats decorated with green and yellow
streamers. From the shore rise cheers and a popping of
rockets. Somewhere a brass band is playing. It is the proces-
sion of some saint being carried by water from one shrine to
another. Before we can find out the name of the saint the
linecar has backed in beside the platform.

It was a big green stationwagon sort of vehicle mounted
on railroad trucks and driven by a diesel engine. We had to
hurry to get off in order to meet at the proper siding the
passenger train coming down the singletrack line. First we
circled the conical mountain on the track the oretrains used.
We stopped over the oredocks. Walter Runge, the engineer
for the company that was repairing the line, stepped out and
picked up a piece of the heavy blue and red rock. "Sixty-
eight percent hematite," he said. "Just about the richest
iron ore in the world. The railroad's still pretty sketchy. It
comes a long way and it takes a long time but it gets here.
These oredocks could have been better designed but the
ships get loaded. There were times when we wondered if
they ever would."

At the edge of the yards our bucktoothed mulatto driver
had to stop the car suddenly to send his black assistant running back to the station to get his orders. The railroad was
operated on the old English block system; only one piece of
equipment allowed at a time in a block. At last the boy

arrived panting with a green slip in his hand and we went off rattling and lurching over the newlaid rails, past bamboo fences and small thatched huts with mud floors and yards planted with scrawny papayas where a few skinny chickens pecked about and dirty children black and brown and grayish white, naked or dressed in rags that barely covered them, rolled and played in the thick dust. One set of houses, freshly built for railroad workers, stood out along the track neat and white with scrubbed tiled floors.

Immediately the town falls away and we are crossing sunseared savannahs that were once planted in sugarcane. Occasionally we catch sight of the ruins of a stone and adobe fazenda crumbling under a bristling mat of vegetation. White and gray zebu cattle with big humps graze on the plain. The railroad sweeps into bare rocky hills scorched and smouldering because this is the season when they burn over the land to have it ready to plant when the rains begin. In the valleys we pass an occasional ranch house with mud walls and tiled roofs set in a bunch of tattered banana trees. As the evening begins to thicken in smoke and dusk the line goes winding in endless curves up a rocky valley. In the distance blue humped mountains rise from smooth rock faces into fantastic cones against the sky.

Walter Runge, a hefty young man from New Jersey who studied his engineering at Rutgers, is pointing out his outfit's work, straightening curves, eliminating grades, laying new rails, reballasting. He makes you feel that this rickety single-track line into the wilderness is an amusing and capricious toy to be coddled and petted and gradually babied out of its errors and vices. Night has come down on us suddenly. As the car stops on a siding he points up into a barely visible tangle of matted trees. "We had a camp up there . . . All over here is swamps. . . The place is full of wonderful orchids . . . Before DDT we had to keep a double payroll because half the men were always down with malaria."

We are waiting for an oretrain to come down. The night is dead silent. A few grasshoppers are making a rasping noise in the trees. From away up the line we hear the whistle of the engine and the rattle of the trucks of the orecars coming round the curves. The doctors are talking about the jungle type of yellow fever which had been found to be carried by the mosquitoes that bred in the little pools of water in the forks of high forest trees. People called it the honeymoon disease because it was often contracted by young men who went out to clear themselves a piece of land when they married. The yellow fever inspectors kept track of it by watching for the bodies of the little animals that lived in the highest level of the rainforest. If they found a lot of dead monkeys it meant that there was yellow fever about. Now that plain yellow fever had been exterminated the jungle type was one of the diseases they were most interested in.

The oretrain goes slambanging past. Now the line is clear. We cross the divide and go lurching and jangling through the night round long curves over singing rails until we roar with siren hooting into the main street of Colatina. Creamcolored stucco housefronts and stores and cafés lit by electric light. The local doctors are waiting to meet us at the station. *Abraços* and *felicidades*. We walk to the hotel past flatcars piled with immense logs of peroba wood. Now this hotel, Dr. Penido is explaining, was an example of how SESP worked. We should have seen it a year ago. Now at least the kitchen was clean and the bedrooms and the dining room and bar. We'd be distressed by the toilet but he was working on that. Gradually. Gradually . . . Keeping a toilet clean was the result of years of education. In the Vale do Rio Doce a privy was a monstrous novelty five years ago.

Next morning we are out early walking round the town. Rosy mist hangs low over the broad sluggish puttycolored river. The bridge was built for a railroad that never got completed; battered trucks are coming across it into town and occasionally a cart with whining wheels of solid planking drawn by a majestic pair of humped zebu oxen. We walk down the cobbled street toward the Health Center. On the way Dr. Penido and Dr. Lavigne, the local chief of SESP operations, proudly show off the market. No rotting piles of garbage as in Rio. The stalls are clean. The vegetables look freshwashed. The butchershop is screened; its marble tables have just been scrubbed. To be sure somebody has left open the little window in the screen through which sales are made. Dr. Penido notes the fact philosophically. The next time it will be closed. "Education," he says in a tone of infinite patience.

The Health Center has an air of quiet gaiety about it. It is an airy little building of gray stone and white stucco, designed I was told by Peter Pfister in the States, with a cool covered patio between two rows of offices and consulting rooms, where people can wait out of the sun and in the breeze. At one end is a playground for children. You can see that people enjoy coming here. Varicolored children are scrambling around on swings and seesaws. People have brought their dogs.

In back was a sample vegetable garden with vigorous rows of lettuce, beets, dill, chicory, carrots, turnips, magnificent tomatoes. In this country they had forgotten about growing vegetables. Beans and rice and occasionally a small gourd called shushu cooked with a strip of sundried beef constituted the daily diet, sprinkled plentifully with dry mandioc flour so that you could make the mess into a ball with your fingers and shove it into your mouth. Now in the town at least people were getting a taste for vegetables. If they proved that they could raise a garden they were given free seeds. Education. The doctors tried to get the schoolchildren into Health Clubs so that they would interest their parents in sanitation and a wellbalanced diet. The trouble was that not all the children went to school and of those that did the great majority dropped out after the first three years.

In the offices they show you their filing system. A simple and usable filing system is the crux of the problem. To produce an island of public health where there has been not the faintest notion of it before, you have to keep a record. That was the best thing the Americans had taught them, the Brazilian doctors agreed, a method of keeping a simple and adequate record without bureaucratic clogging. There are cards for every family in town showing its health record and the results of the visits of the district nurse. There are cards for individual patients. There are cards for each butcher-shop, bakery, bar, restaurant, hotel and boardinghouse, showing its sanitary record, recommendations made, improvements if any.

"Always," says Dr. Penido in his quiet drawling voice, "we try to use persuasion . . . We try to get people to feel they want to improve things themselves. Then when they feel the benefit they become interested."

On the way out we passed a row of humble beatenlooking women waiting in line to get free boiled milk or madeup formulas for their babies. Some of them have shoes but many of them have none. Their skimpy dresses are far from clean.

"Five years ago," says Dr. Penido in his low voice with his sad somewhat disdainful smile, "they were drinking polluted water out of the river and depositing their excrement in the bushes . . . We can isolate the lepers. We can cure yaws with about ninety *cruzeiros* worth of penicillin, we can cure hookworm . . . DDT has malaria on the run. We can vaccinate for diphtheria and smallpox but to have public health in this country we have to produce models that people will copy . . . sanitary islands."

A dark look comes over his face, as if he'd heard something that had hurt his feelings . . . "Now there is TB . . . It seems as if TB spreads out with civilization. When the people lived in little huts in the crannies of the mountains they didn't have so much TB. As we clean up other diseases TB seems to spread."

Across the street from the Health Center stands a very much larger building ornamented with a great deal of carved stone in pompous Manueline style. "What is that?" I ask. Dr. Penido walks on scowling up the street. Somebody else answers the question. That is the lying-in hospital built by the State of Espirito Santo some years ago. A fine building but the trouble is it has never opened. Funds ran out . . . Another Brazilian project.

We walked back to the station down the main street between stucco walls that glowed in the flailing sunlight. At one corner in front of a drygoods store stood a sallow man of middle age with the respectable paunch of a father of a family. He wore a fake Indian feather girdle and a feather headdress and carried a bow and arrow in his hand. Now and then he emitted hoarse fake Indian noises and made wardance steps inside of the drygoods box he stood in. As we passed we noticed that he was barefooted and that the box was full of broken glass. It was some wily Syrian's idea of how to advertise his cotton prints.

The valley was murky and hot that morning. Brush fires burned on the mountains on either side. Clearing land for new coffee plantations. The ranks of shrubby trees I'd been looking at in the hollows of the hills were coffee, the doctors said. In the lower part of the valley the planters were doing very well with cacao; up here it was all coffee. New plantings. Many of the trees were just about to come into bearing. In a few years the Rio Doce would be a great coffee producing region. If . . . If all went well. "Brazil is the land of the future," a Brazilian added bitterly.

The linecar jerked and jounced over the rails. At every station teams of zebu oxen, four five and six yokes pulling in a line, were hauling up the logs of peroba wood from the water's edge. A cloud of reddish dust hung over them. In the middle the river wound broad and sullen under a glaze of heat between rocky islets. Now and then we waited in a siding for a long oretrain to grind heavily past.

We were out of the malaria belt. The chief enemy of man in this part of the valley was a clever little fluke known as a schistoma that spent part of its lifecycle in a watersnail. From out of the watersnail came millions of little wormlike creatures that joyfully sought out the feet of a man wading or the hands of a woman washing and made their way through the pores into the blood stream where they hatched out eggs and produced a highly disagreeable disease known as schistomiasis. Again the preventive measures were privies, sewer systems and pure drinking water because the only way the schistoma got into the streams and ponds where it infected the snails in the first place was through the human faeces.

"In Aimorés and Valadares we'll show you the snails . . . On my way back from the States I stopped off in Venezuela where they are making progress in poisoning the snails. We are experimenting with that method, but meanwhile," said Dr. Penido smiling, "the answer is privies."

In the freight yard at Aimorés we found the SESP doctors' sleeping and laboratory car presided over by a shrewdlooking brown steward named Joaquim, who had some sort of a rising on his chin swathed in an immense wad of bandages and adhesive tape like the false beard of a pharaoh. He served us lunch in the tiny dining section of the car. The doctors said laughing that it was just as well the car was there because the hotel in this town had turned out so hopelessly unsanitary that they had induced the owner to pull it down entirely and start all over from scratch.

In spite of the loss of its hotel Aimorés is a busy little town full of dusty traffic and new building. House building offers few problems in these parts. A carpenter makes around twenty cents an hour. The valley is full of sawmills and every tiny hamlet has a brick kiln. Everybody complains of the expense and scarcity of cement but they have an abundance of cheap tile and brick. On every street we see new brick houses going up with tiled roofs, and well finished woodwork and beautifully laid parquet floors. From the hill which we are climbing to visit Monty's waterworks we see that about half the roofs of the town that straggles out over the valley floor are new. Right at our feet are the new tiny shacks, some of brick and some of the common mud and wooden frame construction, of the working people's suburb which in Brazil is known as a *favela*.

This *favela* is new and the best we have seen on the trip. The houses are in rows and each has a tiny yard and a solidly built brick privy. "Look at all the privies," Dr. Penido is saying with humorous pride. "An orgy of privies."

The Brazilians are puzzled and a little hurt when you ask questions about the *favela*, but to a stranger from the North the *favela* seems the visible symbol of the boundless poverty of the population. With the growth of industry and the caving in of the scanty rural economy people come crowding out of the back country where they lived ragged and barefooted and on the edge of starvation a life as ungarnished in every aspect as the little huts with dirt floors they were born in and dwelt in and died in, but where at least they had space about them and air to breathe. They get work in cities and towns. As a rule they find no housing ready for them and no effort to set up a standard of urban life for them to live by, so they pick themselves out a back lot and put themselves up a shack of what materials are cheapest and handiest just the way they would back up in the hills. They cook on charcoal. They can't read and write so they don't need much artificial light. The women and children fetch water in gasoline tins from the nearest pump, which may be a mile away, just as they would have gone down to the river back home, and they deposit their excrement back of the fence and throw their garbage out on the path just as they always did. The shacks agglomerate into a stinking rattle-trap settlement: a *favela*.

In Rio there are said to be three hundred thousand people living in *favelas*. There's no sewage, no light, no water and very little public order. You come on *favelas* in the most unexpected places. In Copacabana a few minutes walk from the hotels and the splendid white apartment houses and the wellkept magnificent beaches you find a whole hillside of *favelas* overlooking the lake and the Jockey Club. In the center of Rio a few steps from the Avenida Rio Branco on the hill back of one of the most fashionable churches you come suddenly into a tropical jungletown. Under pressure of metropolitan life the *favelas* are even producing a sort of culture of their own. Their religion is the *macumba*. Their artistic and social center the *samba* school. It was only remembering the *favelas* of Rio that you could understand the real enthusiasm under Dr. Penido's kidding manner when he stood looking down with the air of a conqueror on the wellbuilt privies at Aimorés and spoke of islands of public health. You got the feeling that there was more than sanitation, there was the budding of a whole new life, at stake in these islands.

Monty was waiting to show us around his waterstation, ready to explain how the water was pumped up from the river by diesel pumps so that they wouldn't depend on the light and power system that so often broke down. It passed through filters and chemical purifiers. Better water than many towns had in the States, said Monty proudly. Inside the walls were fresh painted and the machinery looked well tended and the tiled floors were clean.

A man was on his hands and knees mopping the tiles as we walked through. I looked at him twice because he was white-skinned and had very blond hair. His face was lined and haggard and dirty. It's a shock to a Northerner in this Rio Doce valley to find the blond offspring of German and Polish settlers living in the same ragged barefoot dirt and degradation as the darkerskinned inhabitants.

"You see," Monty was explaining as he ushered us out on the terrace, "we're all set except for pouring a little more concrete. Then only the cleaning up and landscaping left to do." I asked who the blond man was. "I dunno. He must be a German. I guess they just hire him for odd jobs."

We all stopped on the terrace to look down into the valley. The sun was setting red into the murk behind a scraggly line of ravaged forest on the crest of a cutover hill. Touched with sultry copper glints the Rio Doce meandered with a distant hiss of broken water through rocks and scrubby islands. It looked a little like the Susquehanna below Harrisburg. An oddlooking black bird with brown markings like a butterfly was fluttering about a clump of cactus. Down the path from the waterstation to the *favela,* naked except for a ragged pair of shorts, with a beaten droop to his shoulders, the blond man went stumbling wearily. He never turned his head to look at us. Holding onto his hand was a little towhaired boy three or four years old who was dressed in short pants and a little striped sweater, a sort of grimy replica of what a little boy of his age would be wearing in some distant Northern home. Looking after them I was remembering what my friend the geographer had told me in Rio: "You must never forget that Brazil is the greatest experiment in the settling of European man in the tropics, not always the most successful but the greatest . . . "

"If this town should double in size, and it very well may in a few years," Monty was saying, "this waterstation can still handle it . . . up to fifteen thousand people."

Above Aimorés next day the valley is narrower and dustier and drier. Fires burn more fiercely on the hills. A streaky ceiling of smoke and dust hangs over the river. On steep

eroding pastures that are a network of dry cowpaths big zebu
cattle graze in herds. Gangs are working on the line. Occasionally we have to stop while the section gang ahead
lowers a new length of track into place. The settlements
take on a raw backwoods look. At the little stations where
the linecar has to wait for the oretrains coming down, there
is a great deal going on. There are ferries on the river, flat-
boats that travel on a cable ingeniously propelled by the
force of the current. A shriek of mechanical saws comes
from the sawmills. Carts are bringing in cut firewood for
the railroad or bags of charcoal to be shipped to the charcoal-
burning iron furnaces up the valley. At every siding the ox-
teams churn the dust as they haul the trunks of peroba trees
from the water's edge. At a place called Conselheiro Pena
three men with slender poles are loading the logs on flatcars
hauling with a team of eleven great yokes of zebu oxen.

At a place called Tumiritinga which, so the stationmaster
proudly explains, has just changed its name from Tarumirím,
there is a long wait for the daily passenger train down from
Valadares. Monty and I roam through the ankledeep dust
between the two rows of forlorn low houses of plastered
adobe, looking at the pigs and the scattered garbage and the
open square of sunscorched weeds laid out for the *praça* to
be. "You see," Monty is saying dreamily, "this work can be
expanded indefinitely. We are just in the shape now where
we know how to do things . . . We've had five years to make
our mistakes and to work up a system. We've got the blue-
print and all we need to do now is expand it. At first it was
all by guess and by God as they used to say in the Navy . . .
When my contract expired I went back home and intended
to stay but I got to thinking that this work was about as
important as a man could find to do and I said to my wife
could she stick it . . . with the baby and everything . . . and
she said she guessed she could . . . so back we came. And now
when we're all rearing to go down here and Brazilian organi-

zations are really interested in putting up money for more SESP work, it looks as if the American end was petering out, as if there wasn't much interest in Washington. We are afraid the folks back home are forgetting about Brazil."

In a dilapidated bar an incredibly tattered young white woman with her hair in a ratsnest and her breasts blobbing out of her grimy dress has brought us tiny cups of coffee. A tobacco colored man with a felt hat and a mustache sits at the only other table. Right away he tells us that Tumiritinga had not only changed its name but it had just this day been created a city. They want SESP to come right in. Now that Tumiritinga is a city there'll be money to appropriate for public health.

The siren blows from the linecar. That means that the driver has his orders to proceed. Swallowing the last drops of our coffee we hotfoot it over to the station. Our friend with the mustache follows us all the way to the linecar explaining how much the people of the new founded city of Tumiritinga want help with their sanitation. "You see," Monty nudges me excitedly as we settle back in our seats, "You see, it's like this all over."

The town of Governador Valadares, full of sawmills and dust and new buildings, lies on a bend of the Rio Doce opposite a great battlemented mountain with a smooth granite face of which the top was lost in the level layers of smoke and mist that roofed in the valley. In the crowded freight yards beyond the station we find Joaquim waiting for us with his sleeper which has come up on the passenger train. It is still oven hot from the day's sun in the car, and airless because every space between the tracks is piled high with cut wood for the locomotives, but there is a narrow showerbath where the tepid water washes off a little of the grimed red dust of the valley.

All the way up the doctors have been promising us a good restaurant in Valadares so after everybody has bathed we straggle off up the broad main street, already planted with trees, past a new circular park at the intersection of two broad avenues, still in the excavation stage, to a café presided over by a huge light brown man in a cook's hat and apron whom the doctors say worked as a tailor until it occurred to him that he'd rather be a cook. And a very good cook he turns out to be.

After a great deal of steak and rice washed down by Portuguese wine to the tune of that most ingratiating Brazilian toast *"As nossas belas qualidades que não são poucas,"* we sit a long time talking and smoking. The Brazilians are trying to explain to the Americans, still in a gentle friendly way, that they feel let down after all the propaganda of the Good Neighbor Policy and wartime cooperation by the lack of interest the American people now show in their problems.

"But you don't want American capital. You want to develop your own oil industry and your own iron and steel."

"O petroleo é nosso. That's mostly propaganda," says one of the doctors laughing.

"But everybody believes in it. The papers in Rio are full of it."

"We don't want American imperialism but we do want American interest and help, especially technical help . . . and dollars. We'd like more help for SESP."

"Perhaps what hurts us," says Dr. Penido, "is a certain lack of comprehension . . . I feel it myself with Americans, not with all but with some even at this table. I was two years studying public health at Johns Hopkins . . . Baltimore is a very nice city. I had a very good time there, met many damn splendid guys but I felt a certain lack of comprehension."

He goes on to talk in a dreamy voice about European culture. He lived in Paris as a child. The loss of Paris was something no Brazilian could get over, the loss of that feeling of being linked to the ancient traditions of European culture. The war blacked out Europe. The Brazilians missed the stimulus of an allcomprehending culture. Perhaps that was why they were disappointed in the United States. They missed the stimulus.

The town lights go out. Our immense host brings in an oil lamp and sets it on the big Electrolux refrigerator behind the table.

"There have been a series of disappointments," one of the other doctors bursts out. "After the victory we thought that America would assume a world leadership like the Europe our fathers remembered."

"Without imperialism? How can you do it?"

There is a polite shrugging of shoulders.

"America seems so much weaker in victory . . . But in the story of SESP the important thing is that we have produced a successful experiment in international cooperation . . . SESP would not have existed without the financial and technical cooperation of both Americans and Brazilians. We have proved that it works. We have learned a method. Now we can go on to do great things. But just at this moment in the United States you seem to lose interest."

"We feel," says Dr. Penido yawning, "a certain lack of comprehension."

It is late. We get up from the table and start back to our sleepingcar.

In the morning a small plane came down from the mine at Itabira to pick me up. Now I was going to see where all those orecars came from I had watched jangling round the endless curves of the Rio Doce railroad. As the pilot spiralled up from the airstrip at Valadares to vault the first range of razorbacked mountains we began to note the extent of the devastation of the country. As far as we could see into the murk fires made a red marbling on the cutover slopes. The mountains smouldered like burnt papers in a grate. Pastures along the winding streams showed that fine network of cattlepaths that comes from overgrazing. Houses, usually solitary on a hillock in a valley, were few and far between. Near a house you could usually make out the broad bunched leaves of a few banana trees and some tiny patches of cultivated land. It was hard to imagine how so sparse a population could so ravage the hills, but already the railroads' demands for firewood and the burning of charcoal to cook with and for the iron furnaces and the logging out of lumber for export had gutted the forests of an enormous tract of country. As we climbed again to clear a new set of granite escarpments the valleys below were drowned in smoke. The plane tore into speeding clouds that packed tight and white as cotton against the windows.

There turned out to be no ceiling at all over the airfield at the mine so we had to turn back. When we landed at Valadares again the Brazilian business man who shared the seat with me shouted in my ear, "I was worried, until the pilot told me he was the father of eight. The father of eight must be very careful. . . . I am wondering," he added as we walked with throbbing ears across the field to the shelter, "if as a foreigner you understand the signification of what you are seeing in the Vale do Rio Doce . . . It is climbing a series of steps. First the valley was so unhealthy we could hardly keep up the railroad. The malaria service and SESP make sanitary the valley so that we can improve the railroad . . . America helps Brazil up a step. In the state of Minas Gerais we have the richest iron deposit in the world but to get it out we had only picks and shovels. The American loan buys the machinery to work it . . . Another step . . ."

"But what about the press campaign against American imperialism?"

"That," he said, "is the labor of Communists. Let us go to lunch."

After lunch the father of eight manages to land us on the

hilltop airstrip at Itabira. The mountains all around are still draped in clouds. The drenched air is chilly after the heat of the valley. The quiet man in khaki who comes out to meet us is Gil Whitehead the American manager of the mine for the Vale do Rio Doce Company. "It's too bad that you can't see the Pico de Caué," he says. "I'd like you to see the magic mountain."

While we wait for the clouds to lift off the mountain of iron we drive round the old town that climbs up steep ridges to a suburb of neat new houses for the skilled workmen and to the big concrete hangar that will soon house new machine shops. The valleys below are full of tattered mist. The weather has settled down to a drizzle. The hunks of wet ore shine as they thunder down the shutes into the orecars.

Gil Whitehead is a quiet man with a selfeffacing manner and a slow drawl. Now and then a smouldering sort of humor in his way of talking lets out a sudden flash. He explains how production has increased and how with the improvement of the railroad production would increase still more. For Brazil the iron ore, which was going to steel mills in the United States and Canada where they were using it instead of scrap, would mean dollars in the world market. And when the new machinery came production would really spurt. "Meanwhile," he says, "we are using the only rock crusher that, in these parts, never gets out of order." He points to a little brown man with a sledge hammer trudging along the road outside.

He unfolds a sketch of a projected orecrusher with a system of conveyors down the mountainside to the trucks and the railroad. "We can't be too impatient," he adds dreamily. "When we order machinery it has to come a long way and sometimes it takes a while to get here, a long long while."

The rain has stopped but the clouds hang lower than ever. "Let's go on up anyway." We start up in the station wagon.

As we drive up the broad zigzag road he points out that the road is metalled with ore which is about fifty percent pure iron. "Excellent roadbuilding material," he adds with a short laugh. "There are not many parts of the world where such a road would prove economical. It does here. Iron's all we've got."

As we climb the clouds close about us. Trucks loaded with ore loom huge as they grind past. The stationwagon comes to a stop on a red ledge. We climb out into driving clouds that flap like wet toweling past our faces.

"Here we are just under the summit of Caué. We are now standing on somewhere around two hundred and fifty million metric tons of compact hematite," Gil Whitehead announces. "Since we started in '44 we've taken twenty three meters off the top of the peak. The simplest operation in the world. We blast it down and these fellows break it up."

We are standing under the face of the solid sliced face of the rock. All along it men with hammers are breaking up the great sharp slices and splinters of rock. There are spindling white men and great tall negroes and small compact wiry men of all shades of copper. Some wear sandals and some are barefooted. A few of them have gunnysacks tied around them against the cold or long dirty looped up cloaks. The sledgehammers ring on the dense ore. Here and there little fires of sticks and broken boards glow red in the driving mist.

"It'll go faster when we have mechanical crushers," says one of the engineers who drove up with us.

"In Brazil," says another, "we always have to start from scratch."

Gil Whitehead has picked up a heavy chunk of ore and is looking down at it lovingly. "It's beautiful stuff," he says. "Now that the valley has been cleaned up we can get it out, but it is mighty far from Pittsburgh."

(When the lights go on EDDY JONES *is discovered standing up in his seat waving his arm like a school kid.)*

EDDY JONES: Mr. Lecturer, I want to ask you a question. What effect will that Brazilian hematite have on wages in the Mesabi Range?

MR. LECTURER: As I understand it, the Mesabi Range is a thing of the past . . . Anyway what seems to be happening is that the Labrador deposits are next on the program of the steel companies . . .

EDDY JONES: It all looks to me like a little scheme to get steel without paying American wages. If we insisted on their getting a decent price for their labor down in Brazil they wouldn't need so many doctors . . .

MR. LECTURER: I agree with you. In its present state of poverty Brazil is as open to dictatorship as dry woods to a brush fire. The Communist agitators have plenty of matches. We can't do anything directly about their wages but we can do something about their health. The special public health services are in a quiet way a service to selfgovernment as well as health.

EDDY JONES: To my way of thinking the way to get democracy is to start with decent wages.

MR. LECTURER: In a moment I'm coming to the example of what we might call a democratic type of leadership.

EDDY JONES: I never could understand South America anyway.

MISS SMITHERS: We must try. We really must try to understand foreign countries.

FRED RUFUS: I have a hard enough time understanding my own.

MR. LECTURER: *is desperately pushing on his buzzer. The lights dim. The map of Brazil comes back on the screen. Now the toy plane scoots westward from Rio.)*

CAPTION: *Highway into the Wilderness*

Brazil, you keep reminding yourself as you travel through what limited sections a man can get a glimpse of in a six weeks visit, occupies about half the South American continent and has roughly half the population. Except for the sprinkling of ancient settlements along the great bulge of sea coast thrust east towards Africa the country is all frontier. When you leave Rio in a plane to fly west, you climb immediately over the high coastal ridges and, coasting down into the bumpy air beyond over the knotted snarl of mountains that make up the state of Minas Gerais, you notice right away how few the towns and roads are. You see below you a lioncolored landscape of burned over slopes with tiny green strips of cultivated land spreading up the river bottoms. Rarely, out of a plumy bunch of banana trees, a tiny house with a tile roof shines white as sugar in the slanting morning light. The hills are a tangle of wandering mule and cattle tracks. Men and animals have walked there for centuries.

This infinity of wandering tracks testifies to the still nomadic life of the backlands. A man and his family will live in some little cabin in the hills until the land they work is worn out and then they'll suddenly pull up stakes and walk with their few possessions on their heads for hundreds of miles to find some patch of virgin brush which they can burn over for a new plantation. For cash they burn the larger trees for charcoal. The first few years the scorched forest loam gives them good crops, but the winds blow it off and the rains wash it away and the crops eat it up and after a while they have to move on again. A relatively sparse population has thus managed to ruin immense tracts of timberland.

The co-pilot, a dapper young man from Rio who speaks

very good English, has come back into the cabin and is pointing out the baroque towers of the miracleworking shrine at
Congonhas and further to the north the dark cluster against
a darker mountain of the palaces and monasteries and
churches of Ouro Preto, Black Gold, the old capital of the
state and the center of the gold rush in the seventeenth
century. He explains that the state of Minas Gerais, General
Mines, is one of the oldest settled sections of Brazil, stagnant
now, but — he spreads out his arms — with an immense
future. Far to the north on the indigosmudged horizon, he
points out the clouds that hide Caué, the iron mountain. I
tell him I've been there. "Before it was gold," he shouts
excitedly putting his lips against my ear. "Now it is iron . . .
The iron deposits stretch across the state of Minas in the
shape of a gigantic dollar sign."

He goes back to his place when the plane begins to lose
altitude over Belo Horizonte, Beautiful Horizon, which is
now the capital of Minas Gerais. Spiralling down for a
landing we get glimpses of the regular avenues lined with
trees and the tall white buildings of the city which was
started just fifty years ago on a plan based on L'Enfant's plan
for Washington. Nearer the airfield shine the angular con-
structions of glass and stucco designed by Niemeyer and
some other pupils of Le Corbusier's for a suburban development round the lake at Pampulha. These buildings at
Pampulha are some of the most original and imaginative
works of the newer school of architects in Rio. Unfortunately
the project, suffering the fate of so many projects in this
land of magniloquent blueprints, has received a setback
from a most unexpected cause. The lake was discovered to
be full of snails infested by the wicked little schistoma.
Until some way is found of killing the parasite or the snail,
the development of Pampulha is at a standstill.

After leaving Belo Horizonte you fly west for hours and
hours. The few tiny settlements are invisible from the air-

fields which get more and more rudimentary as you advance into the rolling country interspersed by great plains of the new state of Goiás. After seven hours flight from Rio we are in Goiania. This new capital of a new state is only fifteen years old. It consists of an avenue of feathery trees to the Governor's Palace, some public buildings and a few cross streets of rough stuccoed houses, a new hotel already falling to pieces, and some very nicely printed booklets of plans for the future.

While waiting for a suitable hour to call on the Governor, who had hospitably offered to send me out to the Federal Agricultural Colony the next day on one of his planes, I sat in the tiny bar at the hotel drinking beer with a couple of members of the Goiania Academy of Letters. They had brought along some magnificent booklets describing the plans for the new federal capital of Brazil which was to be established on a high plateau about a hundred miles further in the interior of the state, a plateau that boasted, they told me, a delicious temperate climate, where wheat grew in abundance and where all the plants and animals of the temperate zone, including European man, would flourish.

The development of Brazil had been blocked for three hundred years by the coastal range, by the colonial mentality of a people trapped between the mountains and the sea, they said. The way to break loose was to move the center of the nation boldly up into the plateau. Their eyes shone and their chests expanded when they talked about it. This must have been, I kept thinking, how our early enthusiasts for the West talked and glowed, sitting in some rickety tavern on the site of Washington City, when the subject turned to the Ohio or the great dimly discerned prairies west of the Mississippi. Before modern sanitation and trucks and airplanes all this was a dream; but now, my hosts kept assuring me, it was possible. The federal capital was written into the constitution. It had to come true. By history and tradition and by its racial admixtures Brazil was the best adapted of all the nations of European stock to conquer the tropics. The first step towards achievement would be moving the federal capital.

When I asked whether there was any way of getting to the plateau, they said it would be difficult. You had to go by a small plane to a rather uncertain airstrip. From there it was eight hours horseback up to the site. If it rained, it would be hard to get back. Neither of them had ever been.

"But where does the communist movement fit into all this? Haven't you already got too much government bureaucracy cramping each man's private effort?"

The younger of my hosts spoke up.

"At eighteen I was a Communist, like everybody else. We have malaria and jungle fever and a million diseases, but our worst disease is poverty. Young intellectuals feel trammelled at every hand by poverty. We thought communism was a cure for poverty. It seemed to open new careers for young men of brains. Now I am twentyseven and I have discovered that communism is just another way of dominating the masses. Instead of curing poverty it makes poverty universal. We have got to find other alternatives . . . The Communists now do not make propaganda for communism. They make propaganda against . . . against North America . . . against the rich, against anybody who is successful. In Rio they tell the poor people living in the favelas: 'We will throw out the landlords and you shall live in luxury in the hotels and the apartment houses in Copacabana.' It is simple. It works. Many of our most intelligent men, particularly poets, artists, architects are subject to this illusion. They have not thought the thing through to the end."

"It is up to you North Americans to give us an alternative," said the older man. "During the war the speeches of the great Roosevelt gave us an ideal to fight for. Since he died the United States seems to be drifting. You seem suddenly old and reactionary. We read about the Marshall plan for Europe, but when the Communists tell us it is imperialism we tend to believe them. All we see here is the scarcity of dollars."

"We Brazilians," the younger man burst out, "are a people of noble impulses. We hate war and militarism. We believe in progress. We are a people of grandiose illusions. That is why the communist movement here is like your Mr. Wallace's party in the States. It flourishes in the best society. Many fine people in all walks of life have allowed themselves to be deceived because no one has offered them a better plan."

"Then," said the older man, "there is envy in every human heart. You are rich and we are poor. The Communists play on the envy of the poor for the rich. The cure is a great movement of expansion that will furnish us with new illusions."

He looked at his watch. His voice suddenly took on the plush tones of a master of protocol. "It is time to go. His Excellency will be expecting us to make a short call at the Palace."

Next morning the governor's airplane lands us almost exactly in the center of Brazil. We are standing beside a new gravel road that stretches straight into dusty distance in either direction. Behind us is the ragged airstrip and in front of us a line of great trees that hides the river and all around a rolling country of high scrub vegetation shimmering in the heat. The sun already high beats down on us hard as hail so we take cover under the porch of a long hut thatched with palmleaves. Inside we find a counter and some shelves of groceries and a pale sweatylooking heavyset man with a week's growth of stubble on his chin. Immediately we are all drinking *cafezinho* out of the inevitable tiny white cups.

First thing I ask, "Is Saião at the *Colonia Agricola?*" "He

is," says the pale man enthusiastically. Then he explains
that we still have three leagues to go. We must be patient.
They will have seen the plane and will send out for us from
the *Colonia*. Saião always sends out for people, Saião attends to everything. The pale man turns out to be a Russian, from the Ukraine. He has lived twentyone years in
Brazil. He made big money in São Paulo as a machinist but
when he heard about the colony and the road into the north
he'd moved out here. He steps in back behind a bamboo
partition and brings out a diving helmet. Gold, he says,
rolling his bloodshot gray eyes; he dove in the rivers for gold.
Was he making money at it? One eye crinkles up like a
parrot's and his face takes on that sly look of the peasant on
the steppe. He doesn't answer but he holds up his thumb
and forefinger and rubs them together vigorously.

Before we knew what had happened we were adrift in a
tumultuous argument about the Soviet Union. The pale
man was insisting that Russia behaved as she did because she
was ringed by treacherous enemies. England and America
had always been her enemies. My literary friend from
Goiania brought up the Stalin-Hitler Pact. The Brazilian
judge, who was a small brown sparrowlike man with tortoiseshell glasses, perked up and asked if the Russians had done
right to partition Poland. In nineteen-eighteen the imperialist nations had all fought Russia, the pale man shouted back
fingering his diving helmet in a threatening way as if he
were going to use it for a weapon. We leaned across the
counter and roared at him. Meanwhile an audience was
gathering, an aged scarecrow with a face of stained leather
puckered on one side by some sort of ulcer, a soiled bare-
legged boy with a cast in his eye, a dog, two hens and a
rooster. A pig stuck his snout in through a rent in the
bamboo wall and two tiny yellowfaced children peeked in
beside him. We were all sweating like horses. The pale
man tore the shirt off his damp chest in an agony of con-

viction. It was all lies we were telling about the Soviet
Union. Then he laid his thick forefinger along his nose and
crinkled up his eye with that sly look again and said: "In
all this there is a mystery . . . There is a very secret mystery.
It is true that there is no liberty now but the secret of Russia
is liberty in the future."

"Look here," the Judge asked him, "if you are such an
admirer of the Soviet Union how is it you've been spending
all these years in Brazil looking for gold like a capitalist?"

Suddenly the pale man smiled all over his face. He had
a friend in São Paolo, he drawled, who was a doctor and who
wrote very brilliant articles against alcoholism. This doctor
wrote a whole book against alcoholism but whenever his
friends met this doctor he was in a bar buying himself a
drink. The pale man thrust out his hand laughing. We
shook hands all around and he brought out another set of
cafezinhos on the house.

The cloud of dust that has been coming towards us down
the road turns out to contain a bus. A junglestained paleblue bus bulging with passengers and packages. The bus
stops in front of the palmthatched hut and a few grimy
passengers straggle out to have themselves a coffee. The bus
is on its way to the Colonia. We are fitted in among dogs
and bundles and crates of fowls and the bus starts off grind-
ing and lurching on its slow way through the shabby dry-
season jungle. After a while we begin to pass clearings where
huge stumps and the skeletons of felled trees still smoulder
from the burning over; then thatched shelters, a few half
finished houses of brick. In front of the first tile-roofed
house we see a wattled cage that someone explains is a wolf
trap.

We drive downhill through a broad street of low houses
which are mostly stores. A crazy bamboo shack has a sign
Café Ceres. We pass a billiard parlor. We cross a green river
on a floating bridge supported on clusters of oildrums lashed

together. The Rio das Almas. Everybody points out a small white house on top of a grassy hill. That is where Saião lives.

We are deposited in front of a set of new brick walls which are marked *Grande Hotel Ceres*. We pick our way past the bricklayers stepping over planking heaped with fresh mortar and find that the diningroom and a few small alcoves have been completed, so that the hotel is open for business. The landlady greets us and briskly straightens up a table for our lunch. She speaks English. She comes from the northern part of Bohemia, she says. Oh yes she'd been in the *Colonia* a long time, almost a year.

The place to wash is outside in the yard, two enamelled basins on a soapy board and a gasoline can full of water. The tall unshaven man who is washing his face with a great deal of snorting and sputtering turns out to be a Syrian merchant who sells textiles. Yes business is good, good, good. When we settle down to eat I ask the landlady where Saião is to be found. She shakes her head. He is a hard man to put your finger on. Never stayed in one place. She'd send a boy over with a message.

"He is not here. Dr. Saião has gone to Rio," says a young lighthaired woman, nicely dressed as if for shopping in the city, who walks into the diningroom speaking dogmatic English. She sits down beside us. She comes from Vienna. She has an apartment in Rio. Her husband is a Hungarian. They are settling. If she likes it she will give up her apartment in Rio. If we want to learn about the *Colonia* we must stay many days because it is very interesting. We must come to see her new house. Eventually Dr. Saião will return.

The rosy young couple who walked in while we were talking turned out to be Swiss. The young fellow was an agronomist under contract to the Brazilian government. Did they know anything about the whereabouts of Dr. Saião? Oh no they didn't know anything yet. They had just arrived. Dr. Saião had fixed them up with a house. They had gotten married and had come to Brazil. They both had blue eyes and light curly hair, and fresh pink and white complexions. Their clothes looked crisp and clean. They walked out hand in hand looking into the jungle with shiny eyes.

After we'd eaten the usual meal of rice and beans and meat we strolled around the village of Ceres. The highway cut through the bottom of a wide valley cleared halfway up the hillsides. In every direction among the tree stumps straggled clumps of unfinished brick houses. Everywhere bricklayers were working, framing was going up. You caught glimpses against the sky of the bare brown backs of men setting the tiles on the roofs. That heap of bricks was going to be a moving picture theatre; that one was going to be a bank. Here and there a little house already finished in white stucco with painted shutters stood out bright and neat. On all the hills around the great scraggly trees of the ruined jungle crowded rank on rank against the edges of the clearings.

We kept asking for Saião. "He can't be far" people would smile and say. Everybody was out that afternoon. The American Franciscans who had a little house beside the unfinished church were away on a mission. The young American who ran a brick kiln beside the highway in the middle of town had gone into Annapolis. The Americans who had set up a sawmill down by the river were off in São Paolo.

At Saião's office in the barracks next to the machineshop that kept his roadbuilding machinery in order we tried to get a skinny young engineer to explain some of the workings of the colony to us but he begged off saying that Saião would explain it so much better when he came.

Where the devil was Dr. Saião? One man pointed north, another pointed south. Out on the road at work. How could you tell?

A stocky little man with long blond eartabs combed down

from under a pith helmet had driven up in a jeep while we were talking. Saião was in Amaro Leite. That was a town, a sort of a town. In the north, far in the north. He would be back this afternoon, he announced. *Era certo.* How far was Amaro Leite? The stocky man spread out his arms. *Uma infinidade de leguas* . . . An infinity of leagues.

While we waited the Judge and I went walking along the river. "This I suppose will be the principal *avenida,*" he was saying as we stumbled past wandering trucks through the deep dust. "They shouldn't cut down those trees. That should be the public garden right along the river."

All at once he was seized with a fury of city planning. He pointed here and there among the charred stumps, indicating parks and public buildings. I began to see columns sprouting among the trees, monuments to national heroes, bronze generals on horseback. The little Judge's chest swelled. He began to strut as he talked.

We started across the floating bridge. The sun had set behind forested hills. In the hurried twilight of the tropics a slight coolness rose from the swift mustard green water.

"Soon there'll be a new bridge," said the Judge proudly and pointed to the unfinished cement piers on the riverbank.

At the end of the bridge we met a very tall slender young man with fine sharpcut features and an almost black skin. He wore the usual ragged work clothes. He grabbed the Judge's hand and smiled with all his broken teeth. The Judge asked him how he was doing, was he married yet, were there any pretty girls in the *Colonia.* The young man talked fast and smiled some more and grabbed the lobe of his left ear with the thumb and forefinger of his right hand. That gesture meant O.K. He shook our hands again.

As we walked on the Judge explained that this young fellow had been janitor at the courthouse in Goiania. He'd been starving to death there on eight hundred *cruzeiros* a month. Now he was making fortyfive a day laying bricks.

"The man is happy."

By the time we get back to the *Grande Hotel Ceres* it is so dark we have a hard time finding it. No word from Saião. The dining room is jammed with men eating by the light of two lanterns and a candle. There are bearded men in hunting jackets who look like prospectors, there are salesmen and surveyors and engineers working on the road and the new bridge. Everybody is eating fast and talking fast. The dim light glints in eager eyes, on sweating cheekbones. When I grope my way out to the waterbucket to wash my face by the light of the lantern I see that the man ahead of me, a bull-necked character with a strawcolored beard, wears a large pearl earring in one ear. The night is already cool. From somewhere comes a smell of cape jessamine. Down in the dark valley an accordion is playing and a voice is singing *sambas.*

We are up at daylight standing around outside the office beside the repairshop in the valley with the construction foreman. There are bulldozers and road patrols. The place looks like a construction camp in the States. "No, he's not back yet."

"Yes he is," says the young man from São Paolo. "He got in from Amaro Leite at half past one . . . He'll be along any minute."

"Isn't it early?"

"He never gets tired. He sleeps while he drives."

The man with the helmet and the yellow eartabs drives up in his jeep. "He's back," he says in an excited tone. "His stomach is a little upset . . . He has a slight fever." The men crowd around the jeep with a look of concern on their faces. "But that is nothing . . . For Saião that is nothing."

A sedan drives up with a pretty girl in white in the front seat. A handsome young man in his shirtsleeves slips out from behind the wheel and walks towards us with his hand held out.

"Saião, at your service," he says. He rubs his hand over his

rough chin and adds apologetically that the barber was looking for him. He'd eaten some beans and mandioca flour in
Amaro Leite that hadn't set well. He wasn't quite up to
scratch this morning. He'd be all right. Let's go. He waves
us into the back seat of the sedan and introduces the pretty
girl as his eldest daughter. Her father ought not to be out,
she starts to tell us in remarkably good English, but she long
ago gave up trying to do anything with him. He was incor-
rigible.

Saião is talking to his men. He addresses a few words
directly to each man in a pleasant offhand leisurely tone.
Now and then he taps a man on the arm or lets a hand slide
along his shoulders. When he turns towards us to step into
the driver's seat we can see that he is a good deal older than
he seemed at first glance. His eyes are a little bloodshot from
the late driving yesterday and there is a web of fine lines
around them. He swings the car around carelessly and drives
down the highway. As he drives he leans back over the seat
to tell us about the *Colonia*.

Four years ago there was nothing but mata, the jungle.
This was part of the federal government's colonization plan.
Colonization was not his speciality. He'd spent his life
building roads. His pleasure had been in the fabrication of
highways. In São Paolo mostly. It was the kind of outdoor
life he liked. It was probably from his father that he'd gotten
a taste for it. His father had gone to work for the Central
Railroad of Brazil when he was still a schoolboy and had
worked his way up to be a director. A simple and straight
career, Saião adds smiling with a certain pride. But his father
had never lost his taste for the back country, and nor had he.

How many families have moved in already? asks the Judge.

"Around three thousand . . . This is cellular colonization,
a lot of people crowding around a center . . . "

"The state land office says thirty thousand," interrupts the
Judge.

"That includes settlers outside the *Colonia* . . . What we

need I'm beginning to think is strip colonization, to build roads and settle the land on either side . . . This is our sugar mill." Saião swerves the car off the gravel and up a hill and stops on a grassy knoll in front of another unfinished building of raw brick. "While we are waiting for the rest of the machinery we are going to use the generators to give light and power."

After looking through the mill we walk out among the hills of dark green corn that are sprouting vigorously out of the deep forest loam among the stumps and the charred trees so recently felled. "You see," Saião explains, kicking at a great stump, a good four feet across, "we are not quite ready to use farm machinery. Our machines are hoes and the muscles in men's backs."

"How does one man and his family ever get started hacking down the jungle?"

It is hard the first year, he explains, very very hard. They start out camping under a tree. There is an institution in these parts known as *mutirão*. You get together some food and *cachasa* and a guitar and invite all the neighbors in. They work like fiends all day and in the evening they have a party. A primitive form of mutual aid. All the heaviest work is done that way. The next thing is to put up a shack of bamboo and palm thatch. Then after a year you are beginning to get a little food out of the crops of beans and rice and *mandioca* and sweet potatoes you planted. Maybe you have something over to sell.

As he talks he points out little shacks in the clearings on either side of the valley. Most of these people came from the state of Minas Gerais, to the east, tough people accustomed to living in the bush. They were hard workers if they thought they got results. Here they got results. Rice was very profitable.

"Our land is so cool and moist you can grow rice without irrigation . . . When they get a little cash from a crop they buy bricks and build themselves a better house like that fellow over there." He points out a little white house with an arched veranda, beside a clump of huge trees. "Then they buy some cattle and clear more land and sell the timber to the saw mill and buy shoes . . . Coffee does magnificently here. We are planting Columbian type coffee for the American market. I want my settlers to plant coffee to tie them to the soil. A coffee plantation is a long term investment. Brazilians are too nomadic. They drift all over the continent. They'll clear a piece of land and plant a couple of crops on it and move on. I want our people to stay put . . . "

We drive on through raw plantations of coffee and corn and rice in jagged forest clearings. We visit the hospital and a small unfinished school.

The four things they need to get a colony going, Saião is saying, are: first an all-weather road, second proper division of the land so that each man knew what was his, third a hospital and a public health service and fourth schools for the children. "But what I enjoy most is the road." He shows all his white teeth in a smile. "We are driving a road clear through the center of Brazil."

Already we have left the settlement behind and are charging north up the straight gravel road through the shaggy jungle. Saião drives with one hand, turning back to talk to us as if he knew the road so well he didn't have to look at it. Sometimes he takes both hands off the wheel to make a gesture. The car plunges and swerves but he yanks it back without looking . . . "Here's where we get our gravel. The soil isn't so good. You can tell by the smaller size of the trees. Grazing land to be, but it's full of gravel . . . we get all we need for the road." Whenever he speaks of the road his voice takes on an affectionate tone as if he were speaking of one of his children.

"What do you do," the Judge is asking, "when you get settlers who don't work?"

"When they don't want to work they leave. The others don't like to see idle people around. I've never had to use the police yet . . . or any kind of force. We argue with them, we give them friendly advice. But they have to work to eat. We are not running a home for incompetents. They soon catch the spirit of the thing. They see other people building better houses, buying clothes, making money. Our people are natural colonizers."

We drive north for an hour at top speed. Blue mesas begin to rise up in the distance. Beyond the Rio São Patricio, Saião turns into a construction camp. "Now Papa you can't go too far," the pretty daughter has been saying, "You have that government commission flying in this afternoon." He gives her the look of a small boy called in from a ballgame. "All right," he says, "but at least I can show them on the map."

The construction camp has an up to date thrifty look. The living quarters are on trailers, the woodwork is all done at the *Colonia*. The *Colonia* is his base, Saião is explaining. The repairshop looks neat and businesslike. New lathes and Manley presses. Plenty of tools. The portable generators are humming. Everything is screened, there is electric light, a two way radio.

In part of a shack fitted up as an office Saião strides up to the map on the wall. He points with his forefinger to the mouth of the Amazon. "The object is to open up communications with Pará, our northern port will be the city of Belem. From São Paulo to Belem we have around twenty-four hundred kilometers to go. There are roads from São Paulo to Annapolis. On the new road from Annapolis we've come three hundred and forty . . . nine hundred kilometers of it will be by water on the Rio Tocantins. Landing barges will carry the trucks. War surplus. We are buying them right now in the States."

When he slams the car into the gravel road again Saião

hesitates at the turn as if he had half a mind to turn north anyway. "Now Papa . . . " says the pretty daughter. Obediently he turns back the way we have come. He twists back towards us from the driver's seat with a rueful smile. "You come back in two years," he says. "Then I'll drive you clear to Belem."

FRED RUFUS: That feller's the kind of man made this country what it is.

EDDY JONES: We've got some union presidents in the C.I.O. who are men like that.

FRED RUFUS: I never heard of a labor leader building a road or of doing anything else that was useful.

JAKE JEFFRIES: Mr. Lecturer, do you suppose you could give me that man's address? I ought to be able to sell him some hybrid seedcorn.

MRS. EDWARDS: But if South America is producing such splendid leadership why do we have to worry about their going communistic?

MR. LECTURER: It's not the present danger of communism. It is that using the principle of political leverage it's so easy for any adventurer to take over the government of those countries. That's why it is our friends, the believers in self-government in South America, who are sorest at the United States. They are sore at us because they don't think we have any principles. The attitude of the average American businessman in a foreign country is "Who's a boss? Let's talk to the boss."

Many of our diplomats show the same attitude, in a more refined way. Political tendencies in South America are much more Fascist than Communist, but as time goes on there gets to be less and less conflict between the adherents of the two systems. They help each other against the common enemy which is freedom. Once you've mastered the technique of tyranny it doesn't matter what you call the result.

It was in Uruguay, the one country in South America with institutions and traditions and a respect for civil liberties similar to our own, that I heard the hardest things said about the failure of American leadership.

CAPTION: *The Civilization of the River Plate*

A traveller who has been plodding his way through tropical South America where poverty poisons all human life like an endemic disease, gets the sensation when he lands in Montevideo that he has strayed into some prosperous part of before the war Europe. He's back in the temperate zone. Everybody wears shoes. Working people are welldressed. Skins are light. The men and women you meet on the street have the stocky stubborn look of the inhabitants of Barcelona or Marseilles or Milan, though they are better fed and better off generally than the people of any of those cities are today. The streets are clean. At the hotel the plumbing works, water runs hot and cold in the bath. In the restaurants the people have a middleclass look. It's hard as in the Middle West to tell whether they work for wages or for salaries or whether they are in business for themselves.

Their country the Uruguayans tell you is small, but so is Switzerland they add with a smile. Mostly farms and ranches, sheep and beef country. Montevideo is the only industrial center; as in every South American country the head is too big for the body. But in Montevideo's case, they hasten to explain, the beaches help pay the cities' way. It's the resort area for all the southern continent. People go there to spend their money, especially the Argentines in droves. Maybe they like to breathe the air of liberty, the Uruguayans say with a sly smile. Although Uruguay had as checkered a political history as any of them during the nineteenth century, since Batlle's (they pronounce it Batje) great administration selfgovernment has taken root. The various sectors of the population are well represented in the Congress. There's a flourishing and independent co-operative movement. Labor is organized. There's complete freedom of speech, freedom to campaign, and to publish. Even the Communists can talk as long as anyone will listen. Freedom of speech works both ways. When the Communists tried by gangster methods to close down an American movie that purported to show the seamy side of the Soviet Union, men and women in the audience themselves helped throw the agitators out of the theatre, and when the riot subsided, although it was long after midnight, insisted on sitting through the picture. They wanted to see what it was the Communists were so anxious to hush up.

When they talk about their liberties people in Montevideo have a way of glancing apprehensively towards the waterfront. Buenos Aires on the opposite shore of the estuary is only an hour away by plane, overnight by steamer. Uruguayans don't like the size of Peron's army. They don't like the idea of modernized armies of any kind in their end of the continent. Still, they tell you as if to reassure themselves, that the Swiss have been surrounded by all the armies of Europe for centuries and still have their independence . . . but the Swiss have their mountains. Uruguay, they tell you reassuringly, is the Switzerland of America.

"If we felt the United States was ready to protect selfgovernment, government by the people, of the people and for the people in all the Americas we wouldn't worry about having no natural defenses," one of the Ministers told me. "Unfortunately we don't feel that the United States backs up its friends. We were anti-Nazi in Uruguay when it wasn't any too safe to be anti-Nazi. In Washington they seem to have very short memories. They don't seem to know their friends from their foes. The United States should be our best friend in the world, but North American policy has not been such as to inspire confidence in its friends. That is why the anti-imperialist propaganda of the Communists has made such headway even with us. We would like so much to have confidence in the United States."

In nosing around the town I found myself visiting the rest home of the newsvendors union near the fashionable beach. They showed me their roses and their playgrounds and their outdoor fireplaces for broiling steaks and their clean sunny dormitories and readingrooms. "We did this all ourselves," they told me. "In Uruguay we like to do things for ourselves. In the old days we used to be affiliated with the newsvendors in Buenos Aires but now they let the government do everything for them over there. The *peronistas* have captured their union. They tried to get us to come over to a congress. They had designs on us, but we wouldn't go. We haven't any intention of being sucked into Peron's *descamisados*. In Uruguay there is no workingman so poor that he doesn't wear a jacket."

Montevideo has always been an excellent observation point from which to view events in Argentina across the bay. Traditionally it has been the asylum for political refugees from the sister republic whenever the authorities in Buenos Aires made life too difficult for the opposition. I found people there a little reluctant to speak out too loudly against Peron and his party. Two things frightened the Uruguayans about him: they were afraid his movement might turn to military conquest. An authoritarian republic which would include both banks of the River Plate had for many years been the aim of extreme Argentine nationalists. And second, they were afraid that the mass contagion of the *peronista* movement might afflict some of their own people.

They pointed out that though the appeal to the masses of wage earners of Peron and his Señora was partly demagoguery, it also had a firm foundation in real benefits. The unions which the *peronista* party controlled had, in spite of inflation of the peso, been given a boost in real living standards in return for voting the right way in the elections. As a result Peron's administration was something new in South American dictatorships. Peron had won mass support and organized it skillfully through his party. Mass support had made him partly independent of the army. Of course he had used every demagogue's weapon, fanning every nationalist aspiration and every resentment against North American business and against the old Argentine oligarchy of wealth and land, but in each case he had had real grievances to go on. Their fear was that his movement might spread to adjoining countries where the economic situation of wageworkers was far worse than it was in these fortunate regions of the River Plate where everybody had enough, even too much, to eat, and clothes to wear and a roof over their heads. There was one fact you couldn't laugh off, although the *peronistas* had by underhand methods secured control of the press and the radio before the election and had used money from the public funds for the purpose, there was no doubt that voting had been free and that Peron had a large proportion of the Argentine people behind him.

"We are worried about the *peronista* movement, we don't like his purge of the Universities, we think he's a fascist but a very clever one," said a Montevideo jeweller. "We have to watch and wait. Peron's situation is like Mussolini's before the murder of Matteotti, but Peron hasn't killed his Matteotti yet. Except for allowing a good many bricks and stones to be thrown at his opponents during the *amontonadas* of his *descamisados* he's been very sparing of violence. He's a fox . . . We have to go easy . . . Then too business interests in Montevideo are inextricably linked with those in Buenos Aires; and in our mixed halfsocialized economy here in Uruguay, national interests and government interests and cooperative interests and even trade union interests are inextricably linked with business interests. Montevideo and Buenos Aires are like a pair of Siamese twins. If one of them goes crazy the other one has to be very very careful."

"We'll be curious to see what kind of reception you get from the *peronistas*," said my Uruguayan friends as they saw me off on the flying boat for Buenos Aires. "In any case don't let them pull the wool over your eyes."

CAPTION: *Carnivorous City*

At noon the streets of Buenos Aires are full of the smell of broiling meat. From the old waterfront region of La Boca where in a stench of slaughterhouse swill the sluggish Riachuelo flows past deepsea freighters and fishingboats and dieseldriven rivercraft tied up three deep at the docks, through the long arteries all ajangle with carts and trucks skirting the new wharves and the grain elevators that look out over the earthcolored estuary of the River Plate, to the vast squares and treelined avenues of the business district which converge on the fat obelisk the city's traffic spins around, men and women come stamping down out of stores and office buildings and warehouses and sniff the air hungrily. Most of them had nothing but a few sips of *maté* for breakfast. From every corner under the lightgreen trees drifts the blue crinkling smoke of broiling meat. In a thousand restaurants, rôtisseries, eatinghouses large and small, slabs of steak sizzle on broilers and sides of beef and whole lambs and kids and sucklingpigs turn on spits. By halfpast twelve every table is taken. Rich and poor, bankers and government employees and railroad workers and bricklayers and brokers and roustabouts are putting away great hunks of broiled meat and long loaves of crisp wheat bread with appetizers on the side in the shape of kidneys and entrails and tripe, all washed down with the red wine of the country. While you wait for your steak they bring you cuts of cold ham and salami and roast beef to fend off starvation. No greens. We don't eat cattlefood, the Argentines tell you.

Buenos Aires is the meateatingest city. There are vegetables and fish in the markets but it's around the meats that the throngs collect. You find special stalls hung with carefully plaited intestines and blood puddings and sausages of every shape and size, pink and red and brown and marbled. Other vendors go in for tripe and tongues and brains in enamelled dishes and livers and oxtails and kidneys neatly wrapped in their own fat. Suckling pigs hang in rows by their chins and skinned lambs' heads look at you out of lidless eyes as you walk past.

The Argentines complain that prices are high but you still see cuts of prime beef selling at a peso eighty a kilo, which even at the official rate of exchange, is little more than forty cents. To judge from the crowds people of all classes have money in their pockets to buy with. After the meats the stands where they sell the infinite variety of Italian pastas, spaghetti and macaroni and noodles are the most popular and then those that set out great cylinders of butter and fine local cheeses in the style of Roquefort, Gorgonzola, Gruyère, Cheddar, Edam. Last thing of all the shopper buys a bunch of watercress to garnish his meat with and an armful of flowers and starts for home. As the afternoon wears on and offices close you find people swarming in the huge pastry-shops that have room after room full of round tables flanked by marble counters piled high with layercakes iced in various colors, inscribed with flowers and hearts and topped with marzipan fruits, and escarpments and pyramids of puffs and eclairs and millefeuilles and napoleons stuffed with every

kind of cream and custard. There they drink tea and coffee
and carry the counters by storm before going on to their late
nine o'clock suppers.

On Sunday, for a change, you go out into the country to
eat broiled beef. The Argentine form of barbecue is called
an *asado*. The suburbs of Buenos Aires spread out far over
the prairie, where real estate developments and cottage
colonies are fast eating into the rich farm and grazing lands.
The better off people eat their *asado* in their own country
places set in groves of eucalyptus trees. The poorer people
eat theirs in restaurants and lunch stands grouped along the
roads and round the stations of the suburban railways. But
they all eat *asado*. The procedure is the same everywhere.
The steaks and the ribs of beef and the strings of sausages
and the plaited intestines are broiled over an open fire.
There's red wine and bread and like as not somebody appears
booted and spurred with poncho and guitar to sing the
Argentine equivalents of our synthetic hillbilly songs and
those who know them dance a few steps of the old country
dances. If there's no gaucho, they tune in on the radio for
patriotic ballads of the free life on the pampas.

Buenos Aires is probably the best fed of the great cities of
the world today. The big meals of meat give people a heavy
selfsatisfied air. You can walk for miles through the poorer
parts of town without finding a real slum like Harlem or
South Chicago or the upper East Side in New York. Everywhere the children look uniformly well nourished and
neatly dressed. They all go to school in clean white cotton
smocks. Although the statistics on the relation of wages to
prices are a matter of political dogma, with the supporters of
the present government claiming that wages are running
ahead, while the Opposition insists that they are well behind,
you get the impression that generally inflation has not yet
really endangered the high standard of living. Certainly in
Buenos Aires any place where a man can spend money is

jammed with spenders: clothing stores, pharmacies, department stores, moving picture theatres are full of people. Soccer games and wrestling matches fill huge stadiums. The race courses are so packed with blankfaced heavybodied men in doublebreasted suits that it takes you a halfhour's pushing to get to the booth to place a bet.

In spite of all the talk about the revolution of the *descamisados* Buenos Aires is still a formal selfsatisfied city, a city of welldressed men. The manner of life there is an amalgam of the various ways of living of the great European cities before they were ruined by the wars. Conventions are rigid. Juan Pueblo may take his coat off to prove he's a *peronista* at a political meeting but he can't sit at a café or get into a moving picture theatre without a necktie and even little children have to wear their jackets in public. An American I knew, walking home late one hot night along a quiet residential street, had just taken off his coat and rolled up his shirtsleeves to get cool when a policeman ran after him and tapped him on the shoulder and told him that in Buenos Aires there was a city ordinance against that kind of thing.

Juan Pueblo is the Argentine equivalent of our John Q. Public. In Buenos Aires he's a respectable family man who likes his wife to stay home to mind the children. He dresses well. His clothes are expensive but he buys them on the installment plan. He spends a lot of money on lottery tickets and on the races. He's profoundly sober. Outside of wine with his meals, he rarely drinks. In a café a glass of beer or a small coffee will last him all afternoon. Usually he works a long way from home and has to take a combination of subways and buses and suburban trains to get out to the tree-shaded street where he lives in a tiny onestory house set a little back from the sidewalk with a private yard behind where he can grow a tree or a few flowers in the deep rich soil of the pampas on which the city is built or where, if he has a mind to have a few friends in for a party, he can broil his own *asado* over the coals in the open as the early settlers did when the pampas was unfenced prairie.

He's proud of his city. He calls himself a *porteño,* a man of the port. He knows that greater Buenos Aires accounts for about a fourth of the population of his country. He's proud of its size. He knows that his country is rich in meat and wheat and he thinks it would be rich in dollars too if it weren't for the machinations of American imperialism. He feels prosperous and wellfed. He knows that the city is growing and spreading like a prairiefire over the pampas. If he's lucky enough to own the little piece of land his house is built on it is increasing in value daily and like as not he's planning to sell it and to buy him a couple of lots in some garden development further out where there is still a chance of getting in on the ground floor before the boom reaches its peak. If you tell him it's all specious inflation he's likely to answer that he likes it that way. He's touchy with foreigners, North Americans particularly. He doesn't know much about the rest of the world but he resents the fact that the rest of the world doesn't know much about him. He feels that his country has been treated as a colony by London and slighted and unappreciated by Washington. That's all over now; he's out to get even. Juan Pueblo is feeling his beefsteaks. Buenos Aires, he is convinced, is the finest city and Argentina is the leading nation in the Southern Hemisphere. He likes to listen to orators talking about *argentinidad,* the quality of being Argentine. He may have doubts about some of the members of his government and about some of its policies but on the whole he feels that Juan Peron has made his country a power in the world and he's proud of his president.

CAPTION: *Peron's Trade Unions*

One day the delegate from the bakers' union came by to pick me up at the hotel. He insisted on paying for the taxi. "A workingman can ride in a taxi now," he said. "Before it was unheard of. Go to any factory and you'll see a line of taxis picking people up after work."

When we reached the offices of the Buenos Aires local we walked through a dingy hallway and turned into a high-ceilinged room with stained greenish wallpaper and a long table in the middle. At one end a bulky redheaded individual was pecking at a typewriter. I was introduced to a ruddy sharpfeatured man in a blue suit who'd fought on the republican side in Spain during the civil war. He took me in charge right away. He began by apologizing for the condition of the local. He pointed out the bullet hole in one window and the perforations in the tin ceiling and the places where hunks of plaster had been knocked out of the wall. Hadn't had time to redecorate, he said smiling, since a little shooting they'd had a few weeks ago.

"You think of bakers as peaceful people . . . Actually we are rather violent." He burst out laughing. "But this is a good example of what I want to talk to you about. At the last union convention we threw out our secretary for disloyalty so he came around with a couple of hundred of his gang and tried to storm the office. We fought them off. There was considerable shooting, two killed and several wounded. Now in the old days nobody would have asked who was right and who was wrong. It would have been jail and the police would have taken it out of our hides. Not so under Peron. We were arrested and decently treated and the police judge found it a case of selfdefense and turned us loose. In the old days the working man never had a show."

"Tell him about the *picada electrica,*" said the redheaded man across his typewriter.

"You see we bakers were an illegal association from 1931 up to 1944 when Peron got through a decree giving us legal status. There was no limit to the brutality of the police when they put down a strike. The *picada electrica* is an instrument invented to drive cattle into the stockyards. Used on a man it becomes an instrument of torture . . . We can't go out and tell men who've been tortured by the *picada electrica* to be careful of Peron, that Peron may take away their freedom . . . If the democratic politicians and the gentlemen of *La Prensa* and the Jockey Club had been a little more interested in our troubles then we'd be a little more interested when they say that Peron destroys the freedom of the press. There was never a word in the liberal papers about the *picada electrica.*"

"Look here," said the redheaded man, "we held a convention the other day of our national federation. I tell you it's not a question of the *peronistas* coming over to influence us. They haven't got the personnel. Our boys are over there asking their help. We're going to have to call a strike next month to get better wages. It's been the government's policy to keep down the price of bread so the bakers have had to suffer. Peron has raised milkmen — you don't have to know anything to deliver milk — to a thousand pesos a month while our people who are skilled craftsmen are only averaging three hundred and ten."

"You think you'll get your raise?" I asked the man in the blue suit.

"We'll get it," he answered frowning, "by going along with Peron. We can talk to Peron. We can talk to the Señora de Peron. They aren't ashamed of being seen with working people. Before you couldn't get to talk with an

officeboy in any of the ministries . . . To keep our membership in line we've got to go along with Peron, only . . . " He
put his index finger to his right eye and pulled down the
lower lid. "We've got to keep an eye open."

Out in the shabby hall on the way out a little yellowfaced
man in a frayed collar stepped out in front of me. He had
red rimmed eyes and a week's growth of gray stubble on his
chin. "Illusions," he spluttered in my ear. "Peron's a politician and the worst of the lot. Us bakers are only a few.
Peron only cares for masses he can lead by the nose . . . The
only thing a workingman ever got out of a politician is
promises. When the time comes he'll crack down on us
worse than any of them." Talking fast he followed me to the
street door. There he stopped suddenly, gave a frightened
look up and down the passage and scuttled back inside.

The first thing you see in the office of the Railroad
Workers' medical service is a big sepia photo of Eva Duarte
de Peron. The Railroad Workers have taken over a tall
dim house built by some rich meatpacker at the beginning of
the century, full of stained glass and stucco decorations like a
wedding cake turned inside out. When you are ushered
into the boardroom on the second floor four heavy set men
get solemnly to their feet.

"Of course we are for Peron," says one big pale bull of a
man with the largelobed ears you sometimes see in this part
of the world to mark a trace of aboriginal blood. "Before
Peron the labor movement in Argentina was at the mercy of
the police. Now we are a force." He shoves a big slick paper
yearbook that looks like the yearbook of a powerful U.S.
corporation into my hand. "Read that . . . Take it to the
United States to show them."

He snatches the book back and lays it on the table and
turns the pages with a thick finger and thumb. "You see . . .
the rights of the workingman . . . These are the hospitals

we've bought. If you don't believe it we'll take you to see them. Look . . . ambulances, dental clinics, child care clinics . . . all modern, the finest in the country. When the English owned the railroads they let us die like dogs. A railroad man who got sick starved to death. Now we are a force. One of our officers is minister of foreign affairs. That's a powerful post. You've heard of Juan Bramuglia. He's making a great name for himself in Paris . . . He's our man, an official of the Railroad Workers. We have forty hospitals, a factory for pharmaceutical products . . . No matter who the government is we are going to hold on to our hospitals."

When you visit any of the locals of the Retail Workers' Union the first thing they show you beside the inevitable portraits of the Perons is the photograph of a pale foxy faced youngish man, with his hair brushed back, their minister Borlenghi. He comes from their organization. He holds the most important post in the government after Peron, they tell you proudly. He's Minister of the Interior. The Minister of the Interior controls political appointments and the police.

You have to wait a long time to see Señor Borlenghi at his office in the Casa Rosada. His waiting room is tall and stately, decorated with seals of the Argentine provinces. Groups of politicians in doublebreasted suits sit stiffly on sofas, nod heads together in corners. Talk buzzes about the campaign to put over a new constitution that will establish the rights of labor and the social security laws and the government's control of the import export trade and, incidentally, make it possible to reelect Peron in 1952. Most of the men are young and new to the game. They are waiting for a word with Señor Borlenghi before going out on speaking tours in the provinces.

There turns up an athletic young *peronista* I've met before. "Do you think it's a dictatorship?" he asks me outright. Before I have time to think up an answer, he hurries to tell me he thinks it's nearer democracy than anything they have ever had in Argentina . . . More like Roosevelt and the New Deal. Roosevelt too had his Señora. Mind you he didn't mean everything was done perfectly. It would take time for the *peronistas* to get experience in government. It would take them time to learn their jobs. The oldtime politicians weren't being helpful. The oldtime liberal press was not being constructive in its criticism . . . The Socialists had been so abusive they'd had to close their paper *Vanguardia* down outright . . . Abuse wasn't constructive criticism, now was it?

A secretary has come in to say that Señor Borlenghi is free. Señor Borlenghi turns out to look very much like his photograph. He talks fast and bitterly in a low sibilant voice. He has travelled all around North America, he says. He feels that if our people really knew what was going on in Argentina they'd approve of it. They were being misinformed by the capitalist press and the import-export crowd. *Peronismo* was the Argentina declaration of independence. Before the country had been an economic colony of British and American capital. The working people were going to get their fair share of the country's wealth they had helped produce. I ought to go out to see what Peron was doing for the working people. I ought to go to see what his retail workers were doing for themselves.

All right where was the best place to go?

"Go to see our new resort hotel in the Andes where the retail workers go for their vacations, paid vacations on the employers' time." He gets to his feet. He'll fix it up. He hurries back into his office.

The retail workers' hotel was near Mendoza, a wine-growing center in the eastern foothills of the Andes where it pleases people very much if you tell them their brisk little city looks like a California town. "We are the Californians of Argentina," they answer proudly. There's a great bustle in the retail workers' local because they are getting ready to entertain the Señora de Peron who is coming out to make a speech for the new constitution. Banners are stacked in the corner of the social hall, transparencies are being tacked on their frames.

The union officials are young and full of enthusiasm. They want to show me everything at once. After lunch we set out crowded into an ancient Dodge that turns out to have no brakes. In a park in the center of town an elaborate grandstand has been constructed over one end of a green pond. That's where the Señora is going to speak. The giant faces of Peron and the Señora are already being raised amid bunting between peeled poles.

They point out the posters of the opposition parties. "You see they are free to campaign." They start laughing. "The wind did blow a few of them down during the night."

Then we have to see the immense monument to San Martin, the Argentine George Washington, who set out, they explain, from this very Mendoza to cross the Andes on his famous expedition that joined forces with O'Higgins in Chile and then marched up the coast, knocking over Spanish governors on the way to free Peru and to meet the armies of Bolivar the liberator of the North.

In the museum they point out the first Argentine flag which the ladies of Mendoza sewed for San Martin before he left on his expedition. A tone of religious reverence comes into their voices whenever they mention San Martin's name.

Then we set off for the mountain resort. All afternoon winding over the dry jutting crags of the first Andean range they kept pointing out the course San Martin's army took to cross the mountains. Argentina was on the march again, they said with a shine in their eyes, led by Peron towards freedom from capitalist monopolies, toward liberation of the continent from foreign imperialism, but peacefully, they hurriedly added.

At last we start looping down a gravelly road into a broad valley, green with rows of poplars and eucalyptus trees. Below the pass we climb out of the car to look at the view. They point out far below us a white California style building with a redtiled roof, the new hotel.

The place is called Uspallata. It was in this valley that San Martin stopped to cast his cannon before he marched to the Pacific and now the Retail Workers have bought the whole estate for their resort hotel. That's what Peron and Borlenghi had done for them.

One of the young men waves his hand at the sparkling snowpeaks on the horizon. "Before the *peronista* revolution," he says, "only the oligarchs, only the very rich could enjoy this. Now any member of our union can come and spend his vacation here."

We are eating dinner together at the hotel named, naturally, the *Hotel Presidente Peron*. It is a formal dinner of several courses washed down by first rate red wine and ending up with the usual magnificent Argentine steak. With the asparagus come little silver tongs to pick the stalks up with. I fumble mine and go back to eating the asparagus with my fingers but my hosts all skillfully handle the long stalks with their silver tongs.

"The best," they keep saying. "Peron wants the working people in Argentina to have the best . . . like the oligarchy had it."

They introduce me to a pale young man who is the assistant manager. "We've done this all ourselves," he says. "The architect's plans and the decoration and the management all come from the Retail Workers' Union." Do I think it's a dictatorship, they ask over the brandy and cigars.

After dinner they showed me a suite full of portières and ruffles which they said with bated breath was the Minister's, their minister's. Then they left me to go back to their preparations for receiving the Señora in Mendoza. When I

turned on the light in the room they'd picked out for me to
spend the night in, the first thing that showed up under the
sheet of glass that protected the bureau were the smiling
features of Juan Domingo and Maria Eva de Peron.

CAPTION: *The Corruption of Juan Pueblo*

"Do you think that wages are still running ahead of
prices?" I asked a tall towheaded newspaper man as he
walked along the *calle* Florida brimful from curb to curb
with the noontime crowd.

"Our wages aren't. A newspaper man has to hold two or
three jobs to keep from starving to death . . . That applies
to most of the middle class — the middle class is on the rack
— but the working people still are well off in spite of the
inflation, at least the people whose unions play along with
Peron . . . " We had stopped at the corner of Corrientes, the
avenue that is the Broadway of Buenos Aires. The street was
full of the smell of broiling that came from lines of restaurants and rôtisseries. "We are a sober people but if we get
plenty of meat to eat we think everything is fine," he added.
"Look at this. In ten minutes there won't be a free table.
Rich and poor, bank presidents and government employees
and stevedores and shopkeepers will all be eating their beef
. . . But outside of Peron's private unions the only people
who are really making money are speculators who have an in
with the government and of course some of the government
gentlemen themselves who are opening Swiss bank accounts.
What's the use of talking about it? If Juan Pueblo gets his
belly full of beef every day he's for Peron. No use talking to
him about the constitution."

We were on our way to visit *La Prensa*. The antique
Paris-style offices in the big old building with courtyards

that houses the editorial staff of that venerable organ of liberal opinion have a dark and shuttered look. People talked in low nervous voices. Immediately you get the feeling of being under siege. They told about the attacks of the mob in Peron's last demonstration when *descamisados* were brought into Buenos Aires on trains and buses from all over Argentina. They point out the little park where the open air bookstalls are across the street. Every time there's a demonstration the street cleaning department just happens to dump a pile of brickbats there so that the good *descamisados* will have something hard to throw at the windows.

The mob was against them. It was disappointing how little support they had from the people. Juan Pueblo wasn't interested in freedom of the press. Peron's government had finagled their reserve supply of paper away from them. They were threatened with suits for back taxes. "The sword of Damocles," they said.

In the big entrances that led from the courtyard to the street they pointed out grimly the heavy steel doors they had put in for protection against an attack by the mob during another demonstration.

In the offices of the Socialist Party the atmosphere is even bleaker. No portraits of the Perons on those walls. Their paper *Vanguardia* has been closed down by Peron's government and the press in the basement of the building has been padlocked. In a dim little room beside his offices the Socialist leader talks fluently and well. "Peron has debauched the labor movement," he says. "We have an expression in the Argentine, *un criollo vivo,* a slick customer; that's what he is; he knows exactly what to do to corrupt Juan Pueblo." Handouts everywhere. During his presidential campaign he sent a bottle of cider and a loaf of spongecake to every soldier in the army, champagne to the officers. Their wives got little handkerchiefs with his picture on them. He sent people around on camels dressed as Wise Men to distribute toys to the children. The election was fair, no interference at the polling booths — that was refreshing after fifteen years of electoral fraud — but the opposition parties never had a proper chance to campaign. Peron's fifth columns were in all the unions. He controlled the radio, and censored the newsreels. He had bought up the newspapers. Only two independent papers, *La Prensa* and *La Nacion,* were left and they didn't dare criticize him openly. The Socialist paper *Vanguardia* was the only one that had carried on vigorous daily criticism of the regime and for that reason it had been closed down. The Socialists hadn't been silenced, they had their secret presses that carried on the fight, but people were scared to be seen listening to their orators.

That afternoon I went out looking for a Socialist meeting. At the corner of a beautiful green hillside park beside a flowerstand full of calla lilies I found a car with a loud-speaker. From a stand erected beside it a Socialist campaigner was speaking. He was speaking very well of the dangers of one man rule. The constitution might need changing but not this way, not by Peron. It was spring in Buenos Aires but a little keen Antarctic wind came whistling down the broad streets making listening to speeches a chilly business. He spoke very well but nobody heard him except two mounted policemen and a traffic cop with white cotton dustguards on the sleeves of his uniform and three old ladies muffled up on a bench and a couple of small boys on the way home from school. There were more people waiting for the bus on the traffic island in the middle of the street than there were listening to the speaker.

When we walked away the little Socialist pamphleteer who spent his life getting cracks at the Perons off the Party's secret press seemed pretty chopfallen. "I don't know what's happened to the Argentine people," he kept saying.

Across the street three little schoolgirls in white smocks were looking into the window of a pastry shop. It was hard to tell whether they were looking at the pastries or at the little bittersweet smile on the face of Eva Peron on a poster announcing a meeting in favor of constitutional reform. The Socialist shook his fist furtively at the picture behind the little girls' backs. "Her lies are corrupting the people," he muttered. *"Es una mala mujer . . .* a wicked woman."

A Communist meeting out in a workingclass district near the cemeteries turned out to be larger but it was far from tying up traffic. The Communists were going along with Peron on reform of the Constitution. Their speaker had a good go at the oligarchy and at American imperialism. Not a word against the government. He got the usual cheers for the Soviet Union. Except for the language we might have been in Union Square in the good old days of Earl Browder. My friend the baker whispered in my ear that the Communists had lost all influence in the labor movement; they didn't dare show their faces in the unions. Nothing left but *hijos de papá y mamá,* spoiled boys of the middle class just out of school, broken down journalists, lawyers without clients, doctors without a practice, politicians without votes.

The Radical meeting in a street of welltodo apartment houses and wellgarnished restaurants was more impressive. The Radical Party was the party of the middle class. The middle class by inflation and government regulation was hard hit already and feared worse things to come. In spite of the cold wind a big welldressed crowd was listening intently to a set of speakers who spoke fluently and well, warning against dictatorship and the loss of civil liberties. Argentina had grown to be a great nation under the old constitution of 1853. Now was no time to change it. The crowd listened intently and applauded with passion.

At a windy street corner downtown the Nationalists, as the local Fascists are called, were all out for a new constitution and dictatorship. They had set up an altar to the fatherland capped by a gigantic embroidered eagle. In front of it a dozen boys of highschool age were reciting a sort of a litany which ended with the names of the Nationalist martyrs. They all stood stiff at attention and tried to get the old bloodcurdling Nazi yip into their voices. It was a crowded street, full of traffic. No one was paying any attention to them at all.

Out at the *peronista* meeting in a workingclass suburb everybody seemed to be having a good time. People had the relaxed look of being on the winning side. There was music. Floodlights lit up the portraits of the Perons. The speakers weren't much on oratory but they put on a Punch and Judy show which was a great success. The oligarch got a drubbing. There was a magician and some gaucho guitarists. There was not much interest in the speeches until one of the speakers announced that President Peron was going to see to it that this suburb got a band concert and a free vaudeville show every Sunday. The announcement got a hand. There were a great many young workingmen in the audience and women and masses of children. Juan Pueblo had brought his family.

Every now and then the proceedings were interrupted by an announcement that some lost child had just been found and was waiting for its mama behind the speakers' stand. There was singing of campaign songs. Somebody had coached a group of small boys to shout Per-on, Per-on, Per-on and they went at it with such vim that the Rear Admiral who was the chairman of the *peronista* party had a hard time getting himself heard when he talked about social justice and high wages and the forging of a new Argentina. Everybody was waiting impatiently for the fireworks that were going to follow the speeches.

"When people are getting plenty of meat to eat and have a little money in their pockets, it's hard to get Juan Pueblo interested in the constitution," the *peronista* wardheeler is complaining as we walk down the street toward Luna Park.

He has been telling me that this trade union meeting he is taking me to was to be one of the climaxes of the campaign for a new constitution. Businesses and factories were closed by government order at four in the afternoon to give people plenty of time to get there. Special trains and chartered buses were bringing *decamisados* in from the suburbs and from nearby cities. A block from the Luna Park arena, we meet a pair of mounted policemen, but they have no crowds to handle. Inside the arena the galleries are tolerably full but empty seats are not hard to find. The worried frown leaves the face of my *peronista* guide when he hears the crowds throatily roaring Ev-ita Ev-ita, Per-on Per-on. Won't I join him in the official seats? No thank you. He peels off his jacket as he hurries off towards the tribune.

The tribune stands out in a glare of floodlights, framed with blue and white Argentine bunting. In spite of the evening chill all the officials of the government are there in their shirtsleeves. When the President and the Señora de Peron come in and are seated under vast canvas likenesses of themselves that billowed in the wind a great rhythmic roaring begins. The organized *peronistas* in the stands shout their throats sore and shout again. They listen with tense enthusiasm to the speeches.

Down on the floor of the auditorium the general public moves about listlessly. There is continual coming and going. A man will listen for a little while and then he will start sliding pokerfaced towards the exit. By the time the meeting is half over the streets outside are empty. Only the sidewalk tables of the cafés and eating houses built into the walls of the arena are occupied. At every one sits a heavy set man in a doublebreasted suit or a couple of them, solemnly chewing on a steak or on a triangular meat pie. They sit there eating and drinking, with a shrewd solemn look on their deadpan faces. You can't even tell whether they are listening or not.

Meanwhile *peronista* speeches carried on loudspeakers roar down the empty streets, calling for the new constitution that will make permanent the reforms installed by their great leaders and allow the reelection of Juan Domingo Peron in 1952.

A chill dry wind has come up off the pampas. The loudspeakers carry the rhythmic cheering: Per-on, Pe-ron . . . Ev-ita Ev-ita out into the starry night. All at once there is silence. A shrill scolding voice starts in long breathless sequences, denouncing the oligarchy and the American imperialists who are opposing the new constitution so much needed to establish the rights of labor, social security for the aged and the sick, the firm foundation for a new powerful democratic Argentina. It is the Señora. The shrill singsong scolding voice brings a little shiver to your spine when you remember another shrill voice, scolding over the air not so many years ago: Hitler's.

CAPTION: Prophet of Doom

"How long will it take for inflation to catch up with the high wages?" I asked the financial writer.

"Six months," he said. "In six months . . ." Suddenly he looked up and closed his mouth tight. We were eating lunch at the Plaza in an atmosphere of cocktails and sizzling butter and broiling steak and Paris perfumes and salmon colored draperies. The long nosed waiter seemed to be taking an extra long time to pour the wine. The financial writer was a trim little man with a long wooden face and a small bristly black moustache. A starched handkerchief showed two trim points in his breast pocket.

When the waiter moved away he went on. "I wish they'd buy my paper instead of trying to listen to what I'm saying . . . You can get pesos at ten to the dollar already . . . It is

beginning to accelerate. We Argentines are as accustomed
. . . well as accustomed as the inhabitants of Boston . . ."
There was a malicious twinkle in his eye . . . "to corrupt
government, but I can truthfully say that we've never had
anything like this. In every government a certain number
of deals are made just for the rakeoff, but in this government
it amounts to eighty or ninety percent of everything that
takes place . . . Take this business of the aluminum
plant . . ."

He glanced up and closed his mouth tight as a nutcracker.
The waiter was leaning over his shoulder with the fried
potatoes in a manner that certainly seemed unduly solicitous.

When the waiter had reluctantly moved away an American business man who was an old Argentine hand spoke up:
"This guy, you know who I mean . . . the general . . . is a
feller I used to be able to talk to," he said. "But now I
can't. If I can't talk to him frankly I'm not going to talk
to him at all . . . Too much adulation. And then I have a
notion that the Señora is running away with the show. The
Señora on one side and his financial wizards on the other . . .
She's an extraordinary woman. She's got all the guts in the
world . . . I wouldn't like to mix it up with her."

"What about the aluminum plant?"

"It's just a typical story . . . A bunch of the general's boys
got together to buy an aluminum plant in Italy, out of the
public funds naturally. Everybody was wondering when the
aluminum plant was going to be shipped over. It turns out
now that the plant is a myth and that the *peronistas* merely
put the money in their own pockets. The general had just
decorated one of them for conspicuous faithfulness. He was
so mad he got him up in his office and hit him in the face
with his fist."

"The main trouble," said the American business man, "is
that they made a wrong guess. They held up their prices on
meat and wheat because they thought they'd have a seller's

market when war broke out between the United States and
Russia . . . Well, it doesn't look now as if war would break
out, so they're stuck with a whole wheatcrop and the best
thing they can do with their meat is eat it themselves."

"Very good too," said the financial writer biting down on
a thick piece of rare wellpeppered steak. He looked carefully around the room before he continued. "Inflation is
going to hit the stratosphere." He lowered his voice to a
whisper. "I give the peso six months."

Not only our own waiter but the headwaiter and a busboy
in a white coat had begun to hover about our table. You
could almost see their ears stretching to listen. They continued so attentive to our wants that we had to begin to
talk about the drouth and the horseraces and the real estate
boom.

CAPTION: *Libertarians in Business*

We were walking along one of the avenues lined with sidewalk cafés that branch out from the obelisk like the spokes of
a wheel.

"Right here," my friend was saying, "I always think I am
back in Barcelona. Many Spaniards live in Buenos Aires
for years and never see anything but this street. The café
owners are Spaniards, the clientèle is Spanish. It reminds
them of Spain; that's all they want."

He was a Spaniard himself. Although half his life had
been spent in Buenos Aires he had been one of the most
important journalists of the anarcho-syndicalist movement in
Barcelona during the years of the Spanish Republic. Now
he was associated with a small publishing house, a libertarian
publishing house, he explained, smiling.

He was taking me up to visit the management of the

Federacion de Colectivos. The *colectivos* in Buenos Aires were buses, he was explaining, owned by the men who drove them or by small groups who operated them on shares. Like the jitneys that appeared in American cities at one stage of the lag in transportation to keep up with growth the *colectivos* had appeared when the monopoly-controlled bus company had been unable or unwilling to furnish the rapidly growing suburbs with buses. The *colectivos* were grouped into various lines that gave service to established routes and the lines were grouped into a federation with an elected board of directors. It had developed into a two hundred million peso business.

We were climbing the stairs to the Federation office. "It's amusing how things work out," he was saying. "The great bulk of the owner-drivers are oldtime anarchist agitators or syndicalists from Spain. Of course it's entirely logical because we always believed in individual initiative. We used to talk about seizing the means of production . . . In America we've found it more practical to buy them."

We walked through a waiting room, and a long room with high windows with a board of directors table down the middle of it into the inner office where the officers of the Federation sat talking. They were all of them practical busdrivers or automobile mechanics. No bureaucrats in their organization, they started to explain right away. They had only one paid functionary, a secretary. Their organization was efficient: here was an example of how it worked. The transport corporation which had been taken over by the municipality needed thirteen men working full time to maintain a bus on the road. The Federation did it with three. They had been going twenty years working uphill first against the monopoly that didn't want their competition and then against municipal regulations that tried to drive them off the streets until the authorities found people couldn't do without their service and now . . .

How were they getting along with the *peronistas,* I asked.

"Of course the *peronistas* want to socialize everything. We don't mind supervision by the government or the city but we've got to keep our own administration. Under government administration our service would be more costly and less efficient. After all the citizen wants to get to his work and home again as cheaply and comfortably as possible whether he's a Socialist or a Radical or a *peronista.* Efficiency. That's our great talking point. We hope to convince them. If the government takes over most of us will sell out . . . We are independent men. That's why we can give such good service. Each owner identifies himself with his machine, he lives for it, it's his sweetheart . . . If the state owned it who would care?"

Would they be able to convince the *peronistas,* I asked. Wasn't the tendency all against them?

They hoped so, they said eagerly. The *peronistas* were no more unreasonable than any other politicians.

We shook hands all around and went out onto the street again. I was remembering an almost identical conversation I had with an English truck driver when the Labor Government had been about to take over transportation. He had used the same arguments.

"Will he take them over?" I asked. My friend shrugged his shoulders. That would depend on the political exigencies of the moment.

What did he think of Peron, I asked him as we settled down to a table in one of the Spanish sidewalk cafés.

He paused to take a sip of coffee. "As you know," he answered in a low cogitating voice, "I am a veteran of many years war against authority. Liberty has been my drug . . . But it's as those boys said. The *peronistas* are not very different from other politicians. In some ways they are better because they are new. We can hardly call it Fascism on the

Italian or German or Spanish model. Peron is not all bad. He has improved the moral and material situation of the working people . . . You must remember that all governments have two aspects. From one point of view a government is an organization for plunder and domination but from another it can sometimes be seen to serve certain social ends. It can restore the economic balance. Monopoly capital was too strong. Peron is tipping the scales the other way. Roosevelt did the same thing in the United States. But dictators tend to lose their heads. He has to be watched."

He started to reach for the lower lid of his right eye with his index finger. He caught himself and laughed. "I've lived here so long I'm getting to be a *criollo vivo* too.

CAPTION: *Bountiful Lady*

The ponderous doors of glass and twisted iron open to let us into a large square hall paved with marble. A red-carpeted stairway leads on up to the upper floors of the house. The socialworker who opened the door is a little blackclad man with the manners of a pew opener in a fashionable church. "The Señora de Peron," he whispers, "wants the poor people to have everything of the best." With a discreet wave of his arm he indicates the sofas and the overstuffed chairs and the salmoncolored draperies and the gilt mirrors and the immense bunch of delphinium and calla lilies on the center table. "This house used to belong to a millionaire . . . one of the oligarchy . . . Now it belongs to the Maria Eva Duarte de Peron Foundation. We call it a temporary home . . . Anybody in need can apply to the Señora, any Argentine citizen. This way please . . . They can stay here a week, two weeks till their problems are solved . . . You see this is the office . . . "

The mousy little darkhaired girl behind the mahogany desk starts pulling the cards out of the cabinet to explain the case histories of the inmates . . . A woman with five children whose husband has gone insane, a girl with a baby who came to Buenos Aires to get married and hadn't been able to find the child's father, a widow with a family of seven . . . illness, evictions for nonpayment of rent, traffic accidents . . . "The Señora thinks that spending a few days in a lovely home like this is good for their morale. They all get new clothes, shoes, toys for the children." The socialworker whispers breathlessly. "In the old days before the revolution it was only for the oligarchy . . . Now the Señora wants even the poorest to have the best . . . "

While the girl behind the desk shows us the cards and explains the cases we begin to hear a scuttling of feet and a rustling of dresses behind us. A trained nurse sticks her head in the door and hisses. *"Es la Señora."* A glaze covers the eyes of the girl behind the desk. She begins to forget the details of the cases. She stumbles over her words. The cards keep slipping out of her fingers.

"It is the Señora," the socialworker who opened the door whispers, nervously pulling his necktie with one hand. "She will want to see you. She always wants to see visitors." His voice has a velvet tone.

While the girl picks up the cards in a fluster and lines up the blotter with the edge of the desk we all troop back into the central hall. "She's gone upstairs," whispers the house matron patting a crease out of a sofa cushion. Two nuns are hustling about straightening the flowered carpet. A maid trots through with a dustpan. Meanwhile a photographer has appeared and stands with his camera trained on the marble stairway. Beside him is a sleek young man with a whispy buff mustache whom the socialworker hurriedly introduces as a reporter for *Democracia.*

Of course that is the Señora's newspaper, the largest circulation in Argentina. "She always comes without notice," the socialworker explains in his prompter's whisper. "Her heart is so in the work . . ." The words freeze on his lips.

All at once there comes Eva Peron herself advancing briskly towards us down the redcarpeted stairs, blonde, slender, in a pale gold dress, wearing a becomingly angular magenta hat. Behind her walk two heavyfaced men in doublebreasted suits. Her face is rather sallow. Her eyes are so dark you can't see the pupils. She has small tight lips. She gives each man and woman one sharp attentive look straight in the face and shakes hands unassumingly with a quick almost modest little girl's smile. The photographer's bulb flashes behind us. She asks how we like the house, doesn't wait for an answer and is gone. Only her picture is left, a full length portrait in oils, smiling down at us from the head of the stairs.

The socialworker began to pull himself together a little, panting like a man who's just escaped being run over by a truck. "This way please," he said breathlessly, leading the way upstairs. *"Extra-ordinaire,"* said the Parisian lady journalist opening wide mascaraed eyes and scribbling fast in her notebook as she tottered up over the red carpet on her high French heels. The two Argentine newspapermen from the provinces followed with grave astonished faces. The reporter from *Democracia* came along noting down the reactions of the visitors. The bedrooms were clean, decorated with chintz curtains and bed covers. There were only four beds to a room, flowers on every center table. On every bare wall hung portraits of the Señora and of President Peron. The photographer followed on our heels and everybody had to be snapped feeling the soft beds, admiring the view from the terrace laid out with wicker furniture for sunbaths on the roof, examining the shiny aluminum pans in the white tiled kitchen, chatting with the dazed looking women who were sitting in the patio watching a mob of little children in clean new clothes playing with a whole toyshop full of brand new toys. "The Señora does all the decorating herself. She picks out the toys . . . Everything has to be exactly the way she wants it or it is changed," explained the socialworker. "*Extra-ordinaire,*" sighed the Parisian lady and batted her mascaraed lashes.

Next the visitors were ushered into a long black limousine and taken on a tour. We inspected two more homes, five stories of a warehouse in the wing of a building that had been put up for a new medical school where huge halls were stacked to the ceiling with bedding and blankets, clothing for men, women and children, schoolbooks and toys for distribution in the provinces where people couldn't afford to buy them, cookstoves and pots and pans for the needy. We saw a kitchen being set up for presentation to one of the Argentine Olympic winners. We were asked which of a dozen poster portraits of the Señora we thought did her most justice. After that a home for old men out of town, low cost housing in course of construction. Busts of the President, bronzes of Evita. Everything glittering new and lettered with the names of the Señora and of Presidente Peron. We didn't run into the lady herself again but her picture was on every wall, her face was on every poster. Whenever the photographer got a shot of the visitors admiring the Foundation's good works he tried to include in his background one of the smiling photographs of Maria Eva Duarte de Peron. "It's not a dictatorship," whispered the socialworker in coaxing tones as we started back into town. "It's a great movement for social betterment . . . Say it's not a dictatorship."

CAPTION: *Madame Secretary*

Evita Peron at that time was virtually Secretary of Labor. Each morning in the reception hall of the ministry she received delegations from the trade unions bringing problems for her to solve. This particular morning she has gone to some function or other and is late in arriving for work, but all the officials assure me that she is usually in her office at nine-thirty or earlier.

The corridors and anterooms of the shabby old governmental building are jammed with all kinds of people. There is an excited holiday look on every face. If there are any exceptional security measures they certainly don't show. After a great deal of jamming and pushing we are ushered into a big panelled room with many windows. Round a long mahogany table in the center stand groups of delegates from trade unions. In one corner a mob of young girls in their best bibs and tuckers throngs about an immense bouquet of flowers encased in cellophane. They are the winners of beauty contests all over Argentina. A *reina de belleza* for the year is about to be chosen. Cameramen with flashing bulbs move here and there through the crowd. The place has the air of a Hollywood opening; everybody who is present is anxious to be seen. People keep getting in the photographer's way. It is all highly informal, while they wait people sit on the edge of the long table and chat with their friends. *Peronista* politicians twine their arms around each other's shoulders. Journalists take notes. Around eleven there comes a sudden burst of handclapping and when the crowd parts you see the Señora with a serious attentive look on her face standing beside a small desk full of

papers. People form a ring around her. Those behind crane
their necks to see. This time she is dressed simply in a New
York looking silk dress with a flowered pattern. Her only
jewelry is a pair of long earrings.

Already she is talking fast in a low voice to the men in the
nearest group of delegates. She has a couple of secretaries
to note things down but she runs way ahead of them. She
seems posted on the problems even before the delegates
bring them up. She listens patiently to what each man has
to say. With her secretaries and the government officials her
manner is domineering, the manner of a hostess ordering
the help about, but with the delegates it is level and sisterly.
She always listens to the end. When she answers she talks
very fast in rather a wheedling tone. *"Vamos muchachos . . .
come along boys, let's settle this . . ."*

There are difficult and varied problems; the men from the
meatpacking plants want an immediate raise in wages. There
is a complicated jurisdictional dispute between drug company employees and a union of chemical workers. As they
argue back and forth their voices rise loud in dispute. There
are delegations of schoolteachers, newsboys, shoemakers,
millers, employees of the petroleum industry. Each one of
them wants something. The Señora never loses her friendly
manner of a younger sister who's trying to get her brothers
to agree. Occasionally she'll beckon somebody out of the
group and talk earnestly to him in her soft hissing whisper
in a corner of the room. When a decision has been reached
she calls the Secretary in a loud peremptory tone out of an
adjoining office to tell him about it.

In the middle of a discussion she will suddenly break off
to be photographed in the center of a group of beauty queens
or receiving a bouquet of flowers or meeting a delegation
bringing a check for her foundation. Most of the delegations
bring checks with them. Now and then she will dart across

the room to call some other ministry or the President over the phone. When she catches sight of a friend or a visitor in the crowd she breaks away and runs up to him with a little schoolgirlish questioning look that says, Here I am . . . How do you think I'm doing?

It was three o'clock and she'd seen everybody who was waiting for her before she went off to lunch. In four hours she never paused or sat down.

In the afternoon in another part of the same ministerio she made an appearance in a fresh afternoon dress for a different type of audience. In a small office with red damasked walls were rows of benches packed with raggedlooking women and children facing her desk. Babies squawked. Everybody talked at once. The Señora's desk was set up under floodlights beside a big bronze oversize bust of some hero of Argentine independence. Behind it was a row of small chairs for distinguished visitors. This time it was the French Ambassador and some diplomats, among them the son of the President of Italy. In the embrasure of the windows *peronista* politicians and government officials stood packed together among the folds of the heavy old-fashioned draperies. The corridor outside was full of people waiting to get a glimpse of the Señora. When she finally arrived the floodlights were turned on and there was a great crush of cameramen in the narrow room. Distinguished visitors were posed in an admiring group behind the Señora's handsome blonde head as she leaned over the desk to listen to the troubles of the poor women with their teargrimed children.

"She's too thin," one of the women was muttering aloud. "That woman's working herself to death."

At the end of each hardluck story the Señora reached with jewelled fingers under the blotter on the desk and took out two fifty peso notes. Then she made out with a rapid scratch of her pencil on a pink slip an order for what was needed from the foundation, a visit to a doctor or a blanket or a doll for the baby girl, or a week in one of the Temporary Homes.

When a delegation of merchants appeared with a check in five figures for the Señora's foundation all other business was suspended while the cameramen posed the group. The women and children waiting for attention were pushed back and the floodlights brought forward on their castiron stands. The check had to appear in the photograph. The Señora's white hand was held out to receive it. The leader of the delegation was presenting it with a deferential bow. The check was brandished and the delegation grouped a dozen times before the cameramen were satisfied. Meanwhile the visitors on their tight row of little chairs behind the desk sat blinking from the glare in their faces.

In the middle of the show Peron himself appeared, a bulky jovial-mannered man with dark hair growing close to his head. People clapped and roared and stared at the pair through moistening eyes. While the cameramen peered and shoved in the silvery flicker of flashlights Peron smiled his fatherly smile and the Señora smiled and adulation rose like incense in the airless room.

The President was due to make a speech. He charged out into the hall. The Señora remembered, with a gracious backward look over her shoulder, to ask the distinguished visitors to come along and the whole party worked its way after the presidential couple along packed applauding corridors and crowded rooms to a pair of double doors that opened onto a balcony in an oval auditorium filled to the brim with members of the Federation of Musicians who had come to make President Peron an honorary member of the organization. Pe-ron, Pe-ron Pe-ron, they roared. A small monkeyfaced man in the middle aisle led the cheering, flapping his arms and screwing up his face and writhing in spasms of enthusiasm.

When he got people quieted down Peron began to speak to them in friendly, familiar tones. He talked mostly about how nice it was in the world we lived in, where so many people were busy planning war and misery for their fellow men, to have musicians who spent their lives making their fellow men feel happier. His voice had a warm, confidential note. He raised his left hand and made explanatory gestures, pressing the thumb and forefinger together to clinch his meaning. He was just a modest good fellow trying to explain to other good fellows how he felt. There was no doubt in anybody's mind that those musicians would go away feeling that Peron was on their side.

The President was the first to leave in the middle of the rhythmic cheering that followed his speech. Then the Señora rose to her feet to garner the rest of the ovation. After a few cordial sweet words she made the prettiest exit imaginable, letting herself drop back into the crowd of officials that jammed the doorway, her lips parted and a kiss held out on her fingertips to the crowd below.

CAPTION: *The Man Himself*

President Juan Domingo Peron makes a point of being in his office in the Casa Rosada at six-thirty every morning. If a foreign visitor gets an appointment with him it's very likely to be at seven fifteen or so. Likely as not you'll meet a cleaning man with brooms and a bucket coming out of the elevator when you are ushered in. You walk round many passages furnished in the French official style of the last century, looking down out of the inner windows on a patio with a fountain and flowers and palms; you pass a couple of officers at desks and are let into a waitingroom where a military aid in a white uniform offers you a cup of coffee. You sit there talking about the weather and the horseraces until a phone rings and you find yourself being ushered in to meet the President.

Juan Domingo Peron is a handsome man with even white teeth and a fine burly presence. In spite of a bad skin he has the sort of coarse good looks that show up well in the distance, the good looks of a tenor in opera. He looks much younger than his fifty three years. He's a little overweight perhaps but that is a national failing. You find him sitting at the end of a long conference table in a big bright high-ceilinged room in the rear of the building. He greets you without ceremony and orders up a coffee for you. He has the shrewd longnosed look so typical of his countrymen, the look of the *criollo vivo,* but he has none of the stiff formality of the average Argentine. He has the manners of a man who likes to give the impression that popularity hasn't spoiled him. To put you at your ease he unbuttons the tunic of his general's uniform and says it pinches him. Then he explains that he's only wearing it because he has to receive some Ambassadors later in the day. He laughs. Ambassadors don't like to get up early. You and me we're early birds, he seems to imply. He has a way of winking at you with his left eye and then suddenly putting out a smile. He smokes a good many cigarettes while talking rapidly and fluently with every appearance of frankness. He is thoroughly aware of how his visitor is taking what he's saying.

Foreigners, if they are trying to understand what is happening in Argentina, must look back into the country's history a little, he explains. The Argentines had political independence but economically they were a colony of Britain first and later of Wall Street. Now they had declared their economic independence. To make that stick they had to build up industries and to develop electric power because they were short on oil and coal. The government had to take over the import export business to protect the people because theirs was virtually a two crop country. For a century Argentina had been governed by a small oligarchy of landowners and financiers who worked as the agents for international capital without any regard for the interests of the Argentine people. The Argentine people had overthrown the oligarchy, in a revolution that had fortunately been bloodless. It had come at a time of prosperity when everybody had enough meat to eat. Peron's bitterest critics were making more money than they ever had before. The oligarchs themselves were getting richer than ever. It was the business of Argentines to see that this prosperity was evenly distributed, that the working people got their fair share, that the country as a whole benefited. Argentina was very fortunate that the revolution had been bloodless. It had left no real rancors. There was no real hatred between Argentines. That meant that all sorts of adjustments were possible, peaceful reasonable adjustments. The Communists were left out on a limb because they had no more workingclass backing. There had been no need to suppress the Communist Party although they were certainly Moscow agents because nobody listened to them any more. What he, Peron, wanted, was to build up a third force between capitalism and communism. In building up that force the Argentine people, all the Argentine people from the poorest to the richest had to be considered. That certainly wasn't fascism, now was it? The third force was what Argentina these days had to tell the world about . . . He looks you straight in the face and winks the left eye.

The *peronista* wardheeler was waiting for me at the hotel. His face was all smiles. "You've seen him? What do you think of him?"

I had to explain that all politicians had a way of making themselves pretty charming to visitors. It was part of the art. Of course the President was charming and so was his Señora.

"He's more than that, he's shrewd . . . we call it *viveza*. He's a *criollo vivo,* a slick article, if you get what I mean, a fox . . . If he gets in a hole, he'll know how to get out of it. But it's not a dictatorship . . . Say it isn't a dictatorship."

FRED RUFUS: Mr. Lecturer, I have a question to ask . . . Has it ever occurred to you that Peron may be right? I mean when he claims that what he is trying to do in the Argentine is what Franklin D. Roosevelt did here. Practically speaking hasn't the administration in Washington broken away from control by the people about as much as Peron's administration has. Mr. Truman has the backing of certain trade unions and of certain political machines just the way Mr. Peron has.

MR. LECTURER: There is something in it but you can't push analogies too far.

FRED RUFUS: Our political picture is much more complicated naturally and we have the good old Anglo-Saxon tradition of not letting the right hand know what the left hand doeth that makes it hard for us to call a spade a spade.

EDDY JONES (*interrupting*): You people didn't talk about dictatorship when Herbert Hoover was running his administration for the benefit of big business.

FRED RUFUS: Now Eddy you hold your horses. We're not trying to elect a candidate tonight. We are trying to find the answer to some very difficult questions.

MR. LECTURER: The advantage of trying to see how these things work out in South America is that we can see the same historical processes working out in a different environment from our own.

FRED RUFUS: I hate to say it but it looks to me as if industrial society the world over were headed towards the totalitarian form of state . . . In this country we can do one of two things. We can return to free enterprise and liberty or else . . .

EDDY JONES: Fred, there isn't any free enterprise to return to. What you mean by free enterprise means running the country for the benefit of the directors of the big corporations.

MR. LECTURER: The question you gentlemen have brought up lies at the bottom of everything we are talking about, but if you could both just hold your fire for a few minutes, let's see if we can't get across the mountains onto the Pacific slope . . .

CAPTION: *Between the Devil and the Deep Blue Sea*

When you have bored through the valleys of the gigantic Andes on a tiny train, like a child's memory of a train in a story by Jules Verne, you come out into the stony lands of Chile, that uneasy republic precariously perched on a thousand mile bench overhanging the cold Pacific. The people you meet in Santiago are as different from the Argentines as the people of our San Francisco are from Kansans. East of the Andes, even in the port of Buenos Aires, you have a sense of being in the center of a continental plain. Chile, you immediately feel, is part of an oceanic culture, tied by shipping lanes to the ports of Europe and North America. Since her copper and nitrates are export products which depend on the world market it is inevitable, at a time when the world market is stagnant and sick, that Chile should suffer all the disorders our world economy is subject to. At every street corner in Santiago you meet the political dilemma of our times.

Chile has, like Uruguay, a wellmarked selfgoverning tradition. The trouble is that Chile has not been able to solve the problem of destitution as Uruguay has. Economically Chile and the countries of the River Plate tend to complement each other and should be linked by some sort of close cooperation. Unfortunately the barrier of the Andes and the greater barrier of national pride and tradition and now, greatest barrier of all, the resentment of the Chileans at the thought of being dominated by Peron, keep these nations apart. Meanwhile Chile's bourgeois democracy is engaged in a life and death struggle with a powerful Communist Party, so that you find yourself facing the anomaly that more people have been jailed in Chile to preserve selfgoverning institutions than Peron has had to jail in the Argentine to establish an authoritarian regime.

"What I am trying to do," said President Gonzales Videla barging into his subject without ceremony as soon as I was introduced to him in the diningroom of the Palacio de La Moneda, "is to run a constitutional government between crossfires . . ."

He motioned to me to sit down and eat some fruit. He and I and his aide sat in a stiff row in the middle of the long state diningtable. He himself sipped a glass of hot milk, turning in his chair as he talked. He was a small sturdy man with a hawk nose and a ruddy face and a downright straightforward manner.

"Here we are trying to cope with all the economic difficulties that come from the stagnation of world trade and inflation and unemployment while the Communists shoot at us from one side and the Fascists, instigated by our friends across the Andes, shoot from the other. The Communist movement in Chile is very ably managed, they have shown great cunning in pulling the wool over the eyes of wellintentioned members of other parties . . . It almost happened to me. As you know I was elected with the help of the Communists and tried to cooperate with them. It became obvious that they intended to control my government. I was to be the Chilean Beneš. They were within an inch of taking over the country, so I had to break with them. My problem now is how to find constitutional means to keep the enemies of liberty from destroying the very liberty which has allowed them to become so powerful."

He went on to point out how few selfgoverning régimes were left in South America. Democrats in Chile, and in other Latin American countries struggling with the same difficulties, felt that the United States was not backing up its friends. He wished he could feel that he had the sympathy and the understanding of the United States. Basically the Chilean people wanted the same things the American people wanted.

When I began to say goodbye, he got to his feet to shake hands.

"Well, you're lucky to be able just to write about these things instead of having to take part in them," he said with a wry smile.

One evening in Santiago I was taken to meet Dr. Cruz Coke, the candidate of the Christian-Socialist wing of the Conservative Party whom Communist support had enabled Gonzalez Videla to beat in the last election. He was a tall man with a long wooden face and the large lustrous eyes of a Spanish School "Christ on the Cross." His manner was tense and passionate. He was a Catholic more or less of the school of Maritain. The political atmosphere around him reminded me a little of that around de Gaulle in France. The expression of his face didn't change when he talked. He discharged his sentences at the listener like well modulated small arms fire. He said right away that his quarrel with Gonzales Videla was that in his opinion arresting the Communists and putting them in a concentration camp at Pisagua was making martyrs of them and increasing their prestige among the working people. The law for the Defense of Democracy was neither good defense nor good democracy. The result was that anyone who tried to find a solution to the economic difficulties of the working class was in danger

of being prosecuted as a Communist . . . The whole country
— everybody except the speculators and the very rich — had
been plunged into a state of acute destitution by the rise in
prices and the inflation of the currency. Passing laws had
proved no cure. They had tried to protect wageworkers,
and farmers, in fact everybody's income by law. The result
was that everybody was sinking into poverty together. The
result of the law assuring business enterprises a margin of
profit was that it wasn't any longer to the businessman's
advantage to run his business efficiently because he got his
profit anyway. The continuing inflation had made it more
profitable for a manufacturer to store his raw materials than
to go to the trouble of processing them. If a shoe manufacturer had a warehouseful of hides it was more profitable for
him to go to Viña del Mar and loaf for a year than to pay
men to make shoes out of his leather. This situation was
reducing the capitalist system to an absurdity. A man who
knew a banker could live without working by borrowing
money at ten or twelve percent and buying a piece of land
and waiting for it to go up in value. If he put the same
money into some useful productive enterprise he'd most
likely end a bankrupt.

"Meanwhile the poor devil of an office worker or an industrial worker can't feed his family. Go down to Valparaiso
or into the popular suburbs of Santiago. You'll find people
really suffering. When the Communists go around telling
these people they have a cure for their troubles, it's no good
sending the police after the Communists. You've got to
find a better remedy. It doesn't help telling people that the
Communists are a wicked lot who are trying to take away
our liberties. What does liberty mean to a man who can't
pay his rent or feed his children? He'll trade the liberty to
starve in for a promise of a Communist utopia any day."

The United States hadn't been any help, he went on to

say. His tone was bitter when he spoke of the United States. The worst thing about the State Department's policy all through Latin America was that it had no contact with the people. American officials at the embassies and consulates were afraid of trying to get in touch with the people where they lived for fear of being labelled as Communists and losing their jobs. The fear of associating with Communists among people trying to fight communism was one of the great assets of the Communist Party. To fight the Communists we had to learn to understand their methods and to go them one better. "Why, since the party has been declared illegal many of my Conservatives have protected Communists, helped them to escape, hidden them in their houses, out of mere humanity. Humanity is a good guide to follow in politics as in everything else." Anyway he felt most of the Chilean Communists were Chileans first and Communists after.

When I asked him what could be done to remedy the economic situation, he said frankly that he didn't know. If the United States would only lead the way, he said in an exasperated tone, in democracy as she did in technology, we would all sleep much safer in our beds.

FRED RUFUS (*exploding from his seat*): That's what we get for tossing so much money around during the war. Nobody really likes a spendthrift . . .

MISS SMITHERS: But how can they dislike us so? We only feel friendship towards them.

MR. LECTURER: Everywhere I went in South America I found this same exasperation against the United States on the part of the sort of men who were trying to make government by consent work. Our enemies, like the *peronistas* and the Communists and the extreme nationalists, enjoy having the Colossus of the North always at hand as a bloody shirt to draw a crowd with whenever they want popular support for some selfserving measure. Without American imperialism half their speeches would fall flat. It is our friends who feel a bitterness that it is a little hard to account for rationally. The State Department's policy in the Latin American countries has in recent years been rather fumbling and awkward than aggressive; the American corporations interested in exploiting raw materials in these countries have been more conscious than ever before of their responsibility towards the people they hire to work for them. Part of this state of mind is a reflection of the general lowering of the prestige of the United States that became worldwide when it became obvious that for the second time in a generation, after making a tolerable job of fighting a war, we had made a botch of the peace.

FRED RUFUS: What we have to learn is that each time we make a great political blunder like subscribing to the agreements Stalin dictated at Teheran and Yalta and Potsdam we ruin the lives of millions of our fellow men. We can't expect them to like us for it.

MR. LECTURER (*after gulping at his waterglass*): Santiago, like Madrid, is a city of nocturnal talk. The night I met Dr. Cruz I sat up talking with a couple of newspaper men about dictatorships. The then recent overturn of the elected governments in Peru and Venezuela they agreed were more old style military coups than movements on the new style *peronista* model, but there was some evidence that Peron's adherents on the one hand and the Communists on the other, had some influence on the course of events in Peru. Moreover, that overturn had been aimed at Haya de La Torre's *aprista* party, which the Communists considered their main enemy in that part of the continent. Communists had turned up in important jobs with the military junta. The coup in Caracas seemed to be anti-Communist, but it had created an atmosphere in which only the Communists could thrive.

Think of it, that revolution had been carried out by three tanks. Modern armaments made the seizure of power by military groups almost too easy.

FRED RUFUS: If you'll excuse my interrupting, I want to get my second alternative into the discussion. Centralized power anywhere is almost sure to fall into the hands of a dictator. The cure is decentralization.

MR. LECTURER: One moment please, Mr. Rufus. I was coming to the subject of the function of the army in Latin American countries. In a way these armies are a rather enter-taining phenomenon for a historian. They are a survival of the obsolete military establishments of the Spanish viceroys. They have no real function except to exist as parasites on the bodies of states too poor to support them.

"They are poor devils really," one of the Santiago news-paper men was saying. "I have a brother who is an army officer. He's a nice, kind generous fellow but his training has made him perfectly useless to society. We all grew up in very modest circumstances. My poor mother thought she'd done a great thing getting him into the military academy as a cadet . . . through relations, protections. He got a wretched education. The Jesuits got hold of me and I think they did a better job. There's a stale effluvium of feudal vanities about barracks life that paralyzes the intelligence . . . And when you get to be an officer the pay is very low. Unless you manage to catch a rich woman you can't marry at all. There's all the dreary story of a povertystricken adolescence, whores, clapdoctors, the emptiness of conversations at the military clubs, strutting in billiard parlors, gambling debts . . . When the debts of a group of young officers get too big the only recourse is a conspiracy against the government. You owe money to the tailor, at the café, there's some woman with a wretched brat causing a scandal, you haven't enough in your pocket to buy a bottle of hairoil. If you are bright

and active the road to affluence is a *pronunciamento*. If
your side wins it means position, patronage, sinecures, a
good marriage maybe into a landowning family. You don't
have actually to steal to make money out of government.
Power attracts money as honey does flies . . . If you lose,
things aren't much worse than they were before. A few of
you are shot, the rest are exiled to the regime of a military
prison. Army life is a prison anyway. Then the plotting to
get back begins . . . And you North Americans give these
wretched young men military training. Who are we going
to fight, for God's sake. Nobody wants war less than the
military. In these countries war is still dangerous for the
military. The South American army officer is one of the few
real pacifists left in the world."

We all started laughing. Heavyeyed waiters were turning
up the tables in the wineshop. Outside the streets were
blanketed with white mist off the Pacific. A few rawboned
beggars dressed in dreary rags shivered in the doorways. We
dragged out some small coins which inflation had reduced
to an almost infinitesimal value.

"Our great product in Chile," said one of my friends, "is
not wine or fertilizer or copper; it is the *roto*, the man who
has never had enough to eat and never expects to have
enough to eat . . . But don't you go home to New York and
crow over us," he added half teasing and half serious as we
reached the door of my hotel. "Most of it is your fault. Take
militarism . . . It used to be the British who sold off their
old armaments after each war so that the South Americans
would shoot each other's heads off. Revolutions make
poverty; poverty keeps down the price of raw materials.
Poor people pay more than the rich for manufactured goods
because they can't afford to shop around. Now it's your
State Department that sees to it we get enough dangerous
mechanical toys like tanks and airplanes to keep our civilization down to the level of the edge of the stone age. Nobody
knows what your purpose is. And please don't think that

what I said about army officers refers particularly to Chile. We have a great many sincere and patriotic men in the army, I don't know how they remain so. But what I want you to remember is that each time your statesmen make a mistake, in Paris or London or Washington, a few more children go hungry in Valparaiso."

MRS. EDWARDS *(sighs)*: It's one world all right.

EDDY JONES: If the great corporations who did business in South America had been less greedy in the past we shouldn't have such a terrible reputation in those countries.

FRED RUFUS: Now Eddy you're too smart to keep harping on those old superannuated bogey men . . . This isn't a union convention . . . We are trying to think here this evening not as apologists for business or labor but as Americans . . . As Americans there are more things we agree about than differ about . . . I mean our basic objectives . . . What I'm trying to get across is the idea that the only cure for the situation our friend is trying to explain to us is decentralization. . . . Decentralization applies to politics, to business and to labor . . . It cuts clean across party lines.

MR. LECTURER: If you don't mind we'll take this very important suggestion up when we get home . . . My next lecture . . . Parenthetically I feel that I must admit that American prestige in the world was higher in the days of dollar diplomacy than it has been since our attempt to reform and become the good neighbor.

MISS SMITHERS: Mr. Lecturer, I must protest against this statement.

MR. LECTURER: It may be regrettable but we have to face the fact that the world admires power. Now the power-lovers are flocking to the side of the Soviet Union as you'll notice from the following little scene.

(He presses the buzzer. An airplane view of the sandy deserts blotched with shadows and the dry ridged hills of the Peruvian coast sweeps across the screen.)

CAPTION: The People on the Hill

"You'd better be careful," says the taxidriver, "I wouldn't go up there at night."

"But it isn't night," we answer.

"Well I wouldn't go up there at all."

We stand around the cab shuffling our feet in the deep puttycolored dust. Behind us we see a steep dusty hill marked with a scramble of little flatroofed shanties standing out light against the purplish rock of the mountain and in front of us we look down at Lima, all pale white and dustcolor like a Moorish city with flat roofs and flimsy domes, stretching far into the seaside blur on its arid bench over the Pacific. We hesitate. We are quite a crowd: two European city planners who are getting up a civic plan for Lima's future development, a Peruvian doctor, a journalist and a broadcaster and a painter. One man steps out and we all start straggling up the steep path.

"This hill has always been a hangout of thieves and robbers," puffs the Peruvian broadcaster. "Now squatters have occupied it . . . The story is the first people settled up there because they got a view down into the bullring. They thought it would be nice to see the bullfights free."

As we climb we begin to see, down among the flat roofs and spindly trees, the shaded oval of the bullring opening beneath us. It is Sunday afternoon. The bullfight is beginning. From the bullring comes the brass clatter of a band playing a *pasodoble* and the murmur muffled by distance of crowded people settling into seats. We all stop to catch our breath on a rough stone terrace held together by a few prickly pears.

"The management of the bullring had to lower the level

of the arena to keep people from seeing the bullfights free," the broadcaster continues still panting. "Of course the bull-ring was built by the Viceroy Amat . . . A curious thing about Lima . . . the only history that has remained in our minds . . . is that candlelit colonial romance of the aged viceroy and the actress La Perricholi . . . a world ornamented with pink and gilt cupids and masked ladies carried in sedan chairs orna-mented with pastoral scenes . . . your Thornton Wilder used it in his book . . . " He points down through the sunny haze into the town. "That promenade with the small trees is where high society took its evening walk . . .There was the fashionable convent of the barefooted friars."

His finger traces out streets and buildings. "That's the rococo villa, there where you see the soldiers lined up for mess in the courtyard, where they claim La Perricholi lived . . . of course she didn't live there at all . . . There's the bridge, the one of San Luis Rey, the American tourists say, only it never fell down, about the only thing in Lima that never did . . . Lima's a city that forgets . . . maybe it's because the earthquakes sooner or later bring everything down." The broadcaster starts a sigh but it ends in a little selfcon-scious giggle . . . "An ephemeral city."

We turn our backs to the city and the sea and look up at the cubic shapes of the village above us. There is more order to the houses than had appeared at first. They are built into the mountainside out of carefully laid blocks of adobe. Some of them are of brick and a few are plastered and white-washed. Above doors and windows shuttered with wooden shutters that have traces of blue or green or yellow paint are arbors made of thin poles and roofed with twigs. Alongside the houses enclosures for chickens are carefully wattled out of reeds.

"But these look like the houses of quiet and respectable people," says one of the European city planners. "This isn't a squatter settlement, this is an Indian pueblo."

"The police think different," says the broadcaster.

The painter pushes the beret back on his head and stretches out his hands palms up in a melodramatic gesture. "This is the aboriginal Peru," he says. "Before Lima was the pueblo is."

We start on up the hill, toiling along a stumbly footpath that skirts the side walls of houses and comes out on roofs of beaten mud. We get whiffs of charcoal and garlic from cooking fires. Occasionally a woman with shrouded head or a child with black beads for eyes looks out unsmilingly at us from the shadow of a doorway.

"But where are the men?" the broadcaster is muttering nervously.

At last we see them high up above us. On the steep shoulder of the mountain a group of men is digging. Occasionally the point of a pick flashes in the sun.

The European city planners begin to unlimber their cameras. When we are halfway up the outcropping of slippery rock a short broadshouldered man leaves the group above and comes running down towards us. Under the cream felt hat is one of those broad smoothly modelled faces you see on the portrait jugs they find along this coast in tombs from the times before the Conquest. His black brows are twisted into a scowl.

He comes close up to us, squares his shoulders and speaks slowly and emphatically. "We don't mind your taking pictures for the newspapers . . . But we do want you to get us right. When you write in the papers you treat us as if we were savages."

Everybody talks at once. We are not taking pictures for the papers. These gentlemen are distinguished foreigners who are making up a city plan for Greater Lima. The only journalist is off duty. The man looks at us so hard his brown eyes go into a squint. He listens carefully as if trying to remember every word but he isn't believing what he hears yet.

We are all still puffing and panting from the climb.

"This hill," he says, standing with his legs well apart and his shoulders squared to bar the way, "used to be the hangout of thieves and vagabonds before we took over. We do no harm to anyone. All we ask is to be allowed to live in peace. The authorities treat us like enemies. The police come and tear down our houses, they arrest us and keep us months in jail. See that slum down there where it's damp and unhealthy down by the river. They call that a housing project. That's where they want us to live. We like it up here. We like the air. We like the view and the oxygen. We are all people from the provinces of many different religions . . .

"He means different Indian languages," the broadcaster interrupts in an explanatory whisper.

"We have had to come to Lima as God willed to get work. They drag us down to jail and then they say we are vagabonds. They knock our houses down with the butts of their rifles. Look down there in the gulch." He points with a square brown hand to where two men are laying adobe bricks on a wall. "Look at those two men. Yesterday the police knocked down their house. Today they are building it up again."

"Look, my friend, we have nothing to do with the police or the newspapers," begins the painter in a diplomatic tone, "but since we've come all this way we would like to visit the pueblo. Perhaps if you had time you would show us around."

The man purses up his mouth and looks each one of us in the eye. We all stand still respectfully waiting for him to speak. Gradually the wrinkles smooth out of his brow. He begins to smile.

"We are building a cistern"; his deep voice has become low and confidential, "a tank so that we can have water in our houses . . . Everybody works in his spare time: cooperation. Before we had brought water in a ditch from the hills, good water full of iron and vitamins but the authorities cut it off. Now we have a well and a pump . . . Down there in the slum our enemies come to get our water. The authorities didn't lay in any water so they have to beg us for some of ours. We have bought galvanized iron pipes to pump the water up the hill so that it can flow into our houses. The pipe is imported from the United States," he adds proudly.

Talking he leads the way up the hill. A few of the men digging look up uneasily but when they hear us making approving remarks about their excavation they go on digging. They are short broadshouldered men. Their features, like their leader's, are the features of the polished pottery portraits the archaeologists find in the tombs. Above the emplacement for the tank a trail zigzags to a cross at the crest of the hill. We follow our guide on up and stand breathless beside the crucifix looking out over the buff-colored squares of the city and the white distant streak of the beach and the tall sunbleached islands out in the Pacific.

"Here we had a Christmas tree for the birth of our Lord," our guide is saying. Another thinfaced dusty Indian who followed us up the hill stands hat in hand until we notice him and then makes a little speech: "Gentlemen," he says, "the party who now has the honor of addressing you is the party who is responsible for the establishment of this cross."

By the time we had scrambled down the other path to the village again everybody we met was smiling at us. We were honored guests. "This is our *presidente*," said our guide as a small man in a business suit came out of the first house to greet us. "He knows how to talk to the people down there."

"The gentlemen are making plans for Greater Lima?" asked the *presidente* courteously. "We too have our plans. Perhaps you will include them in your recommendations. This is where we are going to build our church . . . That level square is where we hold our fiestas. We roof it over with boughs. See we've even planted a tree. The last government wanted us to move out into official housing but we talked them out of it. The *apristas* gave us this tree . . . Now we have a new military government and we'll have to explain things to them all over again."

"Military or civil, the governments are all alike," said our guide talking from the depths of his broad chest. "The police come and beat us up with sticks and knock down our walls and drag us down to the city . . . I've seen all the governments. I've seen Leguia and Prado and Bustamante and now it's Odria. I cry *viva* for all the presidents . . . but it's the same police. We are building a *pueblecito* here with our hands and our sweat and the muscles of our backs. Even the mud for the adobe we have to bring up the hill. We leave them alone. Why can't they leave us alone?"

The *presidente* interrupted talking fast and smoothly about how they had already installed electric light in some of the lower houses and about how they wanted a small medical dispensary. "We are not savages . . . we have among us all sorts of people, a couple of lawyers, students, business men, people of some education." He was talking over his shoulder as we followed him down a crumbling trail among the houses. "This will be the avenue that leads up to the church."

"The name of the avenue," said our guide in his chesty voice, "is Avenida Tupac Amarac."

"Tupac Amarac was the leader of the last Indian revolt in the eighteenth century. The Spanish viceroy had him drawn and quartered," explained the broadcaster.

"Yes," said our guide, his voice deep with conviction, "he was our leader."

"Perhaps you can put the name down on the project for the new city plan," the *presidente* rattled on smoothly. We had almost reached the level of the city streets again. "But wait I want to show you a photograph." The *presidente* ran up some adobe steps into a stucco house painted pink with a white trim.

While we waited a half naked man with two gasoline tins hung from a yoke across his shoulders came past us along the path stepping carelessly among the sharp rocks on dusty black feet. His skin showed through his rags the color and texture of old dry tobacco. He looked at us without seeing us as he passed.

"He waters the plants," explained our guide. "He's just come down Tupac Amarac Avenue from watering the tree by the church." He tapped his forehead to indicate emptiness. "A simple one of God but he waters the plants. If they'll leave us alone we'll have trees and gardens on our hill."

"An interesting thought," the broadcaster was whispering in my ear, "we conquered the Indians and little by little very slowly they reconquer us. The Andean pueblo moves into the European city."

The *presidente* had come back with his photograph. It was a snapshot of a jaded old style Chevrolet stalled on a pile of rocks. "The *presidente* owns a car," our guide told us in a voice full of awe. "You'll see it to the left when you turn down from the bottom of the hill."

"This photograph," said the *presidente* in an impressive tone, "is of my car at the highest point it ever reached on the Avenue of Tupac Amarac . . . If the authorities leave us alone I'll drive it to the church."

That night dining in a restaurant with another Peruvian doctor and a lawyer friend of his I was telling the story of the Avenida Tupac Amarac. Halfway through I noticed that the lawyer was taking it ill.

"You like that?" he interrupted. He was a thin pale sharp-faced man with a tense squeaky voice. "You Americans like

to make a fuss about the Indians. You like the idea of getting
the Indians away from us. At one time it might have been
possible but now it's too late" — he let his voice drop to a
strained whisper. "The *apristas* wanted to do that but they
have failed. They are bankrupt because they don't understand what is happening in the world . . . That trip to North
America ruined Haya de La Torre. He came back a Yankee
. . . You Americans have failed . . . The Good Neighbor
Policy almost pulled the wool over our eyes . . . You can sell
us cars for a while yet. You can send us down old women to
chatter about Indians and native handicrafts . . . But when
we have a democracy it will be Soviet democracy and not the
imperialist democracy of lynch law and racial discrimination.
In Europe the liberating wave is advancing. You think you
have stopped it with your oppressive Marshall Plan, but you
haven't. In Asia the liberating armies are reaching the
Yangtse River. All Asia will be freed from Yankee Imperialism. You think China is far away, but for us in Peru China
is not far away. From across the Pacific we can feel the
breath of freedom from imperialism . . . " The little man
was getting more and more excited. His thin nostrils were
distended. Across the plates littered with chicken bones and
crumbled bread and the wine glasses he looked in my face
with an expression of real hatred.

The doctor was a ruddy roundfaced man. He put his
hand soothingly on his lawyer friend's sleeve, and started an
explanation in a cajoling tone.

"Not so bad as that," he drawled. "But I'll tell you why
you will never influence the Indians . . . It is the story of my
cousin Luisito. Luisito ever since the university has been
enthusiastic about the United States. When we were children in school we used to talk about how wonderful it
would be to go to New York and live at the Waldorf Astoria
. . . It was his dream. His *novia* was enthusiastic about the
United States so much so that she went to a Yankee college

for girls. Her family were enthusiastic about the United States so it was decided that Luisito would meet his *novia* in New York and they would be married at the Waldorf Astoria. His father-in-law gave him a car and the new-married couple drove all over the United States to California and Texas and the *parque* of Yellowstone . . . Poor little things, they came back so sad . . . You see Luisito is very dark . . . In my family there is no Negro blood; that I know, perhaps some Indian far back and some Berber or Arab in the peninsula before the Conquest . . . Their car was a Chrysler convertible. They drove with the top down to see the scenery. When Luisito gets sunburned he becomes very dark. They were refused in hotels, in night clubs, in restaurants. They were humiliated. The honeymoon they had dreamed of so became a nightmare. It is hard for a man to be humiliated on his honeymoon. They sold the car and returned desperate . . . Probably now his marriage will be unhappy."

There wasn't much I could answer to that. Certainly we didn't treat the Mexican Indians very well, I pointed out lamely, but they kept on coming in swarms every year across the Rio Grande. At least we paid them better for their work than they were paid at home.

"It is the same here," the lawyer burst out bitterly, "your companies pay them better. They would rather work for an American than for a Peruvian but that is out of ignorance. Soon capitalism will have another depression and the Yankee imperialists won't be able to pay anybody. Then they will see that American capitalism is a failure and they will look across the Pacific to the real Soviet democracies of Asia."

"Meanwhile why couldn't you try to give them a slightly higher standard of living?" I couldn't help asking.

The roundfaced doctor flushed. Now he was as angry as his friend. "Because you won't let us have any dollars. The Yankee capitalists keep all the dollars for themselves or for their imperialist schemes in Europe. In South America the inflation is strangling us. It's only by speculating in commodities that anybody can make any money and that makes the inflation worse. You won't let us import the things we need. How can we improve the standard of living of the ignorant and decadent Indians if we are short ourselves, even of medical supplies . . . And all you do is send down cultural missions to make sweet talk about democracy and silly women to stir up the ignorant Indians . . . We don't want your lynch law democracy. We want consumer's goods."

We had pushed back our chairs and stood glaring at each other round the table while the waiter went off to make change.

"At least you like our cars and our iceboxes," I said, trying to get a smile out of them.

The doctor's face mellowed a little. "For a while we will be dependent on capitalism for manufactured products."

"And for a suite at the Waldorf Astoria?"

The redfaced doctor suddenly softened. "Oh yes . . . " He couldn't help smiling. "Now that would be very nice . . . The Interamericano," he was saying dreamily, "and then two weeks at the Waldorf Astoria."

At the door of the restaurant we parted coldly. As I walked away I could hear the thinfaced lawyer's voice creaking in the ear of his friend.

"Forget the Waldorf Astoria . . . In the Soviet Union they make better cars . . . the Moscow subway . . . They have magnificent hotels and rest homes especially for intellectuals . . . , especially for doctors . . . in the Soviet Union."

MRS. EDWARDS (*as the lights go up*): Well, I certainly hope what you say is mistaken. It gives me the most awful feeling, the idea of being hated by people I don't know . . . It makes one feel creepy.

EDDY JONES: Labor's got to get to work down there. It was

some American labor delegates who first exposed Peron for the Fascist he turned out to be.

FRED RUFUS: Nobody respects a sucker. Strength and singleness of purpose are the things that are respected in this world.

JAKE JEFFRIES: Now I'm just a country boy. All those foreign names got me kinda confused. If I understand it right what you've been trying to tell us is that modern industrial society is so centralized that any upstart can get a disciplined following by giving them an extra egg for their breakfast. He can call that following the Ista Party and can take over the government with three tanks and a little oratory. That's not so very different from what we do at home. Only we do it by herding votes.

MISS SMITHERS (*interrupting with a wail*): I really don't know whether I'm coming to the next lecture or not. It's all so very depressing. Why, I don't expect to sleep a wink all night.

JAKE JEFFRIES: Well, he may not be right, miss. These writers, they make most of this stuff up out of their heads . . . Now let's see if I've got you right. Your idea is that Argentina went socialist or fascist or statist or whatever you want to call it first because it is the only really developed modern country in South America.

MR. LECTURER: Exactly.

JAKE JEFFRIES: Then in the other countries, especially Brazil, things haven't jelled yet. They might go our way and they might go the way of the totalitarian power boys . . .

MR. LECTURER: That's just about it.

JAKE JEFFRIES: It's the same problem we have in the rundown sections of the South and West. In my opinion the cure for lynching is hybrid seed corn . . . If we could get some modern agriculture going in those highlands of Brazil you were talking about and get the majority of folks down there really prosperous, those dictators wouldn't have a chance. They would not only go for our way of life but they'd buy our automobiles and manufactured goods.

FRED RUFUS: What are they going to buy them with?

VOICE FROM THE BACK OF THE HALL: The only way is for us to take more of their exports.

EDDY JONES: Then how are we going to keep up our wage scales?

JAKE JEFFRIES: Or our farm prices? All these dilemmas come home to roost.

MR. LECTURER (*in a salesman's chant*): We will look for their solution right here at home, in my following lecture. Tonight I'm afraid I have to cut our discussion short ... (*He looks at his watch and makes a clucking noise*). Next time we'll throw the discussion open to the floor from the very beginning. (*Still talking he backs out of sight.*)

Dedicated
to a Proposition

III

FOURTH LECTURE

The Country We Came Home To

MR. LECTURER *(rubbing his hands with the air of a man who is trying to make the best of a bad business)*: Ladies and gentlemen, so few people have bought tickets for these last lectures, probably on account of the inclement weather, that the management thought we'd be cosier in this nice little conference room instead of that big old drafty hall . . . So I hope you'll all make yourselves at home while we continue our discussion as informally as possible . . . After getting a few samples of the sort of thing that is happening in other segments of the exasperated world we live in, where disaster has become the norm of human existence, we are coming home to our own problems. *(He turns out the lights and fumbles with the projector.)* Ouch it's hot . . . The management thought it would be more . . . more *intime,* I think that was the phrase they used, if I ran off my own films . . . That feeling of homecoming I felt most intensely one day when it wasn't I who was arriving at all. It was towards the end of the war. I was out at La Guardia Field watching men from the Army Air Force come in on leave, men who had finished their tour of duty in the theatres . . . *(The projector whirs.)* This first reel is rather an old one. *(Mr. Lecturer mutters apologetically under his breath.)*

CAPTION: *A Lump in Your Throat*

The first man out of the overseas transport is a tousled young man wearing a sheepskin jacket open at the throat who trots down the steps with a smile a yard wide on his sunburned face. When he hits the ground he drops on his heels and gives the concrete three quick pats with his hand. He straightens himself up and, lighting a cigarette between shaking fingers, turns to see the rest of them come out. As they run down the steps in their mussed and varied khaki outfits their eyes are big enough to take in all America. One man kisses the palm of his hand and shyly pats the ground with it. Another gives the man next to him a quick nudge. They are all grinning.

They stand still a second looking at the sunny clouds and the airport crowded with planes and the blue strip of Long Island Sound and the shoreline littered with buildings beyond. Nobody says anything.

An airport officer, with papers fluttering off the board in his hand in the fresh wind, jerks his head towards a door in the hangar and starts off. The young men home from all the distant corners of the war pull their shoulders back and take a deep breath and hurry along after him. Some wear sheepskins, some wear leather jackets with Chinese and American flags sewn on the back. A couple have words inscribed in Arabic under the insignia on their breasts. One tall young man is looking a little silly in a sun helmet. A grayhaired officer carries a fat worn briefcase. Another has a Japanese sword.

In a boarded off place they are lectured briefly on the formalities of arrival, on not talking about things they shouldn't talk about. Already the first men are filtering past the intelligence officers behind the desk. Next they talk to a group of F.B.I. men in civilian clothes. Then at the long counter where the customs officers are they stand with twitching fingers waiting for their flight bags to be brought from the plane.

At the same time a detachment of men headed out is filing through the other way with yellow tags on their duffle. The incoming men and the outgoing men look at each other shyly without speaking.

A customs officer takes an orange out of the flap of a flight bag. Everybody looks at it in a puzzled way. The customs officer puts on his glasses, stares at the orange as if he'd never seen one before and then slips it into his own pocket. A smile starts and fades along the row of faces. Somewhere along the line an Italian pottery plate painted with a scene from the Bay of Naples drops out of a canvas satchel and smashes dully on the concrete floor.

Outside, in the lobby where they wait for the bus that will take them across to Manhattan, there's a coffee bar and across from it a desk marked *Transportation*. Two pretty dark girls stand smiling behind the desk marked *Transportation*. "You talk English too?" a very young man asks breathlessly shaking the hair out of his eyes. The pretty dark girls smile some more. "Say Joe, they talk English," the very young man shouts.

"Lord what it feels like to be in a place where things are clean," a boy with a closecropped dark head whispers huskily. They cluster round the transportation desk giggling and blinking as they look at the girls as if the light of them were too bright for their eyes.

At the coffee bar everybody's ordering up milk.

"Did you have a comfortable trip?" a sergeant stationed at the airport who is drinking coffee asks the man next him. "You had real seats."

A blond first lieutenant with an eyebrow moustache turns a poker face toward the sergeant. "All plane trips are comfortable," he says grumpily. He elbows his way back to order up another paper cup of milk.

The crowd is moving away. One bashful looking young sergeant with a pink face is left still standing there. He stutters, but finally he manages to ask, "Say would it be all right if I had just one more shot of milk?"

Meanwhile on the pavement outside there has appeared a liaison officer from the Air Force Distribution Command. He's a first lieutenant. He speaks with a silver tongue. He's telling the newly arrived officers and men about accommodations at the G.I. hotel, about transportation home, about the twentyone day leave they are going to get. What he's saying doesn't go down very well. As the men crowd around him there's a chip on the shoulder look about them. They square their jaws when they ask their questions. They want to know if they have got to go to this damn hotel, when they get their pay, have new uniforms made up; can they start home right away? The lieutenant answers every question in a soothing considerate tone. He's trying to explain that they'll get a break at last. You can see they don't believe him.

On the pavement on the street side of the hangar they cluster together frowning up at the olive drab truck that's waiting for them. It looks too much like the war. They don't like it. A whiff of high octane gas still lingers about the flightbags that are being loaded into the truck and about the men's clothing. When the bags are loaded they pile grouchily into the truck themselves. Driving along the smoothly sweeping parkway into the city they begin to notice that they are home; there is paint on the civilian cars, chromium fittings shine. The people in the cars wear good clothes, there is a wellfed look on men's and women's faces. Crossing the great bridge there are evening glimpses of the river and the wharves, misty beneath them, and of downtown buildings rising in perpendicular glitter out of dusky streets. Long strings of lights are coming on along the river. Lights sweep the pavements outside the G.I. hotel. At the end of the deep street the serried cars and brightcolored taxicabs of the rush hour traffic go hissing past.

The men shave, take showers, borrow neckties, spruce up scrappy uniforms as best they can. The first thing they ask is where can they make a long distance call. Where is Western Union? Some of them have families or friends in the city. Those that don't find themselves out on the pavement headed for places to eat, bars, cocktail lounges.

The long straight streets flare with light and noise under the inkblue faintly starry sky. A man doesn't know where to go first. There is so much of everything. There are so many bars, so many places to eat, you can't make up your mind which one. In the windows of restaurants hams glazed with burnt sugar and studded with cloves stand in solemn rows between piles of great long Idaho potatoes, red snappers and halibut and seabass are stacked on cracked ice amid flower-beds of radishes and parsley. The candy stores are full of colors. At the entrance to moving picture theatres big as railroad stations posters expose acres of pinup legs. From the redcarpeted entrances of dance halls the thump of swing music and smells of dust and perfume leak out on to the sidewalk. And behind all the candy counters, in the glass and monel metal cages of ticket windows, sitting at all the tables, swaying on the dance floors, clicking on high heels along all the sidewalks in front of the bright show windows, letting slender, slick legs be seen as they climb in and out of taxicabs, are girls, American girls, girls in pretty dresses, girls with uptodate hairdoes, girls with kidding lips, girls whose eyes look pleasantly into yours.

Next morning the returnees come trooping into the office of the port embarkation for their orders. They have had haircuts. They have the look of having come out from under hot showers. They are wearing new uniforms. They've lost the chip on the shoulder look. Some of them are a little pale around the gills, a little pouchy under the eyes. Overdid a little maybe. Tried to drink all the liquor up in one night. Some nurse Coca Cola bottles in jittery fingers. They can't stand still. Boys from the same bomber crew lean together in a tangle against the information desk pawing one another like a litter of pups.

"The first thing I did," a lieutenant from Nebraska is saying, "was just to go into a grocery store, just to see the stock on the shelves, that seemed more like home than anything."

"It's the lights that hit me," says another. "I hadn't seen a town with lights in seventeen months."

"The lights and the goodlooking women, my what it feels like to see goodlooking women."

"And being able to sit down at a table and order up what you want to eat."

"I went into a barbershop," says a boy from Brooklyn, "to get a shave. He was the barber I always used to trade with. That barber kept me in the chair two hours and a half. He gave me everything he had including a mudpack and he never charged me a cent."

"When you get out of the service," I asked him, "what are your plans?"

"If I get out," he corrected me grimly, "I want to go to school and then I want to go into business for myself."

When this batch is all assembled the major in charge gives them a talk. He reminds them again not to blab about things they've been told to keep quiet about, not to get drunk in public, to be careful about wearing the proper uniform, about saluting, cautions them about VD and tells them where they can get shoe coupons and gas for their cars, and wishes them a pleasant twentyone days' leave.

The major was a quietspoken Baltimorean who managed to give an air of hospitality to the way he stood behind the counter, distributing the travel orders in their manila envelopes and answering questions about travel time, promotions, change of duty. Like a good host he was interested in everybody. A man whose wife lived in Houston, Texas, while his folks lived in California, was telling his story. He drummed nervously with cigarettestained fingers on the counters while he waited for the major to answer.

"You take your leave in Texas," the major answered after a second, "and your orders will read to report in Santa Monica. That was an easy one," he added.

"When you get out of the army," I sidle up to ask the man with the yellow fingers, "what are you planning?" His answer was almost word for word the answer of the boy from Brooklyn. School; then set up in business for himself. "Let's not talk about it," he added hurriedly. "Bad luck."

The lieutenant who assisted the major was already handing around photographs on glossy stock of men in uniform lolling on the sunporches of big hotels, sitting at tables with starched white clothes in hotel diningrooms, of young men and girls in bathing suits sunning themselves on ocean beaches, or playing tennis in a snowy mountain valley, of soldiers in their shirtsleeves fishing along a trout stream. Those were the redistribution and rest centers they would go to after they finished their leave. The boys looked at them with wide unseeing eyes and went off wagging their heads. They weren't paying attention. The minute each man got his orders he was gone like a breeze out of the door.

EDDY JONES: Lord that brings it home. You were just there looking on but I was one of those guys.

MR. LECTURER: Getting home was a funny business. You

were crazy to see the folks yet you dreaded it too. Your fingers got cold as you sat there on the crowded train looking out of the window and began to recognize the drift of the hills, the way the trees grew along the highway, the signs back of the bleachers at the ball park. You were just a kid when you left; you had grown up since, fast and far, but into a different world from the world your folks grew up into. When you hopped out of the train and saw them all standing there your stomach drew up into a knot . . . You fellows getting home from World War II didn't feel so very different from our crowd getting home from World War I, except we came home mad. The country seems to have lost its capacity for moral indignation.

EDDY JONES: I went away mad, I came home mad and I'm still mad. (*Laughter.*)

MR. LECTURER: I remember a redheaded young technical sergeant with a broken front tooth who was sitting quiet and happy on a couch in the hotel lobby. He went rigid and his face got crimson when I asked him what getting home had been like. He got to his feet finally but he couldn't say a word, only waved his hand beseechingly. For a full minute he stood in speechless agony. Then he blurted out "Oh please I can't . . ." and hurried away.

"Getting home's wonderful, but it's kind of upsetting," a lieutenant off a bomber said, speaking slowly and thoughtfully, when I asked him the same silly question. He was a slender darkhaired man with dark blue eyes and small hands who looked younger than his twentyeight years. His people were Irish. He'd always lived and worked in New York. He'd been home a couple of weeks.

"Of course it's wonderful," he repeated. He had a remarkably quiet way of talking. It was his lack of indignation that surprised me at the time. These young men seemed so much more aloof, though better informed, than we were in our day. "We lived a very isolated life over there way out in tents miles from anywhere only seeing our own crowd and a few miserable Italians . . . New York never looked so good . . . But it was hard getting adjusted. Like everybody I'd formed an exaggerated idea maybe of what a good time I would have. My wife and my parents are probably better informed than the ordinary, at least I think they are, but even with them I find it hard to talk about certain things. Civilians have strange ideas. There are things you can't explain." He paused and took a swallow of water. "I don't think it's that this wartime life has brutalized us. We don't feel we're coming home any different than we went. Only kinder worn out that's all. I don't think we are brutalized. Fellows worry about that. I don't know about the men who have it hand to hand. Most of our killing is a question of pinpoints on the map. You don't think much about people down there when you're four miles straight up. We do certain things that have to be done that's all . . . I don't think it has brutalized us, really. I mean I don't think it has made us unfit to be decent independent citizens. But the way the civilians talk . . . I guess they get it from reading the headlines . . . They seem to think it's all so easy. Making it so easy seems kind of disrespectful to the men who are finding the going so tough over there and who won't come back." He took another swallow of water and looked frowning at the ice in his glass for a moment. "Getting home's upsetting," he said again. "A man doesn't dare plan. If I dared plan . . . It would be a business of my own and a home of our own for my wife and me. But let's not plan . . . It would turn out like that steak . . . Like everybody else I was dreaming about the wonderful big meals I was going to eat when I got home. It was kind of a shock to find I could hardly eat a thing. Must be all that dehydrated food shrinks your stomach up. A friend of mine told me that the night after he got home his mother cooked the most wonderful steak you ever saw about three inches thick. The butcher knew who it was for and had been saving it out for her. He said it looked wonderful when he got it on his plate but when he got a piece in his mouth it tasted like cotton batting to him. He tried to choke it down but he couldn't. His mother cried and everybody was all broken up about it. It made them all feel bad. I guess that's what you mean when you say you've got a lump in your throat."

EDDY JONES: A lot of the guys I knew came home mad at the whole dirty rotten system.

FRED RUFUS: The men I met seemed only to want to get back into what I suppose you call the capitalist ratrace, Mr. Jones.

MR. LECTURER: I've often thought about those returning airmen, so excited about getting home that their heads spun like tops. I've often wondered what they thought about the contrast between their imagining of America on those long, droning missions when the life of a bomber crew was worth somewhat less than a nickel and the America they found when they came to alive and well in their childhood world.

(*Everybody's talking at once.*)

MISS SMITHERS: They've proved wonderful students in the colleges.

MRS. EDWARDS: They don't any of them want another war, I know that.

FRED RUFUS: They still think America is Santa Claus.

MISS SMITHERS: Well hasn't it been, really? Look at the G.I. Bill of Rights.

FRED RUFUS: They'll find out, like they are finding out in England, that there ain't no Santa Claus.

EDDY JONES (*sarcastically*): Except for the directors of the big corporations . . . It's Christmas for them every time they vote themselves another bonus.

JAKE JEFFRIES: New discoveries can be Santa Claus . . . Modern farming methods . . .

MR. LECTURER: Gentlemen, ladies . . . I'm afraid I shall

have to take over the duties of chairman. Mr. Rufus I think
has the floor.

FRED RUFUS: Free enterprise made this country. Without
economic liberty we can't have any other kind of liberty.
Everybody beefs about the wealth of great corporations but
people tend to forget the goods they produce and the services
they perform . . . I'm quite ready to admit that Business is
overcentralized, that Business lost the leadership of this
country during the great depression. Business leaders fell
for this same psychology that afflicts farmers and labor.
When they began to feel the pinch they ran to Washington
for a handout. What these young G.I.'s you're talking about
found when they got home was that they couldn't go into
business for themselves because of the discriminations of the
tax structure against new enterprises. . . . It's almost as
tough for them as for those Englishmen who talked to our
friend here . . . Production of goods is the basis of any society.
When the best advice you can give a young man starting out
in life is to keep away from production and find himself a
racket it is not a very healthy state of affairs, to my way of
thinking.

EDDY JONES: Who's to blame for that, Business or Labor?

FRED RUFUS: I'm not talking about who's to blame. I'm
talking about a condition. Labor is to blame for letting its
votes be bought by every demagogue who peddles a new
handout from the National Santa Claus.

EDDY JONES: While the boards of directors and the traders
on influence are getting away with most of the swag, don't
you think the man who does the work has a right to demand
his share?

FRED RUFUS: Young man, in modern manufacturing the
physical work is becoming less and less important. The real
wealth of a manufacturing concern, and of the nation, lies in
the technical knowhow, in the ability to take some article
we want to produce, say an airplane or a typewriter, to pieces

and to discover the most economical and practical method of producing it. The labor theory of value went sky high with the first assembly line. That doesn't mean that I don't think that skill and even pick and shovel work oughtn't to be well paid. High wages are the basis of our prosperity . . . Maybe what we ought to do is to take our whole productive plant to pieces and try to find some way of figuring the social value — I don't mean the money value, that's mostly bookkeeping, but the value to society — of the various operations and to try to assign the rewards where the rewards are really due . . . We must find some way to encourage new enterprise. New business can't weather the present tax setup which is the result of the famous White House formula: tax and tax and tax, spend and spend and spend, elect and elect and elect. Those young men you are talking about who came home from the war full of illusions about setting up in business for themselves are finding slim pickings, I can tell you. The brightest ones have joined up long since with the big corporate industries and are making their careers inside of the existing organizations. Mighty little new enterprise is being undertaken.

EDDY JONES: If manufacturers were a little readier to take labor into the business as a partner instead of as a wage-slave . . .

FRED RUFUS: You say labor wants to be a partner. I only wish that were true. A partner has to take his share of the responsibility and his share of the risk. Business isn't all profits, you know. There is such a thing as losses.

MR. LECTURER: Gentlemen, perhaps we'd better go on with the program.

JAKE JEFFRIES: I've been trying to get in a word edgewise. I know I'm just a country boy but I'd like to point out that the one place where free enterprise has been flourishing in this country in the last ten years is on the farm. Thousands and thousands of young men without capital have made themselves independent since the upturn in farm prices in the thirties. In spite of a continually dwindling and more expensive labor supply the American farm produces more and, in my opinion, gives a better life to the farmer — of course he has to work for it from dawn to dark — than it has since pioneer days.

MR. LECTURER: We are coming to that, Mr. Jeffries. If you excuse me, I'll dim the lights. I thought we would start with a sample American town.

CAPTION: Sample Town

It's late afternoon of a winter day. You walk along brick sidewalks between gray patches of pockmarked snow, through fog thickened by softcoal smoke. The air smells of machineshops and coalgas. Soot falls gently through the twilight, drips in inky stain from icicles along the gutters, blackens the grime on closepacked frame dwellinghouses, and settles in soft smudges on your face. At the end of every street you can see the spreading buildings of some plant or other, horizontal lines of windows, clusters of tall, smooth stacks spewing spiralling formations of smoke. Often you cross railroad tracks, broad marshalling yards full of clanking freightcars. You are never out of earshot of the hoot and roottoot toot toot of the shunting engines.

"Sure," says the citizen who is showing you around the town, "soft coal and pig iron . . . makes things kinda sooty . . . but I wouldn't want to live anyplace else . . . maybe it's the people."

"Industrious?"

"They shake a leg . . . they like to see a man down at his office at eight . . . Don't forget that in this kind of a Ruhr that stretches from the lakes down across the Ohio River southward more of everything you can think of is produced than in the whole rest of the world put together."

"The Ruhr hasn't worked out so well."

The citizen stops in his tracks. "Out here we're worried about all these problems . . . labor, strikes, all that . . . but we ain't pessimistic. I moved here from Jersey sixteen years ago . . . wouldn't live anyplace else . . . It's the industrial heart of America . . . that's what we are . . . that's why we like it."

Looking through the windows into the lighted parlors the houses don't seem so bad inside. The paint is clean. There are new furnishings and fresh window curtains. Sometimes the mister sits there in his shirtsleeves in a new over-stuffed chair reading the paper while he waits for his supper, or a woman with crisply curled hair wearing a flowered apron is laying the table. The children look wellfed and have bright eyes and pink cheeks. When you reach Main Street and the shopping district the wet sidewalks are full of young people, young men in checked woolen shirts or leather jackets, young women in slacks with white or red or green peasant scarves over their hair. The crowd swirls round the doors of department stores and five and tens and candy shops.

"I don't like Christmas shopping unless I've got money to spend . . . real money like a hundred dollars," one girl is crying to another. "These strikes ruin the Christmas spirit," a man is saying to his wife. "They ought to take the labor leaders out and . . ." "Oh no, just window shopping." "We've come this far," rises a voice out of a group tangled in an argument, "what I want to know is where do we go from here?"

Back in the hotel from a room on the twelfth floor you look out at roofs and factory chimneys and smoke tinged with a rosy reflection of street signs. In the main artery below through a crowd of passenger cars the long dark shapes of trucks and buses move along the bright paths of their headlights.

"Well, what's your answer to the question?" you ask the cub reporter with the baby face and round thicklensed glasses who has perched himself on the corner of the bed with his overcoat draped round his knees. "Where do you go from here?"

"But what does it matter, what we think?" he asks back in an irritated tone. "What does it matter what happens in a dump like this? Everything here is decided by the higher-ups in Washington and Pittsburgh . . . That goes for management and it goes for labor . . . You can't tell me that what people are saying here is of any importance."

The newspaper woman tries to explain the interaction between what people think, say and do out here where the goods and the conflicts really come into being, and what they think and say and do in the central offices where the higher-ups make their decisions, which the people down here enforce. New attitudes filter up, she says, as much as they filter down. After all, isn't this the industrial heart of America?

The cub reporter stares out solemnly through his round glasses aghast with unbelief. "Then you believe in democracy?" he gasps.

"Exactly."

"But why this town more than any other?"

This was a very good sample, the newspaper woman explained patiently; it wasn't a one industry town. Steel accounted for fifty percent but other production was thoroughly broken up into small and varied concerns. There were good industrial relations in one steel plant and bad relations in another.

"All right, all right," said the cub reporter indignantly. "We're a sample . . . I've heard this dump called plenty of things and now it's a sample." He pulled his coat about him and stalked out of the room.

Walking around town, driving out to plants and suburban developments and talking to the taxidriver, the labor organizer, the leading realtor, the up and coming young lawyer, the secretary of the development society, to the seedy character hunched up at the bar in the hotel cocktail lounge, to the young man in a checked suit who's just emptied ten bucks down the drain in a slot machine, to the lady who handles the props at the little theatre, to the plain old steelworker on his way home to Sunday dinner, you begin to get a notion of how this place came to be what it is. Back a hundred and fifty years ago it started with primeval woods and the first settlers floating down the Ohio in arks and keelboats and poling up into the leafy creeks and clearing the timber and ploughing the black soil of the bottomlands and building cabins of logs and mud among the low hills of what was then called the Western Reserve. Painted frame houses took the place of cabins; canals took the place of rutted trails. They began to mine coal and iron and little manufacturies for making farming tools came into being in old barns and sheds along the creeks. The railroads linked the East and West. A man perfected a mechanical reaper and got rich and built himself a tall brick house and a tall brick carriage house and stables overlooking the center of town. There had always been a strong German and Swiss element in the region. Now some leading citizens got together to start a watch factory and brought in Swiss craftsmen. The town with its large population of artisans and mechanics grew and prospered. It was the market center for a fertile farming belt, and the home of a hundred small industries; brick making and ceramics, harness and leather goods, agricultural machinery and metal gutters and flashing and canvas awnings and nails and cast iron furniture and forgings and dies and tools.

The automobile came and World War I and the immense growth of the steel industry. The watch factory closed down and the machinery, bought by Amtorg, was shipped to the Soviet Union. The steel industry expanded with open hearth furnaces and blooming mills and rolling mills. With steel came Negroes from the south and a horde of immigrants from Europe: Greeks, Romanians, Syrians, Czechs, Hungarians, Italians, Swedes, Spaniards, Slovaks, Slovenes, Poles. A local concern that manufactured iron bearings for carts and wagons turned to the manufacture of steel bearings for cars and grew into one of the great bearing plants of the world.

The population changed. The town changed. From a tight little nineteenth century community where everybody knew how old man Saunders had worked nights out in his barn to perfect his bearing that had gone into mass production and made him a millionaire, and how that ingenious ne'erdowell Joe Jones, who was so down and out the boys had to get him a job as janitor at the Knights of Pythias to take care of him, invented the vacuum cleaner that made the town famous all over the world or how old Hopkins out on the county road had lost his farm and ruined his family borrowing money to develop a hard steel bit for use in mining machinery, — where every employer knew the men who worked for him and their wives' first names and the name of the latest baby — , the town became a huddle of walled-off alien groups. The community split a dozen ways.

Out at the bearing plant old man Saunders died, whom everybody had known and criticized so when he built himself a million dollar stone mansion on a hill overlooking the athletic field, — to this day people tell you Mrs. Saunders never liked it and neither did the boys who wanted to grow up just like other folks and instead of one of the Saunders boys a man named Meyer became president and ran the concern which by now had branches in foreign countries, cartel arrangements with British and German manufacturers and all the trimmings of international monopoly.

Meyer got himself a job in the plant when he was mustered

out of the army after World War I, in the tool crib, people tell you . . . "He's a bright cookie allright. He rose up through the entire business, made himself indispensable to the old man and now he's in the old man's shoes." He continually improved the product and the manufacturing process, everything except labor relations. "In the old days old man Saunders knew everybody on the payroll and everybody knew him but this guy, so people who work for him tell you, stalks through the plant straight as a ramrod looking like a Prussian general, never speaks to an employee except maybe to bawl out a foreman because the sweepers aren't keeping up with the litter on the floor of the shop."

Anyway, in labor relations he and his friends who make up the big business of the town tend to line up on one side of the fence, with the steelworkers organization on the other, and the retail merchants and the building trades and the bulk of the citizens in the middle. The situation at the big plant across town that belongs to one of the national steel corporations with plants in a dozen cities is just the opposite from that at the Saunders plant. There the personnel department from complete antagonism in the days before the C.I.O. has switched over to friendly cooperation with the union. Whichever way it works the town and its citizens have lost control of their own destiny.

The local manufacturing concerns have most of them become parts of nationwide empires. To stand up against the great corporations with offices in New York and Pittsburgh the workers in the plants have had to let their unions be swallowed by the great organizations of labor.

Organization has even reached out for the townspeople's less reputable pleasures. An independent citizen can't start a bingo game or install a slot machine or rig up a roulette wheel to fleece his friends with or invite a few young ladies to sit in his parlor and perhaps stroll upstairs with the visiting salesmen without having to do with the operatives of a

quietvoiced little Turkish Greek who lives in a suite at one
of the leading hotels. People tell you that years ago he had
some sort of unpleasantness with the law but that he discovered in time that there was another way around and
patiently and industrially organized the brothels and
gamblinghouses of the whole region into a tight system that
ramifies from the statehouse through townhalls and police
precincts to distribute protection to those who live off man-
kinds' little foibles in return for the cream of the take. "He's
a charming fellow really, one of the city's most generous
givers," people tell you. "He never bothers a law-abiding
citizen. He does it with kindness."

The tendency of nationwide organization is to produce
more wealth but to pump it out of town so that things lose
their early American look of neatness and prosperity. The
softcoal smoke smuts everything up. Instead of a place to
live in it becomes a place to work and to get away from.
The South End across the railroad track where the Negroes
live is a hopeless slum of battered shacks with blackened
hallways, packed one against the other straight through the
block. Southeast, where the Greeks settled round their
church with little onion domes on its towers, and the
Spaniards round their club — and the Romanians and the
Hungarians and the assorted South Slavs — the housing is
a little better but so crowded that hardly a spear of grass
grows between unpainted stoops. Southwest, where skilled
workers and machinists and the foremen in the steel plants
and the officeworkers tend to own their own homes, there
are still trees in the avenues and the houses have green lawns
and backyards. The better off professional people have
tried to get out of the truck traffic and the smog by building
on the small hills to the northward. The really wealthy have
left town altogether and encorporated themselves a private
village in a pleasant rolling piece of woodland outside the
city limits.

"It's not a beauty spot but we have good schools. We've always been great in football. We have a first rate technical high, good hospitals; in care of the blind we are tops in the state; new industries are moving in all the time," says the Secretary of the Development Society. "We're not scared of the future, and we are not ashamed of the present."

"Well here we are . . . You organize to raise wages and prices go up and wages go up and so on. What next?" I ask the big man behind the desk in the bare busy C.I.O. office that's above a furniture store on Main Street. "Where do we go from here?" He's the regional director of the organization. He has ruffled sandy hair and gray eyes and a rollicking manner, half bullying, half kidding.

"Just a minute, please," he lifts a square hand and goes on talking into the phone. One of his staff members has been picked up in a neighboring town for going through a red light and placed in jail until he can raise bond. He's laughing as he talks. "Now you just stay right there George until I call back . . . Don't you think of stirring away from that spot. I've got our lawyer on the job. Hungry, are you? Well, they'll have to feed you. Now don't you go away from there." Everybody in the office is laughing when he puts the receiver down.

"They've got him locked up. That'll learn him not to tear his tickets up. When they get into trouble that's when we hear from them . . . Where do we go from here you are asking?" He leans back in his chair and stretches. "Where do we go from here? That's the sixtyfour dollar question . . ."

In the first place, he starts to explain, people in this country have got to get it out of their heads that the working-man is so hellishly well off. With overtime during the war a man could get by and live a little better than he used to. Yes during that period the steelworker got used to a slightly

higher standard of living. But that had been over for a year
and now, making an average of fortyfive dollars a week,
with the cost of living what it was, men with families were
spending their savings for groceries and rent . . . No, their
war bonds were cashed in sometime back . . . New cars? The
men that had orders in were cancelling them . . . Homes?
Maybe a third, no less than that say twenty percent of steelworkers owned their homes. Some of the veterans who had
bought dumps at outrageous prices were going to be stuck
with them . . . Sure, he admitted that some of the guys had
blown their money in foolishly . . . In steel particularly
there was the kind of man who knew nothing but doing one
operation on a machine. No, he wasn't a machinist because
if something went wrong he just stood there and waited for
a repairman to come and fix it . . . Well he was just the same
outside as he was in the shop. All you could get him to
think of was booze and women or ballgames and craps. You
couldn't get him interested in the union or in buying his
home or in any damn thing. Of course, we mustn't get him
wrong, they weren't all like that, not by a long shot . . .
Those guys were casualties of specialization. The union
wanted them to stand up on their hind legs and act like
citizens. "Well that's our problem."

The phone rang again. He sits up straight and lifts the
receiver to his ear. "The place to see the real steelworker
who is alive all over is in the grievance committee," he says
with his hand on the mouthpiece. "Johnny, take him over to
see the boys at your local after their meeting this afternoon."
Immediately he is lost in what someone is telling him over
the phone.

They call this the All Nations Local because so many
nationalities are represented. It is housed in a brick building that was once a store which fronts on railroad tracks and
the great lightgray bulk of the mills. The grievance com-

mittee meets in the back room. The president, a freshfaced beefy young man out of the open hearth, sits at the desk. A welldressed young man with a thin jaw and large eyes astride a large sharpcut nose sits on the desk in front of him, swinging his legs in their gray trousers creased to a razor edge. He's from the staff. Around them are grouped a number of heavyset fellows with an intent look on their faces. They look like serious family men. In the corner a big sallow man in a leather jacket leans his head against the wall and occasionally lets the heavy eyelids drop over his eyes.

"Where do we go from here?" asks a grizzled Irishman with glasses. "What we hope is that we aren't heading straight into a fight. Prices keep rising. When we reopen our contract next winter we're going to have to have more."

"Some people claim increased production will take care of that and bring a lower cost of living," one man hazards timidly.

The Irishman shouts him down. "That's all propaganda. The newspapers fill us up with that crap."

The big sallow man in the corner who's been asleep opens his eyes and yawns: "Supply and demand," he starts to say.

"Propaganda," shouts the Irishman.

"Well, that's what they used to tell us," the big man trails off doubtfully.

"We mustn't forget that industrial profits have been bigger in 1946 than in any year in history," says the staff man leaning forward from the desk. "Here's the situation in a nutshell. Last winter we had a hell of a struggle to get a raise of eighteen and one half cents. It had taken us two years and four months to get it. That cost the industry somewhere around a hundred and eleven million dollars. To make up for that they got a raise of five dollars a ton that brought them in something like three hundred million and that's how it goes all down the line."

"You won't find that in the local paper here nor over the

local radiostation . . . They're closed to us." A tall gray-haired man with straight black eyebrows speaks in bitter tones. He sits tall and straight in his chair, his long hands with their wellkept square nails resting on his knees . . . "Now in this here grievance committee . . . " he goes on in his resonant voice, "we are pitting our brains against the best lawyers the company can hire in Columbus or Cleveland or elsewhere . . . We don't have no lawyers to present our case. Can't afford 'em. That makes the lawyers sore, they don't like to have a layman pleading his own case. We don't have an education either, we're just workin' guys out of the shop. It's a tough job," he says knitting his black brows. "They've got all the money and the brains on their side and all we've got is the union."

The big man who has been asleep gets ponderously to his feet. "I work in the open hearth. Since VJ Day we've had six hours a turn at the furnaces instead of eight. Can't get the scrap, the company says . . . Can't get the orders . . . We're not workin' full time now. I'm not talkin' about overtime. That's gone. Right now if a man don't work full time he don't break even."

"You ask where do we go from here?" says the Irishman. "We don't want it unless it's forced on us but if they try to cut real wages or to break up the union we're headed into a fight."

"No, no, we don't wanna strike," said the lowvoiced Spaniard who worked at the bearing plant. He was a wizened man in blue dungarees with brown eyes and a sharp pointed nose. It was quiet in the basement of the Spanish club. A few men stood along the bar. A pimply youth with a high-school letter on his sweater was kidding a girl over the phone against the wall: "Got stewed last night. Don't you wish you'd been along?" After she'd brought the beers the black-haired busty woman with deep crowsfeet at the corners of her eyes stood listening to him with her eyebrows drawn together into an expression of tolerant scorn. "Look here mister," the Spaniard who worked at the bearing plant was counting on his fingers, "after deductions we bring home from thirtytwo to thirtyfive dollars. I pay rent thirtyfive dollars a month. I have a wife and boy. We got light, heat, water, groceries, clothes to pay . . . If we work less than forty hours we have to go into the sock . . . you understand, the savings."

He'd been in this country since 1921. His brother had come over first from Asturias in the north of Spain and then he'd come over . . . for the liberty, to escape the military service, of course, he said. Yes he was a little better off than in the bad times but not better off than in the twenties; then your money brought more. He was an American citizen. He was settled in this town for life. The boy was in the technical high taking a machinist's course. At home he and his wife spoke Spanish but his boy didn't speak no more Spanish than a Polack . . . The younger generation they weren't interested in the old countries, they married all kinds girls, all mixed up, growing up as new generation of Americans . . .

"Bah, all generations of men are the same," cried a tiny dusty old man who had been busily putting down one bottle of beer after another and whispering all the while in torrential Spanish into the ear of a round and silent crony whose flopping hatbrim covered his face. The old man, so short his chin hardly reached to the bar, addressed his remark to the company in general and turned up a lined and pointed face dry and brown and brittle as a twist of tobacco with a long twisted nose that gave him a mosquito look. "All men the same," he reiterated in a threatening tone.

A stout fellow down the bar took him to task. He wasn't in no generation with no geedeed yellow Jap or Chinee, he began to mutter. The little man exploded and began to advance splayfooted strutting like a bantam towards the challenger.

"I am a native of Avilés and an independent man," he shouted waving his beerglass unsteadily in one hand and tapping himself on the chest with the fingers of the other.

Somebody stepped between him and his opponent who was four times his size and asked him soothingly where he worked.

"I kiss no man's boot. I work for myself, Antonio Alvarez, natural of Avilés, painter and decorator, at your service." He moved his head forward and brought up his hand as if he were about to remove his hat in a courtly bow. "You can go home and say you have met an independent man." He swept the room with a prosecuting attorney's gesture. "These people are all . . . fodder . . . cannon fodder, factory fodder, trade union fodder . . . fodder." He placed his grimy forefinger against his long insect nose and pivoted back towards the bar until his face was hidden under his crony's hatbrim again.

"*Cosas de España* . . . Things from Spain," said the steelworker shaking his head and smiling. He led the way into a readingroom with easy chairs and a table full of magazines. He sat down and lit a cigarette. "There are two things we think about in the shop to make life better for the steelworker . . . Suppose you had wages go up and down some way with the price of living?" He paused. "Then suppose you had a guaranteed annual wage, a man could plan . . . This way he can't know from one day to the other when he is going to be laid off . . . With security I think we could produce more, now we are always afraid if we finish up an order then we'll be laid off."

That was all he had to say. The rest of the evening he sat silently puffing on one cigarette after another.

Over at the bearing plant local, a new building with an electric light sign, the president, a tall and severelooking young man with a long neck who's recently been elected sits in a swivel chair in his empty office and talks unsmilingly. "We have a real tough proposition," he says. "This concern sets out to be tough all down the line. Now over at the other side of town they'll talk to you like reasonable beings. Just for an example; we had an unjustified slowdown over here a few days ago . . . some little disagreement . . . foreman blew his top and the boys didn't like it . . . Over the other side of town they'd have called the union up about it and we'd have talked to the boys and straightened it out in jig time . . . Here they fired every one of 'em. That's within their rights but it doesn't make for good labor relations. At first we went on the theory that there ought to be some give and take in these day-to-day matters but we soon found out it was all give and no take so now we're as tough as they are. They fight us in the press, over the radio, in notices they tack up on the bulletin board. They could pay for a wage increase out of the money they spend fighting the union. They never lose an opportunity, they even stir up trouble in the plant between different nationalities, between Negro and white. That guy who runs it is a tough *hombre*. I've had to learn to harden up and to be as tough as he is. I'm learning. If business gets tough fighting for profits, we've got to get tough fighting for wages."

Up in the club at the top of the tall bank building businessmen — young men, old men, bald men, gray men — are seated eating whitefish and beefsteak at a round table. The stately whitehaired man with a red face and a flashing Celtic eye who manufactures bricks is talking: "Well I've been in the business since I took over the ruins in 1904. I've been brought up with the men who work for me and I've known them and their wives and their children and their grandchildren. Many of them are Irish, in my business. We've always been Pat and Mike together and we've more or less shared the good times and the bad but now the union has built up a wall between us . . . They were encouraged to do it from Washington for political ends . . . It's heavy work in a brickyard. I know it, I've done it. You don't find many men with stomach for it any more not even among the Irish. Men don't get through the work they used to in a day . . . Here's an example from the building trades. We used to call eleven hundred brick an honest day's work. Now you're lucky if you find an athletic genius who'll lay three hundred and fifty."

"Productivity — going down." The word goes round the table with some headshaking. "The lowered productivity of labor." Men bend their faces over their plates.

"No I don't agree with you," says a small man whose bald forehead rises in a dome above the bar of his steel glasses that point up the way his eyebrows join across his nose. "At least that's not our experience. Productivity with us is up to a hundred and twenty nine percent." He speaks quietly while a tiny smile plays around the corners of his mouth.

"How come?"

"Incentive pay."

"They called it piecework when I was a boy," shouted the rawboned realtor across the table.

"No, this has been worked out since the strike. The gripe on incentive pay has always been that when productivity rose the management would change the rate on the employee to keep him from making too much money."

"Sounds reasonable," says a lawyer flatly.

"The idea was that if a man made too much money he'd go home and not do any more that week," the small man hurriedly explains, "but we have agreed not to do that unless there is some change in operative methods . . . Some of 'em cut their own production by slowing up after they've made fourteen dollars say or whatever they think is enough for the day but we go on the principle that the more money they make the better we like it . . . It's paying off."

"That's certainly not the tale I hear told," says the realtor laughing.

"In the building trades," says the brick manufacturer, "there's one encouraging symptom. Everybody tells us the boys coming home from the services don't want to do heavy work. Well, that may not be so true. In this state there are about fifteen hundred opportunities for boys to learn brick-laying as apprentices etcetera and there are something like five thousand applications."

"Nobody in this world ever worked unless they had to," shouts the realtor. "You can call me a black reactionary if you want to but the only thing that's going to remedy this situation is a backlog of about six or eight million unemployed."

The men around the table stiffen. They are not ready to accept this. "That's going a little too far," someone whispers. There follows a hearty amen. "Now a little recession," someone speaks up. All round the table heads nod. "A little recession might bring both wages and prices into line."

"It wouldn't be a bad thing," says the laywer thoughtfully. "With the demand for goods and services, even leaving the rest of the world out of it, which we have in this country: every railroad car to be replaced, every road to be rebuilt; truck highways, housing, a slight recession might get things into line for a long gradual upbuilding of prosperity afterwards."

"Wages have got to be stabilized first. There's going to be no prosperity on high prices."

"We could get along with the unions all right if they were local," says a heavyset man with knitted brows. "It's the international that's got to go, the international and the closed shop . . . Look here . . . This plant in town, you know the one I mean, has been struck by a C.I.O. Union. It's one of the radical Communist unions. Now the men and women who work in that plant are a hell of a lot more conservative than you and I are. The union won the election by sixtynine votes at a time when the plant was full of outoftown personnel for some war work they were doing. By only sixtynine votes . . . Now there are fifteen hundred and fifty workers in the plant and less than a hundred took the trouble to vote in the last election . . . These unions were forced on the people for political purposes by the New Deal administration. The time has come to get rid of them . . . The situation was produced by legislation and legislation has got to cure it."

The lawyer got up from his chair. "Well I'm just a lawyer struggling along in a small town. I've been engaged in an arbitration between an employer and a union and I've got to leave this pleasant company and go back to it. All I do is tell both sides one thing: 'Keep your sense of humor, don't see bogeys under the bed.' I tell it to the employer and I tell it to the union man. The other feller hasn't got horns and a tail. You try to imagine he has but he hasn't. There aren't any of these problems that we can't work out if we put our minds on them sensibly."

The Secretary of the Chamber of Commerce took me to see a small manufacturer who had eaten lunch at that same round table with us. We found him laying tile in the wall of a new partition in one corner of the shop. He was a gray hollowcheeked man with skimpy black hair plastered down on a bald head. He looked up with an apologetic smile when he saw he had visitors as if he feared he'd been doing something he shouldn't. "We need a partition here. I was just building it," he said. He tapped his trowel on the edge of the box he had his mortar in to clean it off and laid it down carefully. He led the way into the office and sat down at a desk under an old photograph of a man who looked very much like him.

"That was my father," he said, in a modest tone. "We lived in a small town where there was a mine and he got to worrying about a safety door. He was an inventive kind of a man. Our main product is this invention of his. Recently we've had to shut down for some time while we redesigned it to fit different conditions . . . that caused financial complications but now after a very good year it looks as if we might make a go of it."

"We were interested in your labor relations," said the man from the Chamber of Commerce.

The manufacturer looked up sharply. He stammered a little as he spoke. "Well I hope you won't mention this shop in any way so that we can be identified. I wouldn't want to get any of the unions after us . . . A man works in this shop because he likes it. If he doesn't, he moves along. I've had five men come in here in the last couple years to try to organize the men but they never got to first base. So many of my men came to work here for a quiet life, to get away from unions and the wrangling and the dues and the loss of pay through strikes . . . I pay slightly less than the current wage scale but it's more than made up for by our insurance scheme and by the bonus each Christmas. We take about half the profits and divide it up among the employees. We don't worry much about productivity around here because one man doesn't like to see another man loafing around and cutting into profits because he knows he's going to get a slice of them. Well, we're a small plant . . . We're perfectly happy here and we'll get along all right if they'll only leave us alone. You understand, we just want to keep out of sight. If another of those big industrial wars starts up we don't want to get caught in the middle."

"What about the rising cost of living?"

"We think we've got the answer — produce and share the profits."

FRED RUFUS: Looks like you might have run into some of those profit-sharing schemes . . . there are several of them working pretty well out in eastern Ohio.

MR. LECTURER: I'm coming to such a scheme just now . . . Even the union approves of this one Mr. Jones.

CAPTION: *A Profit-Sharing Scheme*

From the small dingylooking office you step through a corrugated iron door into a farstretching cave with pointed vaults smudged with smoke. The light streaks in blue and yellow through openings low in the sides and bellies sharply on the curves of metal cylinders. Up in the gloom above rows of men with tall helmets pushed back on their heads crouch along the tops of the cylinders over the nervous violet flash of welding arcs.

The freshfaced young man from the office who pilots you through explains, whenever there's a lull in the insistent hammering on metal, how the steel sheets are fashioned into tanks. He's from out of town himself but he's married in this section and settled down and he likes it here. He can walk home at noon and have lunch with his wife. If you lived in a big city you couldn't do that. Of course this is a small place and it's a small shop, employs only a hundred men but — he smiles — "we think we've got something here."

Three big grizzled men in worn overalls and tattered, workgrimed gloves are sitting on the edge of a staging waiting for a new batch of steel sheets. They talk in the pauses in the hammering. Sure they think it's working out, they say. It has been going two years. Time to give it a tryout . . . Sure they're all union . . . Steelworkers C.I.O. The system was set up with the union's consent by the boss and the Production Committee elected in the plant. Some staff C.I.O. men came in to work out the details. How did it affect them personally? First thing, they made more money. It meant three paydays a month instead of two . . . Sure they'd had a wage raise when the other steelworkers did but it didn't mean so much because they were getting their cut in the profits anyway . . .

"Let's go outside where we can hear ourselves think," says the young fellow from the office.

Outside he introduces another group. "The thing that makes this system work to my way of thinkin' is there's so much cooperation," says a young man with blue eyes and a long wooden face. "A man don't feel he should do just one job and that only. He'll turn a hand to anything so we produce more without any extry effort. It makes the work pleasant . . . You know in the regular plant a man won't do nothin' outside of his job. He'd be scabbin' if he did, but here we're workin' for ourselves so what's the difference?"

"Strikes, now why should we have strikes?" A fat yellow man threw back his head and laughed. "If there's a pay raise in the industry, the boss and the Production Committee will give it to us . . . Suppose it cuts into profits, well what we win in Milwaukee we lose in Chicago . . . But there won't be any loss. Our production has gone up so we've been able to lower prices even with the rise in wages and in steel sheets."

"We don't like slowdowns either," says the little man with the soupstrainer mustache. "Ain't a man in the shop now who don't keep workin' till the whistle blows . . . except like now when we're waitin' for material or somethin' . . . Loafin' hits our pocketbooks an' we know it . . . If a man ain't on the

job we speak about him to the Grievance Committee and out
he goes."

"When the plan first started," breaks in the young man
from the office, "the Production Committee let quite a few
men go."

"But now most of these guys own homes here and you
couldn't pry 'em loose with a crowbar."

Out along the main street near the railroad station where
the stores are you roam around chatting with the local
people. In the printshop an elderly man with a rockribbed
New England face sits with his hat on the back of his head
and his feet on the desk looking out through streaky panes
at the sooteaten frame houses opposite. After a little talk
about the election you ask what folks around here think
about labor relations at the concern that makes welded tanks.

"On the one hand and then on the other hand, that's how
people think," he drawled after a pause. "It's small . . . a
hundred men, one single product . . . He's the kind of feller
who's always thinkin' up something new. That's his reputation around here. Well he's a rich man and he can afford to
experiment. He invented some process or other over in
Akron that made him a fortune and his father died and left
him a million dollars. The last few years he's been very
socialminded . . . His daughter's socialminded. He can afford
to experiment. They say his business is pretty profitable
right now but the test'll come when things get slack. How'll
this partnership plan work when there're no profits to
divide?"

"It really is a partnership," says the inventor of this particular profit-sharing plan from the end of the luncheon table.
He talks without personal emphasis in an abstracted selfeffacing manner as if he were thinking of something else all
the time. He's a short stooping man no longer young, with
gray hair cropped close. He hunches at the end of the table

with something of the scholarly air of a gopher. "The single most important feature of our plan is, at least that's how I look at it, that we balance our books monthly so that the men in the shop know just where they stand, just like any other partnership. Profits are divided fifty fifty and apportioned out to the men in the shop and in the office in proportion to their rate of pay . . . there's some gripes from a few in the shop because the officeworkers get theirs according to their rates so that if, as has been happening all this year, there are layoffs on account of lack of materials, the salaried workers keep on getting theirs, and the others don't . . . What the people in the shop forget is that the office force keeps on working layoff or no layoff. Anyway there can't be many of 'em worried about it because it hasn't even come into the Grievance Committee."

"How's it working out from a financial point of view?"

"The total profit has increased five times," he says in a casual tone without looking up, "that means that after the split with the men we are making two and a half times as much as we were before the partnership plan was put into effect."

"Do you think this is the answer to the race between wages and prices?"

"Well, we've raised the men's takehome by a third . . . " He pauses. For a second he lifts his eyes off his plate and almost smiles. "And because the men's productivity has gone up — this is a business where labor cost is the whole story; all we do is take a sheet of steel and fashion it into a tank — well because productivity has gone up we've been able to reduce the selling price of our product . . . that's the answer to something."

Our train is late. The early winter dark has closed down on the little settlement. The gusty raw wind driving sleet and coaldust in their faces has driven the three or four men passengers waiting for the train to Pittsburgh into the warm freight office. There an endless argument has been going on between a redfaced man with silky white hair and mustache in freshly washed dungarees who seems to be the freight agent and three grimy men with lanterns in their hands who've come in off the tracks.

The freight agent has something on his chest. "Human nature bein' what it is," he keeps starting out in the manner of a pitcher winding up for a cherished curve. Each time somebody interrupts.

"Wait a minute," the ticket agent with the green eyeshade pushed back on his forehead shouts into the din from his seat at the littered table in the adjoining office. "Has it ever occurred to you that all these strikes and slowdowns might be a blessing in disguise?"

"Funny kind of a blessin'," mutters one man. The others are listening with their mouths open.

"Wait a minute," insists the passenger agent. "Has it ever occurred to you that all these difficulties that curtail production are spreading the backlog of consumer demand out into the future?" the passenger agent continues triumphantly, "so that we won't get a great boom followed by saturation and depression?"

Nobody answers. We have all slumped into astonished silence.

While the men with lanterns and the passengers stand silent ruminating on this novel idea the freight agent gets a chance to let fly with the speech he's been winding up for.

"Human nature bein' what it is," he says in the tone of a highschool orator registering scorn, "you know just as well as I do that when you get a man down you like to kick him in the face . . . Years ago management had labor down and we got kicked in the face plenty. Now labor has the country down and they are kicking us in the face."

"And when did you cease to be a laborin' man, Joe?" the passenger agent shouts from his office.

The freight agent has his answer ready: "Eight hours a

day, I'm a laborin' man . . . the other sixteen I'm a citizen of this community . . . Now human nature bein' what it is . . . "

The crossing bell begins to clang. A locomotive whistles down the tracks. We passengers slide out the door. As we climb on the car we can see through the window the freight agent continuing his oration.

FRED RUFUS: So far so good, but usually it's just when the small manufacturer is about to try out something socially useful that they clamp down on him. What happened to me was that I didn't have enough capital to set up a pension plan. The union clamped down from one side and the banks from the other, so I sold out to a big concern and now I'm a consultant. I make more money telling other fellows what to do than I used to doing it myself, but I don't see how we are going to keep up with the times if we don't have more small plants starting up where men are willing to risk their shirts to experiment in labor relations, or in production methods or what have you?

EDDY JONES: You've been the victim of historical forces. No wonder you're bitter.

FRED RUFUS: Young man, I'm not bitter . . . I'm making more money with less work, but I can't help worrying about the future of this nation.

JAKE JEFFRIES: The future of this nation is sound so long as our agriculture is sound. We can produce enough food for half the world in war or peace.

FRED RUFUS: Suppose a few atomic bombs cut off your gasoline and fuel oil supply for six months.

JAKE JEFFRIES: The weeds would take every farm in the country.

MR. LECTURER: That is why the situation has become so urgent. The more highly integrated industrial society becomes the more vulnerable it is to attack, by enemies without or enemies within. During the nineteenth century the

North American continent was protected by great oceans and by the Pax Britannica. Our economy could just grow like Topsy. Now we have constantly to be in a state of defense, a savage tribe surrounded by other savage tribes. We have allies in the United Nations but you know what Napoleon thought about allies in wartime. This situation has caught us too soon. If there is going to be a distinctive American civilization its foundations have only just been laid.

MISS SMITHERS: That Sample Town you took us to see was hardly a substitute for Florence or Siena, was it?

MR. LECTURER: The first thing a coherent civilization gives its members is a sense of participation. That seems almost lacking in the American industrial town, almost but not quite lacking. In my opinion the great attraction of the Communist doctrine to the young people of the depression generation among whom it made its greatest ravages was that it gave them a sense of participation in history. Do you remember William James' suggestion that the way to abolish war was to give people something more exciting than war? America must find something more exciting than Communism.

JAKE JEFFRIES: We've got something more exciting. That's agriculture.

MR. LECTURER: Travelling round this country I got the feeling that the people who did the work got more satisfaction in farming than in industry.

JAKE JEFFRIES: One reason is that farming is still decentralized. A man driving a combine through a wheatfield is on his own. He's not a robot like a man on an assembly line.

FRED RUFUS: The assembly line isn't the only way industry works . . . There are some mighty interesting jobs in almost any manufacturing plant.

MR. LECTURER: A couple of summers ago I took a trip out to the cornbelt. . . .

CAPTION: *The Most Exciting Occupation in the World*

Green and immense, undulating in low smooth swells to the horizon the cornbelt landscape swings past the windows of the empty club car. We sit talking at a table with our eyes on the quaking green of young corn, frizzly reaches of alfalfa, bluegreen oats, wheat already a little blond here and there where it is beginning to ripen. Across from me sits an economist, a round pale man with round pale glasses. He looks from window to window with pursed lips and taps on the menu card with the point of his pencil.

"Even here in the heart of one of the richest farming sections of the world," he is saying, "you can see on every hand the results of poor farming practice . . . Look to the right over there at the erosion on the top of that bank where the red subsoil shows through the black dirt. It took the prairie grasses twenty centuries to make the humus in that black loam. Look what we've done to it in one century . . . That cornfield to the left; right from here I can see the hunger signs, the red at the base of the stalk that means lack of phosphates, the brownedged leaves that indicate potash deficiency. Not enough nitrogen in that pasture. Cattle paths beginning to show . . . Measure the eroding land against the rising population. Even the population of the United States is beginning to rise against the food supply. Two million births a year . . . Between 1938 and 1946 in spite of widespread war the population of the world went up by something like one hundred and thirty million — almost the population of the United States. How are you going to beat that? You tell me now. You have the floor."

The next morning when I stumbled off the sleeper into the red early sunlight at Coon Rapids the first thing I heard was Bob Garst's resonant voice: "Farming has become the most exciting occupation in the world . . . Something new all the time." He was talking to the elderly station agent. As I stepped up he grabbed my hand and my bag. "Here you are. That's great. Just in time for a cup of coffee before we kinder look around the farms."

"I'm out here looking for an answer to this question: what are you people who grow our food doing to keep up with the increase in mouths to feed in this country and in the entire world?"

"Let's drive around and look at the farms. Maybe we'll find an answer."

Engulfed at once in the sweep and excitement of his talk I followed him into the front seat of his buffcolored Mercury and started busily to listen. He's a large ruddy man with large gray eyes set rather far apart in a large bluntnosed face that seems to be always coming at you like the prow of a ship. He's usually in his shirtsleeves. Suspenders hold up large loosefitting pants. He's a showman and a lecturer but never from any pulpit; he's always watching the man he's talking to, ready to pounce on any useful notion that comes to the surface. He leans back and lets his sentences flow easily and directly from the operation of an alert and interested mind. Raising crops is what he eats sleeps and breathes. Raising crops and selling seedcorn. His conviction is catching. "It's the most exciting occupation . . . it's all developing so fast . . . It's got me so I can't wait to get up in the morning to see what's going to happen next."

The main street of Coon Rapids looks very much like the main street of any other small Iowa town. It's broad and not too clean. Cars spattered with black mud off the back roads are parked along the curbs and in an oblique row in the middle of the pavement. Hardworked trucks and pickups of all shapes and sizes. There are stores and a bank and a movie and a drugstore and a couple of lunchrooms and a billiard parlor where they sell beer. There's the usual filling station on the corner. The buildings are strictly for utility like the clothes the people wear. No frills. A little shabbier than necessary perhaps. Beyond along the railroad you see warehouses and a lumberyard and a white grain elevator and the towering hybrid seedcorn plant newbuilt in red tile with a white trim. We park in front of the coffeeshop and walk in.

Already the counter is lined with weathered men in overalls and denims eating breakfast or picking up an extra cup of coffee before going to work. Hired hands, truck drivers, tractor operators, laboratory workers from the seed plant, small farmers, or owners of hundreds of acres of some of the most valuable land in the cornbelt, they all wear the same work clothes and talk the same talk. An occasional salesman stands out in his pressed city clothes. The jukebox in back yodels the woodpecker song. Pleasantfaced and towheaded, Mrs. White waits on them all with the same serious attentive manner. Eggs and sausage. Ham and eggs. Bacon, hotcakes, many many cups of coffee. Eating my breakfast I sit listening to their talk.

Bob Garst lolls in his accustomed place, his throne he calls it, on the inside seat of a table against the wall. Men who are working for him on his farm or the farms he manages for the seedcorn concern, tenants, associates, competitors, move up, lean over his shoulder, bring up a chair and a cup of coffee to sit for a while at the table. All their talk is about crops.

One man asks about sprays to kill weeds. Another answers boisterously that he's just sprayed eight acres of flax. Ain't that risky? This feller tried it on his corn and laid four rows flat. Cutworms have been at work on the corn in the low spots in the quarter section. Is it better to replant in a late variety or to put in soy beans? A lanky tanned young man finishes his cup of coffee and moves on. A fat man in a frazzled straw hat takes his place. He finds the spray's workin' fine on his fencerows. Bob says he is putting in a dryer for his hay and small grain like the one they use on the seedcorn at the plant. Has an idea he'll dry his oats this season. Eagerly he asks each man what he thinks of the notion. How large should the fan be? What horsepower motor? Men push their visored caps back to scratch their heads, puff on cigarettes, ponder deeply before they answer.

It was a fine sunny morning. The shadows were shortening on the street outside. The crowd in the coffeeshop thinned out as men strode off to their cars or their trucks. Bob got to his feet. "Come along, I'll show you some of the bestlooking farming land you ever saw."

As he slid under the wheel of his car he started talking again. "What we're seeing, is a revolution in agriculture . . . "

As we drove out of town up the hill and through a street of modest frame houses set in green lawns under trees he went on to explain. The revolution started with hybrid corn. By inbreeding it was possible to set desired characteristics and by crossing inbreds to produce the particular kind of corn the farmer in a particular section of the country wanted. Corn in America was the basic product in agriculture as steel was in industry. Improvements in corn had started off improvements all down the line. One of the first characteristics the breeders had worked on was a strong straight stalk. That meant you could use a mechanical picker. The stalks of the open-pollinated varities had been too weak to go through the mechanical pickers without a great loss of ears. Now you not only got an average of twenty percent higher yield but you could harvest your crop much quicker and with less labor. That meant the farmer got more return on the money he invested in the crop and could afford to buy more fertilizer and to prepare his land better, to go in for better machinery, tiling, surface drainage. All that improved the yield again and started the upward spiral in farm production that saw us through the war and enabled us to help feed the world during the period of chaos that followed the war. Higher yields fixed the farmer so he could afford better farming which brought higher yields again. The upward spiral. "In the old days we used to think forty bushels of corn to the acre a pretty decent crop . . . Now I know men who don't sleep nights unless they get a hundred."

His own upward spiral, Bob told me, had started with hybrid corn. He was the son of a merchant in Coon Rapids. He still shows you proudly round the family store, a country general store just on the edge of turning into something more urban. After shopping around at various agricultural schools for an education, he'd married and settled in Des Moines. The depression of the late twenties had caught him in the real estate business. That was no business for a man to be in in 'twenty-nine. He'd already become curious about hybrid corn.

"At first the farmers thought we were crazy," he said laughing. A time of surpluses when corn sold for ten cents a bushel and people burned it in the stove wasn't the best time in the world to interest the farmer in increased yield, but in the long run he'd managed to do it. Since then his life had been selling seedcorn and growing it. The success of hybrid corn had opened his mind to the possibility of all kinds of new advances in farming. It had opened up other people's minds. You used to think of farmers as conservatives, set in their ways, but certainly in the cornbelt farmers now were ready to try new things out. The farmer today did a lot of reading, a lot of driving around to see what his neighbors were up to. "In my opinion the most important thing about all these new developments is that they stimulate people's minds, make them more alert. They are more careful with their crops, they take more pains . . . Now look at this man's farm."

He drew up suddenly at a turning and drove in beside a big old red barn and up a grassy road between two cornfields.

From a rise we could look out over a wide acreage of waving green that reflected at the curl of each shining leaf a little blue off the sky. Beyond, a field of nilegreen oats misted the gentle rise of a broad hill until it met the dim white clouds along the horizon. When we got out of the car meadow larks rose whistling from under our feet. A redheaded woodpecker was chasing another along a fencerow and vanished in a flash of white into some scrub willows.

"This man's farm," Bob went on, "three or four years ago was one of the worst and most rundown old farms you ever saw. It was owned by a man in the Southwest. The man who farmed it was a nice guy but he didn't give a damn. The landlord wasn't interested and the tenant wasn't interested. The land went downhill every year. Now the farm's owned and managed right here in Coon Rapids and the same tenant has become one of the best farmers we've got. There he is," he said pointing to a blueclad figure with a handspray moving through the weeds along a fence on the opposite hill, "spraying his weeds to keep down the cockleburs round the edge of the field . . . Oh we have a lot of fun."

He drove back to the gravelled road and slowly skirted the adjoining section. Beside a magnificent forty acres of oats he stopped to point out distant straw hats and little blobs of white moving through the grain. "This is probably the best oats in the country and do you see what this fellow's doing? He's paying those kids seventy or seventyfive cents an hour to pull weeds out of his oats by hand. His crop's so good he just wants perfection."

"Is it the income tax that makes them willing to spend more money on their land?"

"Sure, the income tax is one thing; a fellow like this will be way up in the high brackets with the crop we're likely to have this year and the prices we'll be getting. So he doesn't worry about how much he spends improving his land. The farmer don't honestly care so much about the money. He likes to make money naturally but it's increased yield that makes him really happy."

We drove on along straight roads through miles and miles of corn. In the seed fields the difference in color and in growth between the male rows that were going to be allowed to pollinate and the female rows that were going to be detasselled made wide stripes of various greens across the landscape.

At a corner in front of a white house set in cottonwoods Bob braked the car suddenly and jumped out. "Look at that," he called back red in the face. "Potash deficiency." I followed him over the fence into the rows of corn that tapered off gangling and pale towards the ditch. "You can tell it at a glance, brown round the edge of the lower leaves . . . This is some of the best land you ever saw but the line of an old lake shore goes through it, tends to be alkaline. If you look you'll find snail shells."

Sure enough when we crumbled the black dirt round the roots of the corn we found little fragments of snail shell in it. "Wisconsin drift," Bob was muttering. "Some of the best soil in the world and this dumbheaded Dutchman won't put on a little potash to give himself a real good stand. He could sidedress right now. It would only cost him a few dollars to get him a crop of corn."

As we climbed back over the fence Bob looked up appraisingly at the clouds that were beginning to pile up behind the hill. "We could use about two inches of rain right now," he said. "Now I don't claim that heavy applications of nitrogen are a cure for drouth but they sure do make your corn crop stand it better . . . And to think that they were telling us when the war stopped that we wouldn't need all those nitrogen fixing plants they built for munitions. Now they are all running full tilt and we need twice as many. We need nitrogen fixing plants all over the country. The air contains all the nitrogen in the world, but building the fixing plants demands a heavy capital investment, the sort of thing the federal government ought to furnish. Clover and the other legumes'll give you some of it but modern agriculture needs a whole lot more nitrogen than that."

As we drove on every now and then Bob looked up at the sky. "We don't need rain so horribly badly but we surely could use a little. Better now than a few weeks from now when we'll be getting in the small grain and be up to our ears in detassellers . . . If you come back then you'll find these cornfields full of every highschool kid in the state. About four thousand of them. We'll have thirteen thousand acres of seedcorn to detassel. It's a problem, I can tell you."

He drove me back through Coon Rapids and out to his own farm a mile south of town. Before going up to the house we stopped at the barn and walked through the gate into a yard where whitefaced steers were munching quietly at some feed in wooden bunkers set out on a concrete floor.

"Now here's something really new . . . When I tell people I'm feeding steers corncobs their mouths fly open and their eyes just about pop out of their heads . . . That's what they're eating. Corncobs put through a grinder with a little high protein feed added and a little bright hay to give 'em the vitamin A they've got to have . . . Every year in the fall when we process our seedcorn at the plant I've been looking at that mountain of cobs and wondering how to get rid of it. We gave cobs to anybody who was willing to haul them away. And it never occurred to me nor to anybody else that they might have food value . . . Well once we got the notion we began to look into it and found that the Ohio Experiment Station has been feeding extra cobs with shelled corn fairly successfully; so winter before last we tried different combinations out with thirty steers in six separate pens, and last winter we were horribly successful feeding, five hundred and fifty head of steers on corncobs and high protein meal. They put on weight at a cost of about a third of what it costs right now to fatten cattle on corn and they gained about three quarters of the weight they would have gained if they'd been fed all the shelled corn they would eat. This experiment is important because if you can feed cattle on cobs, which are mostly cellulose, you can probably use straw and other types of cellulose. Of course it applies only to ruminants but it opens up simply horrible possibilities for cheaply increasing the meat supply ... This summer I'm just feeding nineteen steers as a kind of exhibit. I like to have something to keep the boys interested . . . What do you think of it, Pete?" Bob asked the grayhaired man who walked past with a couple of buckets and a scoopshovel.

"Well, Bob, at first I thought I was seein' things," the man drawled, "but now I'm convinced."

Two hundred miles west and three weeks later a big broadly smiling man named Hans Larson is driving me out from Central City, Nebraska, to show me the crops. It's grain harvest time. Everywhere the dust and whirr of reapers; the big oldfashioned combines towed by a tractor moving with a roar and clatter over the fields, or the new selfpropelled type bright and shiny as toy steamboats cutting a neat swath around the edges of the yellow grain. On all the main roads we meet combines speeding along on trucks. The sunburned crews follow in wellkept cars, part of the army of custom harvesters that starts in the Texas Panhandle and Oklahoma and moves north with the ripening grain, combining grain all the way until the harvest ends far north in Manitoba. The weather is dry and hot. Everybody you meet talks wheat, oats, barley, rye. How many bushels to the acre? The countryside is full of bustle and scurry. If the weather will only hold. No farmer will get any rest until he's delivered his grain to the elevator.

Leaving the Platte Valley Hans Larson smilingly points out a stretch of land that used to be known as Poverty Ridge, used to sell for fifteen dollars an acre but now that they have started using fertilizer the men who owned farms along it wouldn't sell for a hundred. Raised just as good crops as the rich bottomlands.

He stops by the side of the road to point out two fields. In one there is a full crop of heavy bearded barley and in the other the weeds have outgrown everything else. A damned outrage. It was the same land on both sides of the road. These days nobody had a right to make a poor showing in his crops. He'd been explaining that out here in central Nebraska they not only had the depression, but they had the drouth, barely missed being part of the dustbowl, and that in spite of the Platte River that ran from west to east clear through the middle of the state and the known fact that the whole Platte Valley had an abundant watertable eighteen feet or so below the surface. There just hadn't been the capital needed to put in pumps.

Everything was different out here now. This was the seventh moist year, the farmers had money in the bank, they had sunk wells and pumps to irrigate their corn and found they got astonishing added yields by never letting the corn get thirsty. With irrigation and heavy fertilizing they weren't so dependent on the weather any more. The R.E.A. had brought in abundant electric power they could use for pumping when they had to. These abandoned houses we were passing had been vacant for ten years. Folks sold out and went to California. Vacant houses weren't a sign of poverty any more, it was just that the farmers who'd stayed on were cultivating so much more land with so much less labor that they didn't need the extra houses. What caused the change? Irrigation, as crop insurance, and improved machinery and fertilizer and then damn it the farmer was using his brains more than he used to. "And now," Hans Larson said turning to me with a widemouthed smile and the expression of a child being handed a plate of particularly good looking icecream, "We're going down into the Beaver Creek Valley. You're going to see some really luscious crops."

We drove through a forest of densely serried corn so green it was almost black. Hans Larson put on his brakes and took a deep breath. When the leaves stood up straight like that the corn was really growing.

From the corner of the fence a coarse western jackrabbit with ears like a mule was watching us out of glassy bulging eyes. Hans Larson was too busy looking at the corn to notice him. This was corn, he was exclaiming as the jack went lolloping off into the tall grass along the roadside. This was the Choat brothers farm. Clarence, the elder one, only went through high school but he graduated with an average of ninetyeight or something like it. Might not have had so much schooling but he studied his land. He was a smart one. When there was something wrong with a field he analyzed it. He put in earth dams in his gullies and contoured his hills and followed every sound soilbuilding practice. The farm hadn't been much at first, they got it cheap, but now they were getting results. They had three quartersections and an eighty, five hundred and sixty acres that was. Clarence and Elmer handled it by themselves. They were workers all right. They hardly ever had any help. They did a lot of driving.

Looking for the Choats, we rode through their farm in the brilliant afternoon among ripening crops saturated with sun. We found Clarence picking up his windrowed oats with a combine. His small son Garry was shovelling the blond grain into the corners of the truck when his father stopped to unload. The shovel was almost as big as the boy was. It was sweaty work. Their arms and faces were grimed with dust. Now and then they picked off the biting harvest bugs. We managed to get a few words with them shouted above the rattle of machinery while the oats poured out of the spout of the combine.

Clarence Choat was a tall brighteyed young man. He had a way of pausing to think before he answered a question. Not much of a talker. All the time he talked with us he had an eye impatiently cocked up at the sky. He had to get his oats in before it rained. When a man is harvesting oats it is no time for talk.

As we drove away Hans Larson burst out: "When you see a good 'un it excites you. Believe you me when you make crops like these boys do it ain't accidental . . . It's on purpose."

Heading east for the Mississippi River, in another rich farming belt near Freemont, Nebraska, I met a slender thoughtful quietvoiced man who gave me to understand he'd gotten into farming through his banking connections in the bad old depression days when foreclosing was the main thing the banks did. Now Fred Teigeler was in it for its own sake. He spent a lot of time thinking about improving his land. It was a kind of chess game with nature he played. He made a move and then nature made a move.

He drove us out to show off a patch of corn he'd had to plant three times. First standing water had ruined it. Then the wireworms had eaten it. He'd found he could get rid of the wireworms by plowing in a DDT barn spray. Now at last he had a stand. Wouldn't have been possible, he pointed out, if there hadn't been a good shortseason hybrid variety available and if he hadn't known an agricultural scholar over at Waterloo who advised him to try DDT on wireworms. At the present high price of corn it was worth spending all kinds of money to get a crop.

That afternoon we drove over to visit Fred Teigeler's friends at Waterloo, another center of the seedcorn industry. At the offices of the plant we stopped in to talk with the agricultural scholars of the organization. Sitting at the long table in the airconditioned conference room I put to them the question that economist had raised on the train. Leaving the population of the world out of it for the time being, was there any chance of the population of the United States outgrowing its food supply? How much had farm production gone up per man per acre in the last ten years?

They answered it with an example. In the memory of three farm boys sitting at that table when you cultivated corn you used to start out in the morning with a team of horses and a walking cultivator and if you got through six acres it was a pretty good go. Now a man with a tractor could cultivate forty or fifty acres a day and not break his back.

Nowadays a good farmer had to be a machinist and a mechanic. Improved strains were solving many other of his problems, early varieties were pushing the frontier of the cornbelt further north. That meant greater production. There were quickdrying varieties for earlier picking, a variety where the shucks roll back of themselves like the petals of a sunflower leaving the ear bare, easier to shuck. Even in small grains, oats, wheat and barley, where they had to breed by crossing and selection, the breeders were constantly bringing out new varieties cut to fit particular needs the way a tailor would cut you out a suit to measure. Clinton oats was an example. Heavy fertilization, weed sprays, new ways of fighting pests. New crops, new possibilities were opening up. In some ways the advance in agriculture had just begun. Farming was a wellheeled fastmoving industry ready to tackle almost any problem. Everybody wanted to try new things. The farmers were ahead of the experts now.

While we sat there talking a young man in a Panama hat stuck his head in the door in great excitement. They were having a bad time with grasshoppers round Oakland, Iowa. They had sent over for a truckload of grasshopper killer. Some airplanes were just taking off to spray the crops. He was going over to take pictures. This was something new in the cornbelt.

Back in Iowa the corn looked even blacker and denser than it had in Nebraska. Cornfields with milelong rows crowded the roads with their tall closeset waving ranks. A smell of honey came off fields of alfalfa blue with bloom. Everything else was ripe oats. On every farm the combines whirred across the fields followed by their cloud of chaff and dust. Where reapers and binders churned the standing grain, shockers in straw hats followed behind to set up the bundles into rows of shocks. Every man we met was full of the excitement of harvesting a bumper crop. Nobody could stop to talk. Everybody was in a hurry to get the grain into the elevator before the price dropped. Futures were off. There was always the danger of a rainy spell. Some of the grain was so ripe it was beginning to shatter. Men kept looking up at the sky as they worked. The radio had forecasted rain. Round the edges of the fields doves fed on the scattered grain. Occasionally you'd see a cock pheasant in scarlet and stripes picking among the sheared straw. Whereever a farmer had finished his harvest you would find him seated placidly on his tractor turning under the stubble with his big disk plows.

Coon Rapids had a holiday look next morning. At every corner there were bunches of boys and girls of highschool age waiting to earn themselves some money detasselling the seedcorn. The girls wore brightcolored handkerchiefs over their heads and straw hats and various beach outfits and the boys wore all sorts of odd clothes. They were scrambling giggling and shouting into trucks to be driven out to the cornfields.

In the coffeeshop they'd eaten all the eggs. Bob Garst was sitting in his accustomed corner laughing like he'd split about the difficulties of getting seedcorn detasselled. There was no other way than to pull the tassels on the female rows out by hand and they had to do a near perfect job to meet specifications and there was no other labor available to do it. Fifteen, sixteen, seventeen year old kids; everybody knew what teen age kids were like. It was the peskiest and most expensive part of the business of raising seedcorn. He introduced the young man who was in charge of the whole operation. "He's going to lose ten pounds in the next three weeks worrying about those detassellers," he said laughing. Then he added, "There's just time for another cup of coffee, and then we'll go over to take a look at the dryer . . . They'll get it working this evening. That's another thing that's going to open up pretty horribly exciting possibilities."

The dryer turned out to be a long tall narrow building faced with bright aluminum sheets. Bob jumped out of the car and burrowed into the little huddle of men who were helping the furnace expert from Des Moines put the last touches on the oil burner and came out to meet me.

"We've already had the fans going." He turned up a red streaming face after a moment. "We've been drying oats successfully just with plain air so it's going to be that much more successful once we get the heat going. You see this is a batch dryer." He led the way round the bright shining building. "The grain or hay or seed or whatever crop you want to dry is dumped out of a dumptruck into that hopper on the hillside and then it goes up that belt conveyor right into the middle of the upper part of the building where a shuttle conveyor feeds it into whichever set of bins we want to use. So we can handle two batches at once and shoot the hot air first into one side and then into the other."

We stood watching the oats pouring out of the dumptruck into the hopper and speeding along up the conveyor belt. Bob made me take a handful of oats to feel how wet they were.

"We couldn't have built this so easily," he explained looking up, "if we hadn't had years of experience drying seed corn at the plant. Now this isn't what we are recommending for a small or mediumsized farm. This is for a big operation. But as soon as we get this big dryer kind of straightened out so that we know what it'll do and what it won't do we're going to set up a smallsize drying shed for the average farm.

The fact of the matter is that every building the farmer has on his farm is obsolete, barns, corncribs, haylofts . . . All that's got to be redesigned. They were all right for the old scoopshovel, two mules and a plow, backbreaking kind of farm work but they don't suit our really recent machinery. A dryer like this is just a beginning."

While he talked we walked down to the other end of the building. Workmen were still taking away the scaffolding under the front window where the conveyor belt fed in. Others were carting off bits of timbers and cut pieces of aluminum sheeting.

"Here's what it's going to mean. We had a rain last night. Well Viv Bell has been combining his oats all afternoon. There wasn't anybody else cutting, but if Viv had left those oats to stand until they were dry enough to cut there would have been a big loss by shattering and all we'd had would have been a low quality feeding grain. It's going to mean we can get the small grain harvest into the elevator in a very much shorter time. Once we've fiddled with the combines a little so that they can handle the damp grain we'll be able to harvest grain mornings. No more waiting for the dew to dry. We can work all night if we want to because in the dryer we can just take the moisture down to the percentage desired. That means we can get it to the elevator in time to meet high early prices. What it's going to mean in the saving of hay and small seed like clover is terrific. It sounds pretty horribly optimistic but I wouldn't be surprised if this damn dryer paid for itself in a single season."

We stopped beside another truck that was loading dry grain at the end of the building. Bob made me pick up another handful of oats to see how dry it was now.

By the time we get around to the doors in the back where the blowers are and where the last touches are being put on the oil heater, the men are ready with their matches to light the torch. The furnace begins to roar gently.

"Well," says Bob, "you've seen the inauguration of what's

probably going to be a mighty valuable piece of machinery. There'll be adjustments to make. It'll take us a while to learn how to run it."

I follow him inside to peer at the flame. We watch the spinning fan. We feel the hot air sucking through the chamber into the pipes that feed it out under the grain.

As we turn to walk back to the house Bob Garst says in a thoughtful drawling tone, "Less labor, more speed, higher efficiency . . . It isn't going to be so very long before we're going to be able to run the family farm — that means cultivating sixteen hundred acres of some of the most productive land in the country so as to get the highest possible yield out of it — we're going to run the family farm with seven or eight hired hands." He gives me a searching look. "Your question about feeding the population of this planet, doesn't that just about answer it?"

JAKE JEFFRIES *(clapping his hands)*: That was a good 'un. I know all those folks. I kind of expected to see myself walk right out on the screen. But what I missed was the story of flax. I made quite a killin' with a crop of flax last year. Lord, it was murder and a few years ago they used to tell us we couldn't grow flax.

FRED RUFUS: Did you notice something interesting? The people in the postwar world who seemed to be happiest in others countries too were the farmers. In England they seemed to feel the controls less and even in Brazil they were making money. I suppose war is always a good time for farmers, at least for those who manage to keep out of the fighting . . . I wonder if that's so in the Soviet Union.

EDDY JONES: But why aren't these centrally managed farming operations really collectives? . . . Capitalist collectives . . . I'm not a Communist, don't get me wrong, but isn't the collective farming program of the Soviet Union part of the same general trend? Couldn't we learn something from it?

FRED RUFUS: Why not? The central tractor station is a perfectly logical idea, only capitalism does it by assuring the farmer a financial reward that allows the most efficient producers to go ahead and expand their operations. Under British socialism the reward seems to be that the farmer's allowed to go on living a fairly decent life, the sort of life every Englishman is supposed to have a right to, instead of being regimented to the point of frustration. Under the Soviet rules, so far as I understand them, the more you make the more they take away from you and if you don't smile and say Thank you, Mr. Stalin the Great, when they take your wheatcrop, it's off to a labor camp or a uranium mine.

EDDY JONES: Under your great capitalist institutions are the rewards much better?

FRED RUFUS: Damn tootin' they are.

EDDY JONES: But how about working for some big concern that can lay you off at a moment's notice. Even take the case of a pretty high executive. Some new combination is played in the financial management. Suppose he don't go along with the new policy. He's laid off just like the man who rakes the ashes out of the furnace. They treat him better than a poor hunky who can't talk back, but he's laid off just the same and a lifetime's work may be gone.

FRED RUFUS: Are you any more secure working for a labor union? Tell me that.

MRS. EDWARDS: Security seems to be the cry nowadays. People will trade almost anything for security.

FRED RUFUS: Security is only for cowards. Life is risk by definition. We are never any of us going to be secure from death or taxes. My quarrel with people like you, Eddy, is that you are teaching our rank and file to trade for an illusion of security everything a man ought to prize most, independence, the lust for adventure, selfrespect. And your motives are the same as any other politician's motives: to ride to affluence and glory on the backs of the suckers. The only thing the cult of security can give us is a civilization on the downgrade, a policeridden slave state like the Roman Empire in its latter days.

MISS SMITHERS (*in a voice quivering with excitement*): The reign of the Emperor Diocletian is particularly interesting in that respect. The Roman Empire tried to solve everything by bureaucracy and the result was . . . the people welcomed the barbarians to free them from their strait jacket.

MR. LECTURER: There are trends in our corporate industrial society which are working the same way. Unfortunately there are no barbarians left in that special sense of the word. The Soviet Union is barbarous from the humane point of view but from another point of view they have made more progress than we have. They have completed the centralization of society into one governing bureaucracy. If that is the way we are headed they are several jumps ahead of us. In the Soviet Union we have the extreme example of what happens when centralized industry and the centralized state merge into a single tyrannical monopoly. If that's what we want let's go on the way we are going.

FRED RUFUS: That isn't even what Eddy wants. We none of us want that — I mean here in America. Our chance of working our way through to a better society would be moderately good if we could find some way of initiating a powerful movement towards decentralization in industry and in government. I say give industry and government back to the people, where they live, in the small and mediumsized towns . . . Eddy don't you fellows who run the trade unions ever have any qualms about overcentralization? A lot of men in industry sit up nights worrying about it.

EDDY JONES: What can you do when the rank and file won't come to meetings and vote? Honestly in many unions, I don't say in all, we do our level best to keep the membership informed and interested. At the worst we've kept more of the democratic process going than your big corporations . . .

MR. LECTURER: If you will excuse me our time is up for tonight. In my next lecture I am putting on the screen a big business and a big union. After that we can take up the discussion again. *(He drags together his briefcase, his muffler, his coat, his hat, and bolts out the door.)*

FIFTH LECTURE

Two Corporate Organizations

MR. LECTURER: *(after the preliminary coughing has subsided)*: Well, well, I see some fresh faces . . . We are very glad to have you with us ladies and gentlemen . . . I hope everybody has been able to find a chair. We are about to follow around the country the operations of one of the big concerns that mill flour. We start with the raw material . . . grain . . .

CAPTION: *Wheat is King of the World*

On either side of the straight road the ripening wheat flows to the brim of the horizon. Under the blue air of June the bright ears bow and darken where they ripple under the wind. When you stop the car and step out into the roadside grasses meadowlarks fly up from under your feet. The young man from the sampling bureau has climbed the fence and waded out into the wheat. He comes back walking a little pigeontoed to avoid treading down the grain. In one hand he has a bunch of bearded ears. He trails the other behind him combing with open fingers through the dancing ears as he walks. He climbs the fence again. As he comes back to the car he is looking down at his khaki pants with his face screwed up.

"Smut," he spits the words out with disgust.

He brushes the black streaks off his pants. He reaches for a brown envelope off the back seat, packs his sample ears into it and marks down the date, the location, the variety. He crunches one ear into the palm of his hand, puts a few grains in his mouth and chewing starts the car. Three miles down the road he stops again and wades out into the pale glare of another field. This time he comes back smiling.

"Now you're talking," he says. "This is something like."

He holds out a pile of fat golden grains in the palm of a grimy hand. "See the straight clean crease," he says. As he looks up from the second envelope his eyes fix sharply on a white blur that is gaining outline above the horizon. "Thunderheads," he says. "I bet these wheat farmers are worried."

At a brokendown barn the road takes a rightangled turn to the left, then another to the right, then it cuts on straight to the horizon through band after band of undulating wheat. The color's paler here, only darkening to grimy gold where catspaws travel across it in the sunlight. A blur of dust drifts on the wind. When the young man slows the car to look you can hear the whir and clank of a combine. "I thought so," he says. "The harvest has begun. Those wheatfarmers won't close an eye till they get the crop in this year."

You can see a line of trucks piled with thrashedout wheat standing waiting in the hot glare of sun reflected off the corrugated flank of the elevator. Grimed with the dust of harvest the waiting drivers stand in a group in the shade feeling through sweaty overalls the chill of the faint breeze. In the first truck bare brown duststreaked backs move in unison as two men scoop the grain into the hopper. Dust rises. The conveyor belt rattles. The heavy sunlight is reflected sharp as a knife off the rails and batters the boxcars lined up on the siding alongside the elevator. SANTA FE, KANSAS AND TEXAS, MISSOURI PACIFIC, SOUTH-ERN PACIFIC, reads their scaled lettering.

The elevator manager has a square jaw and yellow teeth. He talks through a mouthful of wheat. "Farmers ain't selling. Out of fortyfour thousand bushels hauled into Wichita Falls yesterday only seven thousand sold. They're waiting for the support price."

"Where are they going to store it?"

"It'll get stored but it's first come first served."

In the group of men in overalls, some standing some sitting on their heels in the triangle of shade along the dark sunless side of the elevator, heads are turning towards the west. A lanky man jerks a thick thumb in the direction of the thunderhead making up over the horizon, white as cauliflower above, then rosy, then blueblack below. "Rain," he says and spits out a long arc of tobacco juice. Heads shake.

Meanwhile with dust sticking in patches to his sweaty face the young man from the sampling bureau has come striding out of the little side door of the elevator. Under his arm are a couple of cotton bags of grain with yellow labels on them. He throws the samples into the back of the car and drives on.

When the laboratory men come down to the mill in the morning, they find the bags of sample wheats piled against their groundglass door. They strip off their street clothes and go to work. Their eyes are a little red from having worked late the night before. Outside it is muggy but the air is cool in the white laboratory. The north light pours in clear and gray through the wide windows. There's an aloof out of the world feeling in the laboratory in spite of the hum of stands and conveyors and shaking sifters that comes through the walls from the flour mill. They wash their samples of wheat and mill them in their enamelled model mill. Then the chemists go to work with their test tubes and their heaters and their shining bottles of various colored acids to test out the protein content. At their bench at the other end of the room the bakers mix their dough and work in the yeast and set the experimental loaves to rise in the warm moist air of the glassed rising cupboard.

Meanwhile the director of the wheat survey sits at his desk. He is a tall, skinny man in his shirtsleeves. Last year's map of the southeastern wheatgrowing sections is laid out before him. He frowns when he taps the red areas with his pencil. "These are what we call the bastard wheats," he says. "Beardless types mostly . . . they give good crops and are disease resistant but they are no good for baking. Even the best varieties on the same land vary from year to year. That is why we have to test so carefully and get samples from every wheatgrowing area. We test for protein content and ash and for practical milling and baking qualities. We send reports to our grain buyers in Kansas City and Chicago and Minneapolis so that they know where they stand . . . We make up these maps . . . You see this year's has just started. We only have reports so far from a few counties in Texas . . . The flow's just started into Wichita Falls. Then the Panhandle will begin to move. The wheat'll spread into Amarillo and Wichita, Kansas, till it reaches its climax at Kansas City on the Fourth of July. That's the climax of the winter wheat. You think we're busy now, but you ought to see us in Kansas City on the Fourth of July."

When we walk out onto the floor of the Kansas City exchange a man hurries up and whispers in our ears, "There's four inches of rain forecast for Oklahoma." He tilts his head towards the weather map in one corner of the big hall. To our left the traders in feed are sitting quiet on their benches. To our right a little flurry of yapping and barking has broken out among the scalpers in the wheat pit. Over our heads on a catwalk in front of broad blackboards that cut across the whole end wall boys in yellow scrim shirts scamper back and forth chalking up numbers on a board; prices bid to sell and buy, completed sales marked by a straight white line.

The man who works for the big milling company is explaining as he leads the way: "The grain buyer is the guardian of the miller's cash drawer." He points to the left. "The futures market in feed," he is saying, "gives you a six months forecast on what the miller will get for his offal, that's the part of the wheat that doesn't go for food. That's the special function of Kansas City, because here we have the only feed futures market in the country . . . Then over there at the little desks under the windows we buy our cash grain . . . We have to keep in mind two things outside of the immediate price; what products control tells us about quality and the transit the grain has behind it. We pay a bonus for high protein. Transit's a story by itself."

While we are meeting the buyer at the grainlittered table a man hands him a small tray of new wheat. He peers at the label, stirs the kernels with his finger and hands the tray back in a hurry.

"No thank you," he says.

When the man has gone he mutters, "Yellowberry," and makes a face as if he had tasted something sour.

"Some of this early wheat is too starchy, not the right kind of gluten to make a good loaf of bread," explains the man who works for the big milling company. "We have to watch every detail in this business, always something new . . . that's what keeps us interested . . . There's the weather and the changing quality of the wheatberry and competition in

price and the unpredictable government purchasing . . .
You might say that the government had a perpetual corner
on the wheat market through C.C.C. purchases and the support prices . . . We dance to Washington's tune but we don't
always know what the tune's going to be . . . "

"Did you explain about hedging?" asks the buyer.

"You explain."

"Well, it's like this . . . These showers down in Oklahoma,
they just set up a rise of two points on the board. Now
before the market closes a rumor from Washington may give
a bearish turn to the Chicago exchange and that will affect
us. Well, a milling company doesn't want to be a speculator
so every time we buy cash wheat we instruct our man in the
pit to sell an equivalent amount for delivery at some future
date . . . That keeps our position balanced on the old principle that what we win in Chicago we lose in Milwaukee
. . . That's hedging."

"Now if you want to know about transit," says the man
who works for the big milling company, "we'll go downstairs
and talk to the fellow who handles it."

A ruddy young man who looks as if he ought to be a good
tennis player strides into the office with a bunch of bills of
lading in his hand. "It's simple as rolling off a log," he says.
"Say we buy a carload of wheat from an elevator in Liberal,
Kansas and we want to process it here into flour and ship it
to Springfield, Missouri, we just pay the through rate . . .
The wheat can be processed any place along the way. When
it continues its trip it doesn't have to be the same wheat.
What we do is accumulate a backlog of bills of lading and
use them as we need them in our shipments. Sometimes we
have to buy wheat we don't want just for its preferential
through rate. We sell it right here and use the bill of lading
for shipping out flour. That's what we mean by the transit
behind a shipment."

"Once a man gets into grain," says the man who works for

the big milling company, smiling broadly as we settle down
to lunch in a restaurant round the corner from the Board of
Trade Building, "there's always something new. It keeps
you on your toes."

"Sounds like playing blindfold chess!"

"Well, not blindfold . . . but you've got to know the moves.
You've got to keep the whole picture in your mind. Some
years one of the biggest milling concerns will buy one tenth
of the wheat raised in this country . . . The grain department
guards the cost card. A very small error can have very
disastrous results in an operation of that magnitude . . . All
the time we've got to balance quality and cost against a com-
petitive price for our flour . . . People eat bread all year round
but most of the wheat is marketed in three months. From
June fifteen to September fifteen we eat, drink and sleep
wheat . . . don't have a second to think of anything else."
He leaned back in his chair and stretched his arms back.
"It'll be starting right soon now. It keeps you interested all
right. I wouldn't miss it for anything. I know the company's
interested in a whole lot of other products, but wheat's still
king of the world."

On the wharf at Duluth the wind drives a wet arctic mist
in our faces. The elevator rises huge and black and dripping
above the mahogany water. The long lake freighter lies
alongside battered and vacant as an empty shoebox. Amid-
ships men with welding arcs are working from a scow to
mend some dented plates. On deck a few shivering hands in
variously patched peajackets and dungarees are getting ready
to open up the hatches. A roughlooking crew, windtanned,
with stubbly chins. One of them's the skipper. We ask him
how he is going to clean the holds to take the grain.

"That's easy. They blow in chaff from the elevator. We
had a load of limestone and that kinda battered us up. We

can clean the holds out all right but grain's got to be kept dry. We got to mend them leaky plates."

When the winch starts to haul on the pulleys that move the hatchcovers the old steamboat smell of oil and steam blows into our nostrils off the raw breeze. We climb down a long ladder to the wharf again. The great spouts they call "legs" are sticking out from the side of the elevator ready to discharge the grain. From inside the elevator comes a clanking of conveyor belts and a blast of dry dust.

"An elevator's a dusty job," says the longlegged man in a Stetson hat who's in charge. "If you have hay fever keep out of this game." He turns and looks up at the smooth dark bulk above our heads. "This here's one of the big ones," he says proudly. "I shouldn't wonder if it warn't one of the biggest."

The wheat makes a sound like rain when it pours into the hold in a dun pillar. Dust rises and floats away on the wind. "Dust . . . that's the great danger in grain elevators . . . the damn stuff explodes," says a grimyfaced man with red rims to his eyes talking through a gauze nose pad. "Sooner or later they'll blow up on you."

"Ain't blown up on me yet," says the tall man.

The mist turns into drizzle. In what seems no time at all the holds are full and the legs dripping from the rain are swung back against the elevator. A cheerful whirr comes from the winch pulling the hatches back on. "How soon will you make port?" we shout up at the skipper who's leaning out of the bridge perched over the blunt bow. "We're late starting. "It'll be about seven days to Buffalo."

The superintendent of the elevator in Buffalo was a ruddy big bull of a man. His hands were big and the muscles of his shoulders bulged big under his sweatshirt.

"Sure come on in. Sure it's a big elevator. We can store

a million four hundred and fifty thousand bushels of grain. We'll start the tour at the top."

He walked on ahead, walking on the balls of his feet like a boxer, through the high dimlit cave of the lower story of the elevator bounded with great pipes and hoarded conveyors and the cylindrical shapes of the tanks. There was a roar of machinery and a whir of hidden belts. The place smelled of grain and machine oil and dust. As the big iron box of the elevator rose the superintendent joshed the elderly operator. The operator joshed back. Everybody went by their first names in this mill.

We stepped out on an upper floor among a bevy of huge galvanized funnels. The superintendent explained that these were cyclones to suck the dust and chaff out of the grain. Getting rid of dust was the great problem of grain elevators. The damn stuff exploded and besides it choked you to death. Housekeeping, that was another headache, because the world was full of grubs and larvae and worms that liked to eat wheat just like people did. Dust and insect infestation were the elevator operator's nightmares.

How long had he worked here? Twenty three years. Helped build the elevator, worked on the bull gang and in the mixing house and on the roustabout crew. Not a damn job in the elevator he hadn't done.

We hopped on the one man lift and came out on a house on the roof. It was high and airy up there. The wind blew raw off the graygreen lake. Below was the breakwater and the canal-like arm of the harbor where the freight boats unloaded. Out there along the breakwater was where the boats they used for supplemental storage tied up in winter. The unloading was done with bucket conveyors, lofter legs they called them. Took about eight hours to unload those big babies. The legs took up twentyeight thousand bushels an hour. Out of box cars they could only haul in sixteen thousand: corners, back work with a scoop. No, this year's busy season hadn't begun, it was still all last year's wheat coming in yet. Some Canadian wheat coming in bond from Fort William, Ontario, for shipment overseas. Mostly last year's spring wheat from Duluth.

The other side was the harbor and white lake steamers tied up to gabled wharves and the tangled industrial shore-front of the city. White smoke from a locomotive rose from the tracks below. Pigeons circled overhead. The super-intendent pointed to a figure in dungarees clambering on some staging on the far storage tank. Trapping pigeons. If he had his way he'd let them be, but Minneapolis wanted them trapped. They thought up the damnedest things in Minneapolis.

We turned and he pointed out the covered bridge that carried the great belt conveyor that took the mixed grain over to the mill. About ninetytwo thousand bushels every day. Now we'd work our way down. We started down the iron stairs. This was the machinery floor. Now all these belt conveyors, these were how you moved the grain from bin to bin, it all had to be moved about once every thirty days, maybe oftener in summer if it started to heat, binburning would ruin it. Grain was alive, wasn't it? It had to breathe. Over here under the window the grain passed through sifters to shake out the heavy stuff, the foreign matter you couldn't suck out by air. He opened a sort of box lid. Inside you could see the dancing grain pouring over the conveyor end. He pulled out some hunks of granite, pebbles, a handful of sticks, a piece of a hinge. A feller would be surprised at what they found in the grain: watches, beaten up spectacles, rolls of bills, wallets, jackknives, junk the guys had lost loading the trucks way back on some farm in North Dakota.

Down in the middle story of the elevator there was a board lit by bright electric lights. The superintendent pointed with a proud possessive sweep of his hand to the outline diagram of the cylindrical tanks they stored the grain in. Red and green lights and chalked symbols showed the type of wheat and the number of bushels in each bin. This was a control board. The millers ordered up the mixture they wanted from the mill. It was up to the elevator to get the mixtures right, say forty percent durum forty percent some other strong wheat, ten percent something else. That light showed they were mixing right now in this bin over here.

Naw, the elevator didn't take many men to handle it. Sixtyone including maintenance and loading. They worked three shifts around the clock.

How long did he work?

The superintendent laughed. A grain elevator was a three ring circus. He turned his back on the board. A man had that board in his head even if he was at home and asleep. "If you get into it when you're young you stick to it . . . it becomes part of your life."

When you visit the flour mill next door they give you one of the spare dusters that hang in the office closet to wear and hand you a cheesecloth cap lettered with the company's name The quietvoiced young milling foreman goes on ahead talking over his shoulder as he leads the way between the ranked machines, across the polished hardwood floors. He has a serious, slightly abstracted manner. His skin is very white. The contours of his face have the rounded look that comes from indoor work. First he walks you past the two fifteen hundred horsepower electric motors that furnish power for the far-flung complication of belts and shafts of the seven stories of milling machinery that shakes and rumbles above your head.

"These are the prime movers," he says, his voice deep with respect.

"It is a little hard to follow the process through right in

order," the miller goes on to explain, "because the stuff runs up and down stairs so often . . . The first thing that happens when the grain arrives on the big conveyor belt from the elevator is that it runs through aspirators for a cleaning, then under a magnetic separator to get any bits of iron out . . . then through a milling separator and three cylinder separators . . ."

While he talks we go up in elevators, climb stairs, shoot up and down on one man lifts. Here and there he peeps through a trap into a machine or a conveyor or snatches out a sample in the palm of his hand. Everywhere inside of the system is a hurrying stream of grain, flowing down chutes, dancing on belts, pouring over rollers.

The miller opens a little glass window in a closed conveyor and holds up a handful of wet grain.

"We're running oats for the cereal plant through this part of the mill today," he explains. He pokes his nose down into the wet oats in the palm of his hand. His eyebrows pinch together in a frown. "Excuse me."

He goes to a phone in the iron embrasure: "Hey, Bill, you better come up here, the oats isn't cleaning right . . . Bill is the smutter," he explains smiling again. "He's the man who attends to the cleaning.

"Now after the wheat has been cleaned again . . . " He picks up the thread of his explanation as we start walking down another set of grooved iron stairs, "it lays for seven and a half hours in a tank. That's what we call tempering the wheat. The aim is to toughen the bran and mellow the endosperm. The endosperm is the part we reduce into flour. The bran is the husk. We knock it off in the breakrolls."

We are walking along a row of machines that look vaguely like small upright pianos. "These are the stands. The general principle is that the grain runs through between two steel rollers running at different speeds. It's not ground the way it used to be between the oldfashioned stone millwheels, but it's gradually reduced. We've already knocked off the bran. Next we knock off the germ."

He opens a trap and takes out a handful of soft meal that gives off a rich, wheaty smell. "We sell this separate. It can't go into flour because it is so rich in wheat oil. The wheat oil goes rancid. The germ's really the little embryo plant that's all ready to grow. It's full of oils and vitamins and minerals; there's something in it that increases fertility in animals. They use it on silver fox farms. You know they have trouble getting the foxes to breed in captivity. Recently I heard we had an order for two hundred pounds from a group of ladies in Cambridge, Massachusetts." He begins to laugh. "Same trouble, I guess . . . Now these are all sifters," he points through a forest of oscillating machines masked in canvas that jiggle like African dancers. "It's sifted and bolted . . . bolting means sifting through a special silk bolting cloth that comes from Switzerland . . . Now we've gotten rid of the germ and the bran" . . . He has to shout to make himself heard above the noise of the sifters . . . "Now we are sifting the flour out of the middlings. The middlings are reduced and reduced until we've gotten the maximum amount of flour out of them. What's left is shorts and red dog. We sell these every day with the bran to producers of animal feeds. The price we get for the mill feeds is an important item in setting the price for the flour."

We are back in his little office in the corner of the building. "Sometimes we run off as many as sixteen different grades in a day," he is explaining. "The grade is controlled by what mix of wheats you use and then by the blend of the flours . . . then right on this floor . . . " He points down the aisle, "the blended flours are bleached and enriched with a vitamin and minerals composition to make up for the nutrition we lost by taking out the germ and the bran. After that the flour is ready to slide down to the packaging departments

. . . You don't see many men around. That's one of the nice things about milling," the miller says with a smile. "Not too darn many people around . . . Everybody calls everybody by his first name from the plant superintendent on down . . . A feller likes to work with people he likes."

Back at the plant superintendent's office we found the department heads in white dusters sitting around the wall. The personnel director wore a business suit. A secretary sat at the corner of a big desk with a folder of papers in front of her and her pencil poised.

The plant superintendent himself, a stocky, blue-eyed man with the build and the rosy skin of a prosperous English farmer sat back with his lips thoughtfully pursed.

"Maybe we'd better reconsider that one. Maybe this feller has something," he was saying. He had a way of smiling while he talked and merrily bouncing his words out as if they were tennis balls.

"But it's really a matter for the safety committee."

"Who made the suggestion, this feller or the safety committee?"

"He did, but it's pretty obvious."

"The more obvious it is the worse fools we were for not noticing it before. I move we award him ten dollars . . . Everybody agree?" Heads nodded. " . . . And take immediate steps to move that ladder eight inches to the left . . . It's a safety hazard as it is now. What was the next one?"

The secretary started to read.

"Didn't we have that before?" the superintendent asked.

"Yes," said the personnel director. "We tabled it for further study. I've been over the ground and now I approve of it."

"All right, award him ten dollars and, Maintenance, it is your responsibility to see that screen goes up in front of that rope drive."

"Now there's a whole flock from one feller," said the personnel director. "I don't recommend we adopt any of them . . . he just wants a new suit for Easter."

"Read 'em . . . He may have something," shouted the superintendent.

"We've got to keep our minds open," he went on in a ruminating tone a few minutes later as we all walked down the corridor that hummed and throbbed from the vibration of transmission belts behind the walls. "You know a flour mill's a kind of an oldfashioned business . . . we've most of us been with this same mill twenty years or more . . . the biggest mill in the world but we're one happy family. Milling's still an art. You know the old saying about rule of thumb, that's a miller's saying. The miller tests the flour with his thumb." He held up his thumb and forefinger and rubbed them delicately together. "But we've got to keep on our toes . . . We've got to keep our minds open to improvements."

We were standing in line at the counter. Everybody lined up in the order in which they arrived. We carried our trays to a long table at the end of the room. The superintendent sat in the corner and threw his head back and laughed, "Now let's see who's going to pay for my ice cream." Everybody brought out nickels and a sort of elimination matching tournament began. Everybody shouted and protested. "The beauty of this game," said the superintendent, laughing till the tears came into his eyes, "is that the feller who loses not only has to pay for the ice cream but he has to bring it to us."

The Products Control man lost. "Serves him right," everybody shouted, "he's the guy who's always on our tails in this plant."

After we had eaten our ice cream the superintendent put his hand on the shoulder of a thin man in blue dungarees faded pale with many washings. "You take him over to the cereal plant. . . . He wants to see new developments . . . We may be a lot of stick in the muds over here where we mill out the flour, still muddling along with the steel roller process they invented seventyfive years ago . . . " He laughed and slapped his knee and went on. "But over there in the cereal plant new things are coming up every day . . . And that all takes packaging. Packaging is the nubbin of breakfast cereals manufacturing and it's getting to be that way in flour, too, in domestic flours. The modern housewife doesn't even want twentyfive pound bags. No room in the modern household for the oldtime barrel of flour sitting on the floor of the kitchen cupboard . . . You take him through your bag of tricks. Show him all the skeletons in all the closets."

"All right, Charley," the thin man said and we started out across the railroad tracks.

The cereal plant turned out as full of sideshows as the midway at a carnival. There were boilers for softening the grain, hot rollers for roasting and crushing it, big conical kettles travelling on an overhead trolley, steamers for cooking the paste that was pressed through great metal dies, a shooting gallery where the puffed cereals were exploded in guns. The place smelled of steam and hot wheat and burnt sugar and roasting flour. Mountain ranges of biscuit flour and chocolate cake mixes travelled slowly on conveyor belts and disappeared in bright stainless steel hoppers.

We stopped in the laboratory where young men fresh from college chemical courses checked each product once an hour, twenty-four times a day.

"What happens if they spoil a batch?"

"Goes to the dogfood man . . . But our business," said the young man from Purdue, "is to check things before they get to that point . . . We bake the cakes and make the biscuits. We test all the ingredients as they come in and the products as they go out in bulk and in packages . . . Here's an example." He waves a little scribbled slip of paper under my nose. "One of the boys just found six bags of the wrong kind of cocoa in a perfectly good carload. If that had gone in a whole batch of cake mix would have been ruined . . . that's what they pay us for."

The lower floor is the packaging floor. The products slide down chutes and tubes. From the bright merrygorounds of the packaging machines long processions of boxes brightly colored and printed with sharp lettering to catch the eye proceed in regular files through the room. The packages bob and pause under the delicate flexing stainless steel fingers that do the sealing and folding in of the oiled paper. Way at the end they are grouped into cartons and the cartons start on their own progress through sealing and stamping machines until they dive into the chutes that take them to the loading platform.

"In breakfast cereals," the guide is saying, "packaging is very important. The product has to be kept fresh and free from moisture. Then there's eye appeal."

We are walking past a stalled machine. The boxes wait in a queue on their track like people lined up to buy theatre tickets. A young man with a streak of oil on his nose has his face poked into the middle of a tangle of rods and levers. The tip of his tongue is between his teeth and he's trying with a small screw driver to pry loose a bit of torn printed stock from under a roller. Beside him another man is collecting the bashed and damaged packages in a handtruck . . . "Delicate machinery means first rate maintenance . . . In plants like this the maintenance men are the most expert and are the best paid personnel."

We are walking alongside a moving conveyor. The cereal packages are passing through a gate. "This is a metal detector. If any metal . . . screws, nuts, tiny flakes of steel, has dropped into any package this light goes on and it is ejected . . . Then we have girl inspectors along each of the lines. This and the small packaging department over in the

flour mill are the only places in the plant where we use girls
— outside of the office, of course. We just use them on the
day shifts. On the night shift we use disabled veterans. They
have worked out very well. They like the work. They don't
mind night work . . . Maybe you'd like to talk to one of our
inspectors?"

The inspector is a quiet spinster with very clear gray eyes.
She used to be a schoolteacher, she says, making her voice
heard above the rhythmic thump and clatter of packaging
machinery and the rustling of conveyor belts overhead. Now
she's an inspector of packaged cereals.

Funny, in college she had majored in Latin, natural
enough because her people were Scotch . . . "You know the
Scotch, they like to be scholars." She had intended to teach
Latin but the opportunity hadn't turned up. She'd been
here more than seven years now. She had been elected shopsteward. If a girl has a grievance she takes it up with the
foreman and if he can't see it she goes to the business agent
of the union . . . Everybody sits down and talks it over. So
far nothing's ever even gone to arbitration . . . management
and the union leaders are all pretty reasonable people . . .
The only complaint she had was that a woman didn't have
much of an opportunity for advancement. No way of getting
up over a dollar twentysix an hour. Maybe some day there
would be supervisory positions open to women.

Over in the small packaging department under the flour
mill we sat down to talk to another group of girls at a table
in the little lounge in front of their locker room. Out among
the machines where endless streams of flour were packaged
into small bags it was too noisy to talk.

They were mostly blonde and Polish. Their mat Slavic
skin looked yellow under the dusting of flour. Most of them
had worked five or six years in the small packaging department already. Even if they got married they came back. Oh
yes, they liked the music every fifteen minutes out of the

loudspeakers that blared above the metallic clanking and thumping of the packaging machines, particularly when they played Slavic tunes . . . their national tunes . . . They giggled . . . They liked that. It was monotonous work, just one or two movements in time with the rhythm of each machine but it was better since they started team work. Two or three girls worked as a team on each machine . . . They had a minimum basic wage and then piecework above that. Oh yes, everyone of them said they liked piecework better, especially in teams . . . a chance to make better money . . . the time moved faster with teamwork.

But why were they being asked all these questions? Was something the matter? A couple of them began to huff and puff and toss their heads a bit. The stout matron of the lockerroom reassured them. Only a man writing an article for a magazine.

"Will he be taking pictures?"

"And me looking a sight with flour all over my face."

Giggling and shrieking they all ran back to their machines.

Only men worked in the big packaging department where they filled the hundred pound cotton or paper bags which took up the main stream of flour out of the mill. The foreman proudly exhibited a new machine that did the whole operation: filling, weighing, shaking down the flour, sewing up the top and pushing the bag off onto a conveyor that carried it to the loading department. All the operator had to do was to stretch the mouth of the empty bag between stainless steel arms that held it steady while the flour poured in.

Over in a corner the oldest type of machine was still in operation. There an old man with a seamed and raddled countenance inserted the bag under the flow of flour, waited for it to fill, weighed it, sewed its mouth by hand and lifted it off onto a truck. When we stopped to talk to him he looked up from his work with uncomprehending redrimmed eyes, like a disturbed woodchuck's.

How long had he worked here?

Thirtytwo years.

What kind of jobs had he had?

Always the same job. His eyes snapped impatiently. He didn't like the interruption. What the hell does this guy mean asking me these questions his eyes were saying. His hands, thin and angled like claws under their covering of flour twitched with impatience to get back to his machine. The flour had filled the deep ridges in his cheeks.

"Wassa matter? Ain't he good job?"

"Sure, sure."

He lowered his angry rodents' eyes and scurried back to his place. Already the flour was spilling out on the floor. We stood beside him a moment but he didn't look up again. He had fallen back completely into the tense cycle of keeping up with the flow of flour out of the spout.

(As the screen goes blank MR. LECTURER *gets to his feet and starts to walk up and down in front of it.)*

When I started on this trip I thought all I'd need to do was follow the wheat through from the harvest to its appearance packaged on the grocery shelf. But it turned out to be not so simple as that. The concern I was studying had other ramifications. Some of them resulted from the use of byproducts and some of them resulted from expansion of the financial structure of the corporation. Up to nineteen twentynine the company had concerned itself principally with milling out flour. As in many other developments in this country that year was the turning point.

New Era financing had pumped up the economy like a balloon; it couldn't hold any more hot air so it burst. In the typhoon that resulted not so many men of affairs had the sense to hold their hats, keep their shirts tightly buttoned and plan for the future. Those that did found, when the wreckage of the great depression had been cleared away, the future not nearly so black as it had been painted.

A group of men brought up in the traditions of this famous old milling company, decided it was better to expand than to contract; at least expansion would give them a run for their money. Corporations were on the market at bargain prices. So they spread out. They took in a company on the Pacific Slope and a feed concern in Detroit and decided to go to work to sell flour from coast to coast. Flour was a substantial basis for any business — no matter what happened people would go on eating flour in some form or other. They figured on some anchors to windward; byproducts of flour and feed, byproducts of the mechanics of the packaging machines, byproducts of the knowledge and abilities of the men they hired to work for them. They created a corporation capable of taking many protean shapes. This corporation has proceeded on its way, containing within itself the not entirely digested shapes of other concerns like an anaconda after a meal.

The management discovered for one thing that animal feeds were about as important in their business as human feeds. In the old days, so one of the old millers in Minneapolis told me, they used to dump the offal into the Mississippi River. The offal was the bran and red dog and middlings, everything that wasn't white flour. Oldtimers still called it offal, but it wasn't wasted any more. Now nothing was wasted not even the dust. The offal used to form banks in the river that fermented and sometimes pretty near choked up the channel. The neighbors complained. Eventually the city got a public health service that put a stop to dumping in the river, but meanwhile an old man with a horse and wagon had taken to fishing the offal out and hauling it off to sell to people that fed hogs. That was the beginning of the millfeeds business.

In Detroit when I asked him about the history of millfeeds the president of the feeds division of the corporation spoke with a reminiscent twinkle in his eye. The joke was that this feed concern didn't start with grain byproducts at all. It started with a trainload of beet pulp. In those long ago days before the first world war a certain Detroit engineer found himself one morning the owner of a trainload of beet pulp. This gentleman was essentially a designer of factories for the refining of sugar from beets. He was something of a grainbroker too, a man who had his finger in many pies. In the course of a brokerage operation he was caught with this beet pulp on his hands. There was no sale for it. The sugar market was in one of its moments of glut. He had an idea that beet pulp ought to make good feed for dairy cattle. The experts in the agricultural colleges said it wouldn't, but in the end he and his friends found a way of processing it so that cattle would eat it, and started a company that became preeminent in dairy feeds. From dairy feeds they branched out into feeds for fattening steers and hogs and chickens and dogs and rabbits and even for mink and silver fox. The manufacture of feeds demanded a great deal of experiment in animal nutrition and for that purpose they started an experimental farm near Detroit. "The thing to do is to drive out and look at that farm."

MR. LECTURER *turns off the lights and starts up his projector again.)*

CAPTION: *Byproducts*

"We are rather proud of our Holsteins," says the farm manager as we walk through the quiet clean black and white barns between the ranks of quiet clean black and white cows. "Now this is Our Girl . . . " He pats a particularly large cow on her protruding hip bone. "You see she's not a show type, but there's a chance that she'll make the national record for milk production this year. You see we have to prove to our customers that the increased cost of a balanced ration pays off. We're meeting price resistance. The days during the war when people were begging us for feed are gone. Now we have to prove our point. Our best customer is the dairy-man who keeps a careful and accurate record."

We walk out past a little recess in a white wall where a calf is having his photograph taken. "We take all their pictures," the Manager says tenderly, "we keep a record . . . Now this animal had an interesting history." He points to a glass case of bones displayed on velvet in the corridor out-side the farm office. "You see our research men save the skeleton when an animal dies or is slaughtered. They can tell a good deal about the nutritional condition from the calcium content of her bones. Look, this cow here gave 187,000 pounds of milk in twelve years, an average of twenty quarts a day. During that time she consumed a carload and a half of feed, half a carload of beet pulp, two carloads of hay and a silo full of ensilage. Some machine for processing farm products, eh?"

We follow him into a little building full of rabbits in cages, pink noses throbbing against wire mesh. "The prob-lem," he is saying, "is the same for any animal . . . a question of finding the nutrition formula and learning how to make it out of ingredients that are commercially feasible. Most of our rabbit feed goes to the coast . . . Los Angeles ate six mil-lion pounds of rabbit meat last year . . . Now pigs . . . "

We are walking along a series of pens squirming with Hampshire sows and their litters. "Fertility, health and live-liness of the little pigs are the main things we work for. If the farmer can raise four more pigs per litter than he usually does he can produce a hundred pounds of dressed pork for three dollars less. That makes it worth his while to use our feed . . . Now over there are the chicken houses. We've developed a broiler feed that produces fifteen pounds more broiler per hundred pounds . . . Our chicken farms have resulted in some interesting sidelines, such as the sale of chicken blood and chick embryos for laboratories."

"It was just luck," the executive from San Francisco is saying as he drives us over to the airport, "that our division didn't bring a chemical plant along when we were taken into the corporation. The founder, that old engineer we were telling you about, did a lot of worrying about some tanks he accumulated of a substance known to the trade as Stepan's Wastewater, which was left over from processing beet pulp. He wasn't a man who liked to see things go to waste. He discovered that you could use Stepan's Wastewater as a base for the production of monosodium glutamate, the famous Chinese flavoring agent. Due to financial technicalities that plant was taken over by another concern that operates it now . . . Of course our own corporation produces MSG too. You'll find them making it in Keokuk."

Keokuk turned out to be an old Mississippi River town, full of sunbaked memories of sternwheel steamboats and Mark Twain and Joseph Smith and the early Mormon settlements. There in the ancient brick factory of a rural patent medicine concern the corporation had set up, early in World War II, a plant for the refining of starches.

"This operation," says the lively young engineer in charge, "is certainly a far cry from the oldtime mill where you waited with a team of horses while the miller ground your wheat out into flour. Our business here is to extract the starch from the inferior flour that's known in the trade as 'second clear.' It is largely a question of producing a slurry of starch and water. We spin that in centrifuges to throw off the starch. That leaves us gluten, another valuable by-product, and on the chemical end monosodium glutamate and glutamic acid hydrochloride. The production of ergosterol, vitamin D, is a separate proposition."

"How are you able to work out job classifications in such a different type of work from ordinary milling? It's the same union, isn't it?"

"Yes. Everything depends on working out a chart of job classifications locally. Setting the job descriptions was an intricate piece of labor relations work because when we started out nobody was familiar with this sort of operation . . . We had to set up an elaborate advancement chart. We had to have a clearcut basis for determining qualifications . . . The job descriptions had to be all written out in the clearest possible language. All new job openings are posted. The man who is qualified by seniority gets a chance but, if he can't do the work satisfactorily, other men are tried out down the seniority list until somebody sticks. The union has so far backed management up loyally once the qualifications have been established. Conflicts that arise are talked out in the labor relations committee. The labor relations committee also handles the profit from the Coca Cola machines, they use it for parties or for buying uniforms for the ball team or sending people flowers if they get sick or if somebody dies . . . I suppose you'd call that the social side of the committee's work. It helps make the employees feel that they belong to something they have a part in, that they aren't just being sweated by a soulless corporation. As processes change and new jobs appear, job descriptions are worked out in detail. The chemical industry is an evolving industry. You'll get the last word at Kankakee . . . "

CAPTION: *The Triumph of the Dial*

The new fatty acids distillation plant you see on the screen erected along the railroad track just outside the pleasant elmshaded Central Illinois town of Kankakee is even further removed from milling. Instead of the bustle of people and machinery, and the dust, and the loud voices, and the kidding and horseplay of an oldtime flour and feed mill, the plant at Kankakee is as quiet as a college hall during a final examination. The airconditioned rooms of the office wing are tinted in deep blue and tan. It's more like walking into the Museum of Modern Art than an oldfashioned factory. Out back beyond the long low office and laboratory buildings you can see the fantastic shapes ringed with catwalks and wreathed in piping of the great stills.

"The plant is a pipefitter's dream," says one of the engineers who is getting it into operation. "We have miles and miles of different sorts of pipe." He smiles a quiet smile. "Pipefitter's nightmare I'd call it," says another glumly.

"Now you probably want to know what fatty acids are. Well, the simplest way of putting it is that when you split off the glycerin from an oil or fat, say soy bean or coconut oil, you have left a string of fatty acids which are distilled off under various chemical conditions at various heats. There are demands for all sorts of fatty acids in soap and detergent manufacturing and in the paint and varnish industry and the demand is growing. What we aim to do is to custom make fatty acids as the demand develops. First we've got to learn to run this damn plant."

"How do you get your personnel?"

"We've had to train each man for his job. The engineer in charge is a fatty acids man and the supervisors have had experience in chemical plants of course, but it's a little like setting a man who's accustomed to playing the piano in charge of a very complicated organ. A chemical still is not something you can put into operation overnight . . . The men under the supervisory level we find have worked out best are farmboys . . . A man who has run a tractor on a farm is likely to be a resourceful fellow. He's had experience patching things up with baling wire. Men who have been garage mechanics or run their own filling stations work out well. We have to have men with initiative."

The supervisors were young men not long out of college chemical courses. They spent their time anxiously watching dials, working out pressures and temperatures, doping out the causes of burst pipes and unsuccessful runs. They all looked thin and haggard from long hours of work. There was a little of the atmosphere of one of those amphibian teams out in the Pacific dumped out too soon to cope with the realities of oceanic war. "A plant like this," one of them said, "looks very pretty on paper but you have to run it for a year before you start to find out where the bugs are . . . It takes it out of you. We've had a time explaining to our wives why we got home so late nights."

"Of course there's been a certain amount of turnover," said the Personnel Director. "Some people just don't like the smell. We try to make men feel at home from the first day, try to get somebody to eat his lunch with a new man. We get his supervisor to spend plenty of time explaining the job. We find the first day is very important. We don't fire a fellow at the first shot, either. We like to give him two or three swings at the ball. We always interview men who want to leave to find out what the trouble is. Wages too low? Work too hard? Don't like the other men? We feel that as the methods of industry change personnel relations have to change too . . . We hope to keep a little ahead of the game."

"The better designed a plant is the more sensitive it is," said the plant superintendent. "The more sensitive it is the more skilled the personnel needs to be."

The surprising thing to a layman about the new flour mill in the industrial section of Los Angeles that we visit next is that it looks from the outside very much like the chemical plant at Kankakee. The very tall young miller from Salt Lake City who is explaining it to us, as we stand out in the honeycolored sunlight of Southern California looking up at the tall tanks and the gleaming aluminum pipes, uses that same word "sensitive."

"This here's a real sensitive plant," he is saying in his low drawl, in the tone of a doctor describing a sickly child. "It is a flour mill designed by a firm of engineers accustomed to designing chemical plants . . . What they have done is to turn the oldfashioned flour mill inside out so that practically everything except the control room is out of doors. The elevator has been treated the same way. They think that is the answer to infestation and the dust hazard. You see those great aspirators . . . well, the story of this mill is that the flour is sucked by air from process to process. The whole operation is pneumatic. It's strictly a pilot mill. They've had something like it in Switzerland on a small scale but this is the first one in America." He is talking loud and fast now: "We are pioneering a new era. The engineers are redesigning the equipment as we go along. I tell you this is worth while. I was so anxious to get in on it I transferred to this job at my own expense without advance in pay. This is the first radical change in milling since steel rollers took the place of millstones."

When I asked the man who had for many years been at the steering wheel of this entire enterprise about the importance of the mill his eyes lit up immediately.

"There have been only two improvements in the art of milling in our time . . . " he started eagerly to explain. We were sitting in the Olympian quiet of his airy panelled office on the top floor of the corporation's office building in Minneapolis. Through the windows you looked out over the gray downtown squares of the city towards the factory chimneys and the tall cylindrical forms of clustered mills and elevators that fringed the skyline along the river under the clear pale blue Minnesota sky. He was a whitehaired man getting on in years. He had recently retired as president of the corporation but you could see by his manner as he talked that all his thoughts and dreams were still in the business.

"The first," he said, "was made back in the last century, the discovery that you could reduce flour better if the rollers didn't touch, and the second is the use of air as a classifier of the flour. The pneumatic system is getting a thorough trial in the mill you saw at Los Angeles. That mill I hope is only the beginning of great developments. Milling has been a traditional art . . . Now we have to get out from under the weight of tradition and precedent. We have to keep telling ourselves that there must be a better way. We want to replace the rule of thumb by the rule of the dial. The miller won't need his thumbs any more. We've cut off his thumbs. The dial with its little pin keeping a record on graphpaper is going to prove a far better guide for future progress than the oldtime miller's thumb. There'll be no thumbs in the flour milling of the future."

A VOICE WITH A GEORGIA DRAWL: Will you excuse me Mr. Lecturer if I interrupt . . . I understand interruptions are in order . . .

MR. LECTURER: Quite . . . Maybe you would introduce yourself. I believe you are a newcomer in . . . er . . . our little circle.

JIM OVERTON: My name is Jim Overton . . . you can set me down for a Georgia cracker . . . I'd like to know what those nice millers we've just been seein' and hearin' about are goin' to think about havin' their thumbs cut off.

MR. LECTURER: I doubt very much if they have been consulted . . . Now that young man from Salt Lake City is going to be perfectly happy watching a dial. He evidently read the signs of the times. To my way of thinking the question of our friend from Georgia uncovers the stumbling block that stands in the way of participation of even the lower ranks of management in the fundamental decisions of the great corporations, decisions that affect the lives of every man working in the industry . . .

JIM OVERTON: Do you folks mind if I tell you a little story? I'll make it short . . .

When I got out after four years in the navy, I went lookin' around to find me a job. I thought of one of the big national corporations, that had a particularly progressive and liberal reputation. I had a long talk with one of the executives — a very splendid gentleman he was. He described an empire of salesmanship and manufacture scattered all over the country. "We're gettin' so big," he kept sayin', "that what we've got to do is tighten up our communications. We've got to centralize. We've got to train a group of young men who'll be loyal to the company first. We'll keep a man a few years in one place and then move him somewhere else. We want him to learn every aspect of the business. Then if he makes good we'll bring him into the central office and make a top executive of him. . . . " But that was just what I didn't like about the navy, I tried to explain to him. I don't want to be just a pawn on a board, I told him. I want to be a citizen of these United States. To be a good citizen of these States I have to be a good citizen of my home town first, and then of my own home state of Georgia. I want to grow up with my part of the country . . . If I'd liked the other kind of life I could have stayed in the navy.

FRED RUFUS: There could be another way of arriving at those decisions. There's the tendency towards centralized power and there's the tendency towards local autonomy. The advantage of local autonomy for the plant or the sales office or the regional branch is that it promotes that individual personal initiative that built this country up . . . Every man makes mistakes, but mistakes aren't so dangerous at the local level as they are when through bureaucratic machinery they cripple the whole organization. What I say is give every man a chance to make his own mistakes . . . Of course there are some operations that are much better done from a central office. Buying of raw materials say, that has to be centralized. The continued development of our society hinges on hitting a balance between personal initiative and the logical advantages of centralized control . . . The danger is that the men on top of these great organizations keep going off into the stratosphere. Yesmen appear around them. A palace guard grows up and a whole mesh of bureaucratic routine that prevents the big brass from understanding the feelings and the needs of the men who are really doing the work.

MR. LECTURER: What I have been trying to point out is that the leaders of industry and of the trade unions haven't got much time to make up their minds. Do you want power or do you want a good society? We were all brought up in a world where a favorable climate existed for free institutions. One reason why we were able to develop so far in so many different ways in this country was that we lived in what was more or less a friendly world. Now we have to go on experimenting and developing in a world where the men who have seized political power hate and fear everything we stand for, where all the basic rights and duties of men which we take for granted are called into question and denied. Time's running out on us. Whether we can save some sort of free enterprise will depend on whether we can keep our social structure evolving and improving so that enough people continue to feel citizenship in it. A man whose personal initiative has been taken away is no longer a citizen, he's a serf. Citizenship isn't entirely a matter of a decent minimum wage or of going to the polls every four years.

MRS. EDWARDS: Isn't that what Congress ought to be worrying about? Businessmen are so busy.

MR. LECTURER: Laws and regulations follow somewhat clumsily the changing outlines of the social structure. The political structure of the nation will inevitably follow the social forms set by Industry.

JIM OVERTON: The reason so many young people have lost faith in the machinery of liberty is that they don't see how they can fit themselves into it. It's not entirely a dollars and cents proposition. What they want is a feelin' of wellrounded citizenship, I'm goin' to try to set up my own business in my own home town. I know it's a crazy thing to do but damn it I want to feel like an American.

FRED RUFUS: What you've been saying comes mighty close to home young man. I had to think out the same problems you did during the period when I was deciding whether to let my factory go or to go along with it into the great corporation that ate it up . . . I may have made the wrong choice. The trouble with my life now, is that since I gave up the plant and fixed myself up a fine office as an industrial consultant, I can't get my feet back on the ground. I'm in that stratosphere you people have been talking about, the stratosphere of the overpaid. That's why I've been so patiently sitting in on our friend Mr. Lecturer's sometimes rather cloudy ramblings . . . *(People laugh)* because I don't want to get lost in that stratosphere.

MRS. EDWARDS *(pipes up)*: What I kept wanting to ask about that milling company was, if those manufacturers are so clever, why don't we get better bread in this country. The average commercial bread tastes like blotting paper. Did you know that bleached white flour gave dogs fits? *(More laughter.)*

EDDY JONES *(breathing excitedly)*: Fred, let me ask you a question? If your manufacturing plant had been taken over by a national trust really operated in the public interest instead of by a corporation working for the imaginary interests

of some nebulous investors and the real interests of a preda-
tory board of directors, wouldn't you have been willing to
go along?

FRED RUFUS: That's a very good question, Eddy. The
trouble is that it is my considered opinion that, at his present
stage of development, it is not in the nature of man to
operate any business really in the public interest. The habit
of domination and exploitation of the weak by the strong is
too deeprooted. Maybe it's not so much the fault of the
strong as it is of the weak, who are pushovers for the magnetism of leadership. I don't mean that there aren't currents
of real public spirit in most men. There are even a few men
who will sacrifice everything for the good of the community
as they see it. But most of us are made up of a tangle of
personal ambitions and rivalries. Our right hands don't
know what our left hands are doing. We are driven by the
need to support our families and to keep our heads in the
air above the shoving and elbowing mass of our fellow men
. . . I spent some years in Washington during the war and I
came away with the feeling that there was more real public
spirit among the ordinary businessmen of this country than
there was among the professional public servants. Personal
vanity seems to play more of a part in Washington than it
does in business. In business we make mistakes and we admit
them and correct them, or else we get the sack. I met so
many wellintentioned men in Washington whose usefulness
was destroyed by blind vanity. A public official never dares
admit he made a mistake.

MR. LECTURER: That's all true, Mr. Rufus, but there's
another side to the picture. There's the eagerness with which
people subordinate themselves to a master plan or a dominant idea.

MRS. EDWARDS: Couldn't we harness that enthusiasm to a
drive to make democracy work?

MR. LECTURER: I'm thinking of the sort of selfless passion

with which men throw themselves into advertising and selling . . . Of course everybody likes to do things they know how
to do well, but there's a sort of dervish enthusiasm about
American salesmanship, a complete abnegation of the critical spirit that always amazes me when I run into it . . . Incidentally spending a few days with advertising men and salesmen in this country makes the dervish enthusiasm of the
Russians for the particular brand of patent medicine their
government is selling more understandable . . . Let me show
you a scrap of an afternoon I spent with an intelligent young
man who was selling for one of the big packaged food concerns. Although he was still pretty young he had worked for
seventeen years for the same concern. I followed him on his
rounds that afternoon.

We drove out through shaded streets between green lawns
and shrubbery. The white dwellings, spaced far apart, were
reached by curving driveways. "This is my home town but
I'm just learning to appreciate it," he was saying; "I didn't
have no part of it when I was a kid, kinda grew up in
the back lots. I wanted to be a ballplayer but I had
to go to work . . . old people to support. Working for
this great concern has been like a college education for
me. I never did get through high school. I grew up kind of
a gutter character. Now I can look people in the eye in any
part of town, if you get what I mean . . . Nice part of town
. . . residential," he added as he steered round a corner into
another wider avenue with a strip of green grass and flower-
ing trees down the middle of it. "When I was a young feller
this would have scared the daylights out of me . . . Of course
if you've got a name and a product and a solid concern back
of you a man would be a fool if he couldn't sell. The name
does half the job for you. What a name means to the women
in this country . . . Now you see this is still a nice residential
neighborhood, not so rich but nice."

The grocery where he stopped his car was on a somewhat

shabby corner. Three dogs were dozing outside on the dusty pavement. The window was scrawled over with the prices of items in white paint. When we went in the swinging doors a sleepy housewife was pushing a fairhaired child in a wire cart between ramparts of lettered and packaged groceries.

"Heigh ho Silver!" shouted the salesman trying to break up the afternoon quiet a little.

"He's got saddleburns," answered the grocer, grouchily. Gradually the salesman cheered him up with talk about going to the lake. Keeping up a constant chatter about fishing and boating he walked along the shelves inching the packages of his firm's products forward a little, setting the lettering so that it would catch the light. He pulled a package of stickers advertising special items for Father's Day out of his pocket and placed it tenderly in the grocer's hand. Then he ran back out to the car to fetch a brightcolored cowboy cutout.

"Now we'll fix them up for you, George." He bent the cutout along its dotted lines and set it on a breakfastfood box. "Nifty, don't you think?" George grunted. "How's business?" he went on, offering George a cigarette.

"Not bad," said George. He let a corner of a smile get started on his face.

While, still smiling, George attended to the young woman with the child, the salesman hurriedly built a pyramid of breakfast food packages in the center of the store. Under his breath he whispered, "I think I can sell him on this offer of a baseball bat for every sale of fifteen cases. I can get him on getting that for his boy. I'm letting him off easy this time . . . Next time I'll hit him over the head with a big order."

The next stop was at a little family grocery kept by a man and his wife. As we went in the salesman pointed out where they lived across the street in a white frame house. We had hardly stepped in the door before the wife started complaining that she'd tried the new cake mix and she didn't like it. "It tasted good but the cake came out all soggy like. It looked like putty. I did cook it careful — all the right heats and everything, because I like your products. I did so want it to be right, but how can I recommend it to other people if I can't get it to come out right myself?"

"Now you do something for me, Mrs. Kovak. You try it again and just see if you don't get it to come out right," said the salesman in a pleading tone. Meanwhile we were helping Mr. Kovak move cases of groceries around his crowded little storeroom in back. The salesman was trying to make room for a new display of breakfast foods.

"Oh me," said Mr. Kovak, running stubby fingers through his gray hair. "I ain't got room for another thing."

"I'll tell you what I'll do, Mr. Kovak. I'll call up the jobber and get him to take back those big packages. If the big packages don't move, we'll take them off your hands ... "

"You see," he added when we went back out to the car. "They're nice people but they've got their hands full. They're putting their boy through the University. If some kinds of stuff don't move we just take it off their hands."

"Now watch this feller. He's a character," he said as we walked into a big newlooking grocery store around the corner on a shopping street busy with traffic and buses. "He's got two stores and he thinks he's the king of the cats."

This grocer is a darkhaired youngish man with a bright, sparkling black eye. While he kids a customer from behind the cash register, the salesman looks eagerly around the shelves to spot his products. While he is going over the storeroom, the grocer comes from behind and grabs him by the shoulders.

"What's on your mind?"

He shakes hands affably. "I see a nice spot for my display."

"Say, where's that baseball bat you promised me? The kids are yelling for it. It hasn't come yet."

Meanwhile another salesman handling a detergent has come in and tries to buttonhole the grocer.

"How do you do, sir?"

"I do as I please . . . No, I can't handle all these new items. It just makes cats and dogs."

The grocer comes back to the flour products salesman and gives him a wink. "Now about this cake mix offer . . . What are most of them setting the price at?"

He is distracted by a small boy who wants to buy a nickel cup cake. He comes back and stands over us as we pile up the special trial sale boxes of the cake mix.

Meanwhile the girl with yellow hair who is sweeping out the store has come up . . . "I hear you are giving 'em away," she says. "I sure want to try that new cake."

"Sure we're giving 'em away for thirtynine cents," says the grocer. "Want to see me make a sale right now?"

He waltzes up to a lady who stands frowning over a little pencilled shopping list. "Here's the biggest value in the store."

She looks at him with round eyes.

"But my husband's on a diet. I don't bake any cake."

The grocer comes back to us after waiting on her. "This'll move," he says. "What do you want to bet I've cleaned the whole order out by Saturday night?"

"How about passes to the ballgame?"

"You gave me two passes already on that other deal. Now I want two seats."

"Okay. If you sell the whole lot by Saturday I'll give you two seats."

"Two seats beside the two passes?"

"Okay."

"Well, you just watch me."

With the bright new shiny packages of the cake mixes in his hand the grocer advances on a customer who is pushing a load of groceries out on a glider. After he has totted up her bill on the adding machine he says, "Now let me add thirtynine cents for this special offer of cake mixes."

The woman stares blankly. Her eyes travel indecisively from the grocer's face to the packages of cake mix to the bills in her pocketbook and back again. "But I didn't intend to bake any cake this week . . . "

"You'd better try it, honestly," says the grocer, looking in her face with his sparkling black eyes. "They'll be gone by the time you come around again. This is just a few packages on a special introductory offer the salesman just brought in. Two packages for the price of one plus one warm dime."

The woman's eyelashes began to flutter. "Only a dime more? Well, I guess I can afford that."

"Can't afford not to," said the grocer jovially.

The cake mix goes into the bottom of the big paper bag under the other groceries.

On his way out the salesman takes his hat off with a flourish to the grocer through the glass. "I guess he wants to see that ballgame," he says and lights up a cigarette. "It's all give and take," he adds in a philosophical tone as he gets back behind the wheel of his car. "No use trying to high pressure people. You help them out and they'll help you out."

FRED RUFUS: That fellow knew his business.

EDDY JONES: Just imagine what kind of a country we could have if we had people putting that amount of tact and enthusiasm into getting people to work together in the public interest, instead of working for the interests of some few financial wizards up in that stratosphere you were talking about.

MR. LECTURER: There's a kind of abnegation about salesmanship, the sort of thing you usually associate with religious enthusiasm. It frightens me to think how easily our salesmen could be set to peddling *Pravda* and *Izvestia*.

FRED RUFUS: That's where I think you are wrong. You said yourself that it was the means that counted in a democracy more than the ends ... That young man's ways of doing things make to my way of thinking for far better Americanism than strike pickets going around with clubs intimidating the men who want to keep on working to support their families.

EDDY JONES: Maybe we do use a little gentle persuasion with a club now and then to keep the scabs from going to work: it is no more than your friends taught us with their hired thugs in the old days.

JIM OVERTON: I'm a Truman Democrat, ladies and gentlemen, as you have probably guessed but I still think every citizen ought to be protected against violence. In my opinion a workin'man's got as much right as anybody else to make his own decisions.

FRED RUFUS: Even without the fear of being beaten up if you guess wrong, it's hard enough to give working people, or any other kind of people for that matter, the courage to make decisions for themselves. We have to face the fact that most people are scared to death of decisions. A lot of people would rather be bossed than boss themselves. That weights the dice pretty heavily in favor of the sort of men who like to do the bossing, whether they are high financiers or labor leaders or Communist Commissars.

EDDY JONES: Isn't that because we all got our training in the capitalistic ratrace? (*sarcastically*) That's what you call it, Fred.

FRED RUFUS: They've had socialism in the Soviet Union for more than thirty years. That's a generation of men. Unless the news we read in the papers is entirely false the struggle for personal power is more violent and deadly there

now than it was in the beginning . . . We've had Christianity
for nineteen centuries and a half but still very few of us
follow the precepts of Jesus.

MR. LECTURER: That, in my opinion, is the unique virtue
of the Anglo-Saxon system of equality under the law, and its
practical formulation as a method of government by the
founders of this republic. The United States Constitution is
based on the pessimistic view that no man or group of men
can be trusted with power. Power has to be diffused and
doled out a little at a time; it is in the hands of representatives who have to go back every few years to meet their
electorate face to face. It is a system that works very im-
perfectly, but it works better than most. We must not forget that the norm in human affairs is the frank exploitation
of the governed by the governors.

EDDY JONES: But we Socialists believe in representative
democracy. We believe it ought to represent the real needs
of the people instead of the financial interests.

FRED RUFUS: The greatest financial interest is now the
Executive Department of the United States Government.
With the immense growth of the taxing power and the
power of financial control the administration in office is very
nearly able to control the electorate. The first aim of any
administration, I think you will admit, is to perpetuate itself in power. The second aim of any administration is to
make itself comfortable in power. I defy any man to spend
a few months in Washington without coming away with the
impression that government workers now constitute a class
in the Marxian sense — dedicated to their own class interests
— just as the managers and executives of the great automobile companies, say, constitute a class . . . A new class of
trade union executives is just growing up. Eddy you hang
around the top C.I.O. or A.F. of L. officials for a while and
even you will see the earmarks, just as you'll find them
among the brass hats in the Pentagon. The sort of men I'm

speaking of do put in a lot of work for the organizations they represent, and few of them are entirely devoid of public spirit. In all of these classes you can find men who will on some occasions subordinate their own careers to their idea of the interest of the American people, but it was your own Karl Marx, Eddy, who taught us that in the end it was the mass interest of any particular class that predominated over the individual virtues or vices of its members.

EDDY JONES: We have always admitted that democratic socialism would take education to put across.

FRED RUFUS: The trouble is that you are educating your people the wrong way. All you are teaching them is class war and it's not class war that is going to save us from that shot in the back of the neck the Reds use to eliminate their opponents. They'd probably shoot you, Eddy, before they shot me.

MR. LECTURER: In the trade unions as in the corporations you have two conflicting currents. You have the current that makes for selfgovernment and the current that makes for dictatorship. Let's take a look at a trade union . . .

CAPTION: *Farm Boys in Industry*

"As I was tellin' you," E. K. Bowers was saying, as he wedged himself into one of the small chairs in the hotel room in Gadsden, Alabama, "I was a farm boy raised on Sand Mountain in Blount County. Well I never knew nothin' about unions nor nothin' like that, but in July 1936 I'd gotten married. I was runnin' a little crop on halves. There was nothin' to it but to come to work down in Gadsden . . . My daddy told me I'd better not come down but times were bad and I was desperate."

E. K. Bowers was a longlimbed blackbrowed young man of

the old black Scotch-Irish mountain stock. As he talked he stretched his legs out on a second chair. Then he tumbled off the chair and sprawled on the bed.

"A feller can talk better if he gets hisself comfortable," he apologized in a smiling drawl.

"In them days you couldn't hardly get in the rubber plant unless somebody recommended you. There was a highway patrolman who was a friend of mine and when he carried me over there he said, 'I want you to promise you won't mess with no union.' At that time I didn't know what the union was. I made him that promise. It was the only way to get a job. That was the time the United Rubber Workers was just tryin' to get a start. They'd set up Local Twelve with twenty or thirty guys. Well I went to work there but conditions were terrible. I hired out at thirtytwo cents an hour. Every day or so they'd run somebody out of the plant. A big bunch of thugs would come down the aisle after him akickin' his ass as fast as his feet hit the ground. Well I just kep' my mouth shut. I was inspectin' tires then. We just had three or four days work a week and as soon as I finished I'd light out for home up the mountain. I'd made that promise and I didn't join up. I got a big blackjack and kept it in my toolbag just for self protection. In 1936 when Sherman Dalrymple — he was president of the international union they organized in Akron — came down he tried to address a meeting and they beat him nearly to death. The law didn't do a thing to help him. They had to drive him clear to Birmingham before he could get any medical help. Well they beat the union down. It went plumb out of the picture in 1938 . . . They laid off any man who had anything to do with the union. I just stayed out of the way. In 1943 the Rubber Workers sent in another organizer. By that time I'd been through a whole lot. Every time a man seemed to be making too much money they lowered the piecework rates. They'd fire a man for being late twice. It was bondage, that's what it was. I decided we needed something. The steel union was already organized so when I heard there was an organizer for the rubber workers in town I went in to see him right here in this hotel. 'Boys,' I said when I come in the room, 'I'm not sure I want to join the union but I want to talk about it' . . . Well there was twentythree on my night shift and next morning I had seventeen signed up. I carried them cards in next day. Those organizers just about went crazy. Now it only takes eighteen members to form a local. They brought back the old original charter and you'll see it on the wall. An election was held in 1943 under the War Labor Board and we won three to one."

He heaved himself up off the bed.

"Let's git a move on," he said.

Going down in the elevator he went on: "They froze wages the next day. After that everything we got was through the War Labor Board. Management and the union set up grievance committees to handle problems for the people," he said as we climbed into his lightgray Nash. "The Rubber Workers had an educational program. They sent me up to the Highlander Folk School for a four weeks term in labor relations. Then in '46 I went to the University of Wisconsin for a two weeks course. That was the year the local elected me president. I served till last May."

We are still driving up the broad main street of Gadsden. There is the bus depot and the filling stations and the lunchrooms and the dingy moving picture houses with glaring cowboy posters and the jimcrack clothing and furniture stores. Passing the courthouse E.K. points out the hall where Dalrymple was so badly manhandled for his pains when he tried to hold that meeting thirteen years ago.

Crossing the bridge over the slow green winding Coosa River we find ourselves abreast of a police car. The policeman raises his hand and looks our way and grins. Bowers waves back jauntily.

"Looks like there had been a change in people's attitude."

"There's been a change all right . . .If we have a problem now, we call up the Chief of Police. If he has a problem he calls us up. We'll go around to see him later."

"What do you think caused it?" I'm asking him.

"I'm just a farm boy," he says and winked. "I wouldn't know."

We are over in the industrial suburb of East Gadsden, driving along a street of small new white houses set among mown lawns and trimmed shrubberies.

"Mostly rubber workers here," E.K. is saying. "The plant's just a few blocks." He draws up to the curb in front of a row of yellow brick stores.

The local is in the corner store. An elderly man is sweeping cigarette butts and chewing gum papers off the cement floor. There are a few vending machines and a softdrink counter. The inner wall is plastered to the ceiling with posters advertising local merchants. One corner is piled to the ceiling with yellow chairs to be used at the meetings.

In the office we find a quiet spoken slender man with glasses, named Thompson, the present president. Proudly he points to the framed union charter hanging on the wall. He says he has worked in the plant since 1933 when the A.F. of L. made its first efforts to organize rubber. There'd been a change all right. The worst time in his opinion was between the passing of the Wagner Act and the Supreme Court decision. The hearings before the La Follette Committe had helped. The government had brought pressure on the rubber industry during the war. But the company didn't really call off its dogs till a cease and desist order was served on them by a federal court.

"A lot of them people was misled," said E.K. "There's been a complete reverse among the people of this community in about four years . . . Of course we've got eighteen hundred voters now. In the old days only two or three hundred took the trouble to vote. We put on a big campaign and got up a fund to pay back polltaxes so that the boys could vote."

A squarebuilt man with close cut light hair came in the office. His name was Jim Huey. I asked him if he noticed any change in Gadsden. He smiled. "I surely can see it," he said, "because I've just come back after an absence of several years." He added that he'd first gone to work in the rubber plant for twentyfive cents an hour. He'd gotten interested in the union way back when the A. F. of L. was trying to organize rubber under the N.R.A. "Many a day I didn't know whether I'd go home to my wife and children or end up in the hospital . . . Finally I got laid off along with everybody else who had talked union. I went out of town and got into construction work during the war. When I came back after we had a union and some sort of security I went up to the superintendent and asked him 'Do I look like an outlaw to you?' 'No,' he says. 'Well I'm the same now as I was in 1936.' "

Had there been any change in management personnel in the plant?

No, management was about the same, explained the union president, but policy seemed to have changed. There was a new labor relations man. In the old days what they told you was, "If you don't like it there's a barefoot boy waiting at the gate to take your job." Now they behaved more like reasonable men.

As we talked other men strolled into the office and added a phrase now and then: people in town looked up to Local Twelve now instead of looking down on it. The working people had credit with the merchants; in 1935 only five percent of the rubber workers owned their own homes, today certainly over half did.

"The bankers and merchants think something of us now that we've got money to spend and the politicians talk sweet as sugar now that we're usin' our votes," said a tall young man in a red hunting cap who had just come in.

"We tried to show 'em that we were responsible citizens of the community," E.K. summed it up. "We cut out wild-cat sitdowns. We showed the company that if they'd stick by their word we'd stick by ours."

Jim Huey drives us over in his fine new car to the plant you see stretching in long oblongs of glass and concrete and brick under the sparkling winter sunlight. The four huge chimneys are letting out coils of black smoke into the blue winter sky of the Alabama foothills. Inside a hot sickly spicy smell hits our nostrils. "That's the rubber smell," says E.K. "You get used to that first thing."

In the vestibule you notice a box marked Suggestions. Was there much interest in the suggestion program? There was during the war, they answer, but now any really good suggestion meant men laid off. Not much interest in that.

Walking through the plant with its huge spaces of gray light threaded by overhead conveyors carrying strips of rubber to the tirebuilders, or bulky halfbuilt tires on their way to the hot ranks of moulds shaped like oversized watches, or the crisp finished product moving in a long slow line towards the inspectors, we stop now and then to chat with some man E.K. knows particularly well. Each time I ask how much things have changed in the last ten years.

"It's a different place," says a whitehaired man who is trimming the little ends left on the finished tire when it comes out of the mould. "It's not the wages. It's working conditions are so much better. Now the foreman treats you like a human being. Before he acted like a slavedriver. I wouldn't go back to the way things was not for any amount of wages."

We find a blacksmudged Banbury operator sitting on a truck eating a sandwich from between waxed paper. The Banburies, he explains, are the big hot chopping machines where the rubber is melted and mixed. "There just ain't no comparison"; the words come in a rush; his blue eyes flash in his lean blackened face. "Before we had a union it was just simply hell. Now workin' in a rubber plant may not be heaven but a man can feel some selfrespect."

In the tube department we find a burly popeyed colored man operating an electric truck. E.K. explains that the colored people and the women are all in the union. "It's nicer now," the colored man purrs in his slow molasses tones, "we make better money. About a third of our people own their own homes. Before the union hardly any of 'em did."

"We haven't quite closed the gap in wages yet, but we hope to do it," E.K. apologizes. "Equal pay for equal work all down the line is what we're workin' towards."

"Yessir Mr. Bowers," purrs the colored man cheerfully.

On our way out we stop in to say goodbye to the people in the labor relations office. "If you people will give me a job, I'll go to work inspectin' tires first thing Monday morning," says E.K.

A company man looks up from his desk in surprise.

"Sure enough?" he asks. E.K. nods. "Well, I'll be damned."

As we walk out of the plant E.K. starts to explain in an undertone, "I been away from home on different kinds of union business for the better part of a year. I've got to get back in the good graces of my wife and kids and I've got a farm to look after. Sure enough I'm goin' back to work."

I've been asking him to drive me around the outskirts of town to see what kind of houses the people lived in who worked in the rubber plant. "I can only show you a sample because we got people living in thirteen counties in our local. Some of 'em live on their family farms. Others have bought little farms of their own. As I was tellin' you, I do some farmin' myself."

He drives the Nash fast out a broad highway, crosses over red dirt roads through new developments and doubles back into town by another highway. Everywhere he points out the rubber workers' houses. Most of them are one story, or story and a half houses, small but sparkling new. Some have gardens or a peach orchard of a couple of cultivated acres off which cotton has recently been picked. Some own adjoining filling stations or country groceries.

About fifteen miles out we turn in beside some new fencing and drive up to a white newpainted house on a hill. We find E.K.'s friend hard at work out in a freshly cleared pasture. His son is helping him load out saplings onto a truck. He and Bowers kid back and forth. He wasn't so strong for a union at first, it comes out, but now he says he wouldn't go back to the way things were, not for a million dollars. He works on the midnight shift because that gives him some daylight to work on his farm. From where we stand he shows us with the sweep of an extended arm how he is filling his gullies with brush, and his new fencing and the work he's done on his road and points out the Hereford cattle he's just bought that are cropping the new green pasture and another field where he grazes his neighbor's horses. He has only owned this place a few months. He has two hundred acres along the highway and up the wooded hills. It will take a pile of work to get the place productive and paid for. As the man stands there beside us in his leather jacket with heavy work gloves on his hands and his legs apart bracing himself a little against the chill winter wind you can see in his eyes under bent brows the fields of alfalfa he is talking about for next year, the fattening calves, the new barns, the hoglot, the future full of hard independent work and private personal satisfaction. "I guess I like farmin'," he winds up.

"Me too," says E. K. Bowers.

CAPTION: A Community Changes its Mind

Back in town I made a round of calls on leading citizens.
The elderly politician who held a state office in Montgomery
wouldn't let himself be drawn out on the subject of labor
relations. "As far as I can see," he drawled vaguely, leaning
back in his swivel chair among the calfbound tomes of his
law office, "relations are highly amicable . . . highly amicable."

The Mayor explained the city's program for parks and
playgrounds, and improved school facilities and brought out
a paper showing how wages of city employees had gone up
in twelve years, and how municipal services had improved.
The population had doubled in that time. On the walls of
his office he pointed out photographs of new swimming pools
and of Governor Folsom, of himself posed with Mr. Truman
and of Franklin D. Roosevelt, "one of the greatest men that
ever lived, sir" . . . The Mayor laid the city's growth and
peaceful labor relations to the splendid class of people, sir,
to be found living up in the hills and valleys of northeastern
Alabama, sir, but he admitted that the fact that labor had
been willing to cooperate in all civic projects had greatly
helped him in trying to give the city a progressive administration, sir.

A young attorney who handled a certain amount of business for the unions said he'd felt real ashamed of the things
that had gone on in Gadsden during the years they were
fighting the union. Management and the local citizens and
some of the working people themselves had seen red because
they had felt pressure was being put on them from the outside. Maybe they'd felt they were being intimidated. The
population around here was pretty independent. You could

lead them but you couldn't drive them. One thing he could say was that people had been willing to change their minds. In the last few years the Rubber Worker's Union, for one, had done an outstanding job in public relations. They had inaugurated a practice of asking the Mayor and leading citizens to their anniversary dinners. They worked on the Community Chest and Red Cross drives. When people got to know the union representatives personally, to eat at the same table with them, they soon discovered that they didn't have horns and a tail.

Yes, indeed, said another attorney, eagerly, labor peace has been the making of Gadsden. The feeling against unions there had been particularly bitter because back in the early twenties a violent strike had ruined what was then the town's most important industry, some railroad car works and repair shops. After the strike failed the shop had burned down one night and public opinion had blamed the strikers. The railroad had never rebuilt the repair shops but now there were two flourishing industries on that very site. The picture had changed completely . . . In his opinion a decrease in juvenile delinquency had gone along with the increase in wages. One of the reasons Allis Chalmers had brought in its great agricultural machinery plant was that the city had a reputation for good labor relations. The Rubber Workers had taken the lead in all that. Now anybody starting up a new civic enterprise went to the Rubber Workers first.

The pretty blonde lady in a winecolored dress with a lace collar who was secretary of the Etowah County T.B. Association said that and more. She said the Rubber Workers had never failed to help in any way the Association asked. The Rubber Workers was the only union represented on the board. If they thought a thing was for the good of the community they'd pitch in and work . . . Here was just a little incident: the Business and Professional Workers Club

wanted to get hold of a wire recording machine. The union
had one that they used to teach public speaking. When nobody else would loan them one Mr. Bowers came down with
the Rubber Workers machine and ran it for them, although
he had tickets to a ballgame that afternoon and wanted to go
awful bad . . . "People appreciate things like that . . . People
feel a lot kinder towards unions on account of Mr. Bowers,"
she said.

"Sure the Rubber Workers have been well led both
locally and in the international office in Akron," admits the
man from management's side of the fence I find smoking a
cigar on the davenport in the lobby of the hotel, "but we
think the company's done a good job too. It takes two to
strike a bargain. Fundamentally good labor relations consists of two men sitting down to argue reasonably across a
table. There has to be mutual respect. If each of these men
is able to carry out what he agrees to then you can go places
. . . We've all of us had to learn a lot of new tricks in the last
few years but I guess it hasn't done us any harm."

Back in Washington I went around to see a labor statis-
tician who had the reputation of being a man wellposted in
union affairs. In his dim office piled high with filing cases
and mimeographed sheets I was asking him how good a
sample of the C.I.O. organizations the Rubber Workers was.
"Of course it's not the most dramatic of the unions," he
answered, "but it may be one of the soundest. When the
C.I.O. was being established they led the way with their sitdown in the Goodyear plant and their famous picketlines.
Since then it's been . . . What's the quotation about 'happy
is the people that has no history'?"

From the beginning they had an oldtime American type of
leadership, he went on to say, with the advantages and disadvantages that implied. There had only been two Inter-

national Presidents. Sherman Dalrymple, the first, was a man of great personal magnetism and an eloquent speaker, but with little of the urge for personal aggrandizement that often went with that particular makeup. He had been appointed out of the Goodrich local by William Green and then had been elected by their first convention when the union was organized on selfgoverning lines under the C.I.O. He was a thoroughly honest selfsacrificing kind of man. He never would take an adequate salary. He was the son of a hotelkeeper in a small West Virginia town and had been a Captain of Marines in World War I. He had the same general background as the backwoodsmen from the hilly Appalachian states who poured off the farms into the rubber shops during the early boom days of the industry. During the second war Dalrymple had been dead set against any labor man's seeking exemption from military service. A lot of the Rubber Workers' prestige out in Akron was due to the fact that Dalrymple and Buckmaster, his vice-president, showed themselves during the war to be patriotic Americans of the old back country stripe.

When Dalrymple retired, partly on account of ill health brought on by the terrible beating he had suffered down in Gadsden, his vice-president, a man of somewhat similar character, though less the emotional orator, was elected in his place. Leland Buckmaster came from the Firestone local. He'd been raised on a farm in southern Indiana and had studied to be a schoolteacher before he went to work in rubber. These two men had given the rubber workers a grassroots type of leadership. They didn't give the militant romantic leadership some labor leaders did but they were both men with a profound sense of personal responsibility. "They have kind of set the tone for the organization. You'll see out in Akron. Although the industry is decentralizing, Akron is still the capital of rubber. Akron sets the tone."

CAPTION: *Rubber Workers International*

In the limousine driving into Akron in a cold drizzle from the airport on my way to visit the international office I met a tire salesman. "Lord what a dump," he was grumbling. "I have to come here once a year and I always dread it. The climate's terrible. There's nothing to do in the evening but go to hear hillbilly evangelists . . . The company does its best to make us happy while we're here, but I sure don't look forward to Akron."

I asked him where his home was.

"Florida," he answered proudly, "where the labor unions don't run everything and there's sunshine all the year."

I found the international office of the union — its full name is the United Rubber, Cork, Linoleum and Plastic Workers of America — in a small uptodate building which the union owns and operates. I asked the men I met there the same question I asked in Gadsden: How are the Rubber Workers fitting in with the rest of the organizations that make up American community life?

"Well," the general tenor of the answers was, "we're not so sure how the companies feel, but things have certainly changed a great deal since the days of the great sitdown when we put out the longest picketline in history in the zero cold; that was a real nasty fight with the community against us, but now we're in the city council and the Community Chest, we're in about everything in this town except the Portage Country Club . . . We feel the Rubber Workers are part of Akron now."

Mr. Buckmaster was out of town that day so I spent the afternoon talking to two young men from his brain trust, one a scholarly individual from the University of Chicago, who was Research Director and the other a young man with the build of a football player who was only two years out of Harvard. He had no labor background at all. As he put it he was continuing his education. He had come out and found himself a job in a rubber shop and then had gone to work for the union because he wanted to learn what kind of a country he lived in. I found myself devoutly hoping that more sharpeyed young men from the colleges were doing what this young man was doing.

When I told them I understood the Rubber Workers had had no history since the first famous sitdown, they both got to their feet. History had been popping and sizzling all summer. They'd just come out of a knockdown and dragout political campaign. It had come about probably because Mr. Buckmaster hated so to play politics. The average labor leader spent as much time mending his political fences as any wardboss. Mr. Buckmaster was the sort of man who believed if he did what he thought was right, the rank and file would understand without too much explaining and would back him up. In the long run it had worked out that way but it had been nip and tuck. Last summer the opposition had managed to unseat him as president.

A radical faction — politically they were supporters of Henry Wallace — grouped round the president of the Goodrich local, had captured the executive board at the national convention the year before and had gotten Buck-master removed on a pretext and had come within an inch of taking over the leadership of the international. All the summer of 1949 had been spent in desperate electioneering in the locals. At the September convention Buckmaster's supporters had won a clean sweep. The next job had been to weed out the Communists and near-Communists who had taken advantage for the Party line of what was basically a political fight staged by ambitious personalities trying to get into positions of power. Communists were something Mr.

Buckmaster knew a good deal about. In fact, he was one of Phil Murray's most trusted advisers on the Communist issue.

The next day I met Mr. Buckmaster at his office. He turned out, as he'd been described, a tall quietspoken retiring man with glasses. His manner of talking was that of the principal of a good rural high school. He'd pause a long while before he'd venture an opinion. There was a certain amount of quiet Hoosier humor in the way he put things. Obviously he was not a man given to broad generalizations. One of his favorite ways of turning off a question was to answer in a slow low tone, "I don't know enough about that to say."

He took me out to lunch, with some union officials, at the Portage Hotel, which he explained was an old hangout of folks from the Rubber Workers' office. Although the place was crowded, the waitresses hovered solicitously about the long table we occupied in the middle of the dark oldfashioned coffee shop. It was obvious that they thought the world of Mr. Buckmaster and his friends. He was explaining that it was in this Portage Hotel that the convention had been held that switched the Rubber Workers over into the newly formed C.I.O. He told how William Green had sat there with tears running down his face. He pointed out the circular seat in the apselike depression at the end of the room in the center of which John L. Lewis used to plant himself when he came to Akron during the strenuous days of the sitdowns.

Back in the office I was introduced to some members of the staff. There was a square sallow slowtalking man who had charge of compensation and the unions' campaign against occupational hazards. His name was John R. Kumpel. He was born and raised in the Illinois coalfields. When he was fifteen he went to work in a mine. When he was twentyone he came to Akron attracted by the higher pay in the rubber shops. "I saw so many men injured when I was a boy in the coalmines that I've always been interested in the prevention of industrial accidents," he said, looking up from the mass of papers on his desk. When the 1944 convention set up a Compensation Department, Dalrymple had put him in charge of it instead of hiring a lawyer. He wanted a man who really felt it in his bones. So compensation and occupational hazards had become his life work. "We can't all be Mexican generals, you know. Some of us have to attend to the details."

"We have managed to cut the accident rate just about in half. Ten years ago we lost from sixteen to seventeen percent of man hours worked through accidents. Now, for rubber tires and tubes we have dropped to six and nine tenths percent."

As I got up to leave his office he said in an oddly apologetic tone, "By the way, I might add that I'm a Republican."

Fleet Perrine, the man who ran Buckmaster's campaign for reinstatement in the presidency, is still the union's General Organizational Director. The post corresponds to Promotion and Sales in a manufacturing concern, and has internal political implications besides. He sits at his desk with an energetic and forceful air, looks very much the sort of man you would find in a similar position in industry. Only the large knotted hands clasped over his desk betray the fact that he once worked in a rubber shop.

"We don't raid other unions," Mr. Perrine was saying. "We try to stay out of a place where they've got a union. Rubber is pretty well organized and so is linoleum and cork. Plastics is the new field. It's a rapidly expanding industry with some immense plants but a great many small plants too, some of them even family shops set up in garages and old barns. It's a job to go after those birds." Outside of the drive for recruiting new locals it was the district organizers' business to service the local unions all over this country and Canada. Especially they furnished time study men the locals called in to help in disputes on job evaluation. The management man made his study and the union man made his and if the two of them couldn't agree they took it to arbitration. A great deal of the time they did agree. The union time study men came right out of the shop, they were picked to take courses in time study work. "We'd rather have men out of the shop than hired experts, they have the thinking of the working people."

CAPTION: *Akron the Tire Builders' Town*

Going down in the elevator I asked an elderly man who had the burly look of a rubber worker whether Akron was a good place to live and raise a family. "It didn't used to be. Everybody thought they'd come here and make big money in the rubber shops and go along home. The companies used to threaten that if we brought in unions they'd move out and turn Akron into a ghost town, but now it looks to me as if the working people got along better here than they did in most places."

I kept thinking of that as I walked along the main streets between the broad show windows of department stores, well stocked with goods that had quite a metropolitan air about them and particularly when I drove out through the residential districts where there seemed to be no dwellings worse than the big old frame houses with broad porches set on lawns along treelined streets that were considered a prerogative of the middle class a quarter of a century ago. These were nearly all the houses of rubber workers. Nearly seventy percent owned their own homes, I'd been told. There was an air of space and ease about them that expressed very patently the fact that the average hourly wage of their owners was a dollar seventythree.

In one of these houses, on one of those suburban streets on the wooded edge of town, I sat in the parlor talking to a baldheaded man in his shirtsleeves. He worked as a tire-builder in a rubber shop. When he apologized for the appearance of his house and yard, explaining that he'd been so tied up with community business recently that he'd let everything go to pieces, I couldn't help telling him that his house looked better than most of the places my friends lived in. He laughed and said he guessed he was pernickety. Maybe it was because his dad was a Scotchman. His dad had worked for thirtyfive years at the Goodyear plant, as a foreman, and had never seen any need for a union. In spite of his bringing up he said he certainly saw a need for a union. "If we could only get our people out to the meetings. Our local has thirteen thousand members and we consider it a good turnout if we can induce two hundred and fifty to come to a meeting . . . " You could correct a lot of things if you could keep the interest of the rank and file. A good union newspaper would be worth more than a lot of flowery speeches of Johnny-come-latelies who were looking to their own personal gain more than to anything else. "We should do more to sell the union to the rank and file and to the community at large . . . I put us down as a sales organization."

Suddenly he looked at me and grinned. "You've guessed it by this time. I'm a Republican in a Democratic town, but they let me live," he said. The union was pretty powerful in local politics, he went on, they had seven members on the city council. The mayor was still a Republican but he couldn't have been elected without labor support. Akron used to be the bosses' town. Now it was a working people's town. He'd been putting in a lot of time recently campaigning for the Community Chest. He'd been called in when collections were lagging in his local. "The charitable work benefits our people more than anybody else in town. I feel they should pitch in and support it."

Next afternoon I sat in on a session of a grievance committee at a mediumsized tire plant on the other side of town. At one end of a T-shaped table sat a slender young man who did time study work for the company and a big curly haired Syrian with a voice like the bull of Bashan. He had worked his way up in the plant to be an official of the union local and had been hired over to be a spokesman for the management, so it was explained when I was introduced to him. At the other end of the table sat the negotiating chairman for the union, a tall bulky darkhaired Swede with a quiet judicial manner that would have done credit to the Supreme Court. Beside him sat the union's time study man. Leaning back in their chairs against the opposite wall were several shopstewards and the president of the local. The union men all wore their workclothes. It was a slategray afternoon of sleet and rain lashing against the windows. The steampipes hissed and rattled. There was a good deal of yawning. The lights were on in the darkpanelled conference room. The discussion proceeded drowsily, enlivened by gusts of heavyhanded kidding. Most of the men were smoking and seemed to be enjoying the warmth and comfort of the conference room, and the feeling of sitting back and stretching out their legs on the company's time.

The cases under discussion nearly all involved seniority. There had been cutbacks in the labor force during the summer and now men were being rehired. As each man came back there had to be some reshuffling of jobs to conform with seniority rules. The union men brought up a couple of safety problems, a leaky steampipe, floor clearance in front of an elevator.

When the labor relations director ushered me in an argument was going on about some man who was getting slack in his work. "I'll bring my little boy in tomorrow," roared the company spokesman. "He can make that much money standing on one foot."

"What happened to this guy?" asked the labor relations director, laughing.

"It's a new type machine," explained the union president.

"You can't run a farm and do a job in here at the same time," shouted the company spokesman.

"Last Tuesday we explained that what a man did outside didn't count," replied the union president in a tone of exaggerated patience.

They couldn't seem to decide this case so they went on to the next. This was a case of job selection by a man being rehired. The man wasn't satisfied with his rate.

"What do you want me to do, pay him six hours for an hour's work?"

"I'll tell you what's happened," said the big negotiating chairman soberly. "The job has changed since we put the rate in."

"All right," said the labor relations director. "We'll check the rate."

"Now there's this fellow doing light work over in the tube room. He thinks he ought to be paid at his old rate before he got hurt. Now he's just getting the day work rate."

"He can make more money stayin' home," roared the company spokesman.

"But he wants to make a little money to buy crockery to sell for Christmas."

"Next thing he'll come over here with a tin cup."

Everybody burst out laughing.

"All right. All right, here's another. Let's get this one before anything else," said the president of the local in a pleading tone . . . "We all get a lot of hell from the people outside that isn't working," he added ruefully, scratching his head.

This seniority business was as much of a headache for the union boys as it was for management, said the labor relations director as we settled down in his office again. It cost the company a lot of money every month changing men around, training them for new jobs. It was a headache but they had to live with it for the life of this particular agreement. The truth of the matter was that a lot of problems were coming up in labor-management relations that just couldn't be handled like a game of poker. Take pensions, for an example. That big Swede the negotiating chairman was as levelheaded and fairminded a man as you'd hope to find. He wouldn't run for president but he did a grand job on the grievance committee. If only there were more like him. Some of the union officials were torn between their own good judgment and the fact that they had to bring home the bacon to their constituents. They forgot things weren't like wartime any more when the sky was the limit. Now competitors were cutting prices. Management had to keep down costs.

When the Syrian came back to the office I asked him if the men didn't resent his switching to the management side of the fence.

"Well, they do and they don't," he said. "We've gotten to the point where we can kid about things and not get so mad at each other. To tell the truth in Akron there just ain't the bitterness there was."

That night I had dinner at a new drivein restaurant a little out of town, all glass bricks and floodlights outside and white and red plush decorations in the style of Dorothy Draper inside, with a professorial little man from Vienna, very much the type of Herr Doktor you would have met in the old days meditatively drinking coffee with whipped cream on it at a café on the Ring or addressing a class of serious young proletarian thinkers in one of the handsome Socialist apartment houses so soon to be battered by shellfire. He had escaped to this country with his family in the thirties and found himself living in Akron with a job in the

Public Library. He had seen Akron in industrial war and during the period of cooperation when we were all fighting a common enemy and in the present period of organized bargaining. I brought out my dogeared old question: Had Akron improved as a city to live in since labor attained citizenship.

He must go back a little bit, he explained earnestly. It was difficult for a European arriving in America . . . American life was so raw. Life had none of what Europeans considered the alleviations of culture, the little trimmings that made the days pleasant. At first he had thought Akron was dreadful, a honkytonk boom town jerrybuilt for a few years to be abandoned when industry moved somewhere else. Akron will be a ghost town, people said, and nobody seemed to care. How could he live there? he used to ask himself. But then in watching the development of the relations between labor and industry and between labor and the community it had suddenly come over him that he was seeing the beginning of a civilization. Everything was brutally fluid and changing. That was the excitement of American life. Now he feels that Akron is his home. In the very few years he has lived here he has seen the city grow and change, from a battleground become a community, right under his eyes. He knows he mustn't be too optimistic, but there is more satisfaction in the beginnings of a beginning than in anything else in the world.

(MR. LECTURER *lets himself drop into a chair at the end of the conference table and takes a long drink of water.*)

As I was saying, ladies and gentlemen, it's the hardest thing in the world to describe a social process while it's going on. I hope I've managed to transmit to you my feeling that it is possible to go to work on our society and direct its course but that first we must study it carefully and dispassionately.

EDDY JONES: What's wrong with that last picture? It looks to me like a tolerably accurate picture of a democratic well run union, a little on the conservative side perhaps.

MR. LECTURER: Did you notice one thing? The unions are having the same difficulty in getting their members to go to meetings that corporations have in holding the attention of their stockholders or political parties trying to drive their voters to the polls. They are all fighting the apathy of the average citizen. At the same time they are holding a club over his head. I was very much shocked to hear the answer a man who had seemed to me a pretty progressive officer of one of the union locals gave when talking about sitdown strikes. One of the old timers asked him if he'd be in favor of beating up scabs if they should have another strike. "Sure," he said, "after what they did to us I wouldn't have no scruples." . . . Now you can't enforce selfgovernment with a club. That sober national president of the Rubber Workers Union had to build himself a political machine to keep in office. You can't encourage individual initiative by rigging a political machine.

There are two sides to this trend towards dictatorship. On the one side you have the apathy of the electorate and on the other you have the urge to dominate of the powerhungry individuals who are always ready to climb — booted and spurred as Jefferson used to say — on the backs of the rest of us. If you could cure this civic apathy — and some of it is more fear of consequences than it is apathy — you'd go far towards finding a cure for the weaknesses of selfgovernment. There are a great many people in this country, in the trade unions, in the corporations, in local and national politics, sincerely sweating day by day to make selfgovernment work. Something must be done to make them feel they are all working for the same common cause if they are to have the courage to stand up against club rule and machine rule.

FRED RUFUS: What we've got to have in this country is

something that will give people back the feeling of being the masters of their destiny.

JAKE JEFFRIES: Work is the only way, doing work they understand the importance of . . . Now farming is a pretty speculative business, but the farmer can see that his work counts.

EDDY JONES: You farmers have had a boom period. Now you are starting in on a period of overproduction again, like the late twenties. How are you going to feel when you go back to burning wheat in the stove?

MRS. EDWARDS: We are all agreed that we are in for controls. We want controls administered by the people.

JAKE JEFFRIES: Of course, if we go on taking government subsidies we are going to have to take government controls; the question is how to get the local boards to take the initiative.

MRS. EDWARDS: Isn't it time we decided what kind of society we wanted, and started to take steps towards getting it?

MR. LECTURER: The trend at present is towards massive bureaucracy in industry and in government. At present, as Mr. Rufus suggested, we exercise very little more control over our President than the Argentines do over theirs. They both trade in the same type of demogogic appeal based on the vote of working people somewhat forcibly massed into unions. By habit and tradition the President of the United States has to be a little more careful to give the impression of obeying the law. I happened to be in Argentina during the 1948 campaign and it was laughable how easily you could have interchanged the speeches that were being delivered by Mr. Truman and by Mr. Peron. You couldn't say that of the Opposition. The Opposition in the Argentine was dealing with realities and made much better sense than our Republicans did . . . We must admit that political thinking in the United States has been bankrupt for a number of years. Our basic difficulty in my opinion lies in the fact that we have slipped from one type of obsolete thinking — I mean the oldfashioned laissez faire capitalist thinking, which never did really apply in this country because so much of what we called free enterprise grew out of windfalls like the discovery of oilwells, or handouts by the nation like free land to the railroads — to a camouflaged socialism which is equally obsolete. Politicians and worthy persons orating in forums (even as you and I) toss around dogmatic statements from one book or the other more or less indiscriminately, on the theory that any stick will do to beat a dog with. As Mrs. Edwards so aptly said we must know what we want and look around for ways of getting it. That will require a renewed formula for selfgovernment.

FRED RUFUS (*jumping to his feet*): First we've got to throw the rascals out. Inflation and ruin . . .

JAKE JEFFRIES: Excuse me, Fred, I'm not worried about inflation. In my opinion money in the modern world is only a bookkeeping proposition. The important thing is, no matter how you measure the buying units, for the producer to get his fair slice of the pie and the wageworker his and the distributor his and the speculator — he still has a useful role to play — enough return to induce him to risk his cash . . .

FRED RUFUS: If you'll excuse my interrupting, Jake, that's just what we are complaining about. The government controls the value of your money. The administration is able to auction off the slices of your pie to the highest bidder in votes and campaign pledges.

MISS SMITHERS (*with a wail*): The way the great offices of the state were auctioned off at the end of the Roman Republic. Good gracious, it looks as if we had reached the point where all the popular democracies of the past went on the rocks.

MR. LECTURER: If we could be left alone between the two oceans as we were a hundred years ago we could eventually muddle through to some sort of solution as we did in Civil

War times. But we are not going to be left alone. We cannot afford a civil war between Management and Labor even if it never came to a Gettysburg. We are going to have to find our solution under fire, under fire by particularly destructive weapons in the hands of particularly fanatical opponents who are determined to stamp out the spirit of liberty on this earth . . .

FRED RUFUS *(interrupting)*: And you and me with it, brothers and sisters, don't forget that. I might add that if all we can do to fight the monolithic slave states abuilding in Asia is produce a slave state of our own we won't be much further ahead, now will we?

A MAN WITH A FOREIGN ACCENT *(who has sat all evening taking copious notes on the discussion, raises his hand. He has a thin scarred face and a wispy, drooping mustache. He wears a monocle and a dinner coat)*: Beg pardon, please . . . one moment only . . . This confusion would account for the alternations in the American policy that are so puzzling to Europeans and Asiatics alike. The American government, particularly through your Department of State, talks everything for the people, but practically it shows only scorn and contempt for the people. Where in any of the wartime deals with the Soviet Union made behind the backs of the peoples concerned has there been any regard shown for the American principle of selfdetermination? The American government makes great speeches about wanting the backing of the democratic men and women in the Western World, but how does it treat the displaced persons? What has it done for the refugees from Soviet tyranny? Why is it easier for a Fascist or a Communist than for an honest democrat to get a visa to the United States? If the American people believe in selfgovernment and practice it why are their true feelings so ill represented by their government?

MR. LECTURER: That is a most understandable question, sir, and one that makes any good American feel thoroughly

ashamed of himself. In my opinion we have brought ruin on a large part of the world and find ourselves in danger of attack today largely because we forgot once too often that our basic principles were things not of words but of deeds.

EDDY JONES *(getting to his feet and crying out in a voice almost tearful with earnestness)*: Jeepers Crow, ladies and gentlemen, I don't see why democratic socialism isn't the answer. We've just had an example of a trade union that has solved two very urgent problems successfully by democratic means. Why doesn't the answer for America lie in democratic or, as Mr. Lecturer pedantically insists, selfgoverning trade unions on the one hand and selfgoverning cooperatives on the other?

JAKE JEFFRIES: I'm just a country boy, but I thought you Socialists wanted the government to operate everything.

EDDY JONES *(laughing)*: I'll settle for the cooperatives and the trade unions.

FRED RUFUS: Eddy, you people make me sick. Top dog will continue to be top dog no matter what name you call him by. Management will have to manage. You fellows really don't know what you want. All you are capable of doing is stirring up class war and class hatred. Any wily politician or any totalitarian machine can take advantage of you. Haven't you learned anything from the fate of the Socialists in Spain or in the Balkans or in Poland or in the Argentine?

MRS. EDWARDS: Let's stay home, Mr. Rufus, and see what we've got to do here, please let's stay home.

MR. LECTURER: The work of this country is done by a tangle of pyramiding corporations, most of them run from the top by small groups of powerful men much the way the Communist Party (that great international corporation for the capture of political power) is run from the top. Opposed to these corporations, representing the interests of the wage earners about to the same degree as the financial top layer represents the interests of the investors, has grown up a tangle of pyramiding unions, some of them tolerably self-governing and some of them dictatorially administered by bumptious czars. Out of that welter of corporate interests comes the great bulk of our national activity, of production, of wages, of conflicts. Small business struggles on, oscillating on the edge of extinction like the Indians and buffalo.

FRED RUFUS (*interrupting*): At this rate if it is to continue it will probably have to be preserved in reservations and national parks. (*laughter*)

MR. LECTURER: Now no human arrangements are perfect, but even with all the loss of time and energy in pulling and hauling between management, and labor, and government impinging on every section of the economy with taxes and subsidies, the present parallelogram of forces performs tolerably well in producing goods and services and wages and rewards. If only it would go on working as well as it does now. From the long term view the picture is not so bright. We are drifting towards a dangerous merger of political and economic power. The people become more and more apathetic because the problems are too much out of their grasp for their understanding. Nobody knows which wheel to put his shoulder to. The cure lies in increased participation. Participation in local selfgovernment, unit by unit, in all this complication of hierarchies would tend to cure the apathy which is the worst disease of the masspro- duction economy.

The problem is, of course, how to bring it about. There are a few hopeful signs; profit-sharing devices, suggestion systems, the management labor committees we had in war- time, the growth of the cooperative idea in enterprise. They are frail straws but they exist. I believe and hope that they reflect a new set in the wind, but I have to admit it is hard to tell today whether these hopeful signs I see are the last vestiges of a vanishing habit of selfgovernment or the new budding of its renewal. There comes a point in every man's life when he must take the risk of believing. I believe that our salvation depends on our making a stand and recklessly investing all our hopes and energies in these vestiges and renewals.

MRS. EDWARDS: When do we start? We mustn't forget that the repeal of prohibition seemed hopeless until enough sensible public spirited men and women got together and made their weight felt. Why not start an association for the revival of selfgovernment? I'm ready to pay my dues right now.

FRED RUFUS: Mrs. Edwards, we've got enough wellintentioned organizations in this country, all collecting dues and sporting celebrities on their letterheads, to save the world and several of the planets besides . . . But before we mount our snow white steeds and ride off in several directions at once, let's find out where we want to go.

(*A squatfaced young man with slicked back black hair who has been sitting beside a girl in a raincoat with pixie glasses jumps to his feet. He stands glaring at Mr. Lecturer out of gimlet eyes.*)

THE CHINESE STUDENT: The unknown person who is taking the liberty to address you, ladies and gentlemen (*he begins in correct but slightly lopsided English*), is a Chinese student. At the risk of making myself objectionable to the present company and to the secret police who will wish perhaps to transport me, I cannot hold back my speech. The Chinese people long ago loved the American people because they came as missionaries of the bearded God. They were simple childlike people who taught keep your ears clean and marry only one woman and be kind to everybody and the bearded God will make you rich. Many Chinese tried the formula and were successful. That was in the old days of my parents when everybody hoped for justice and peace. But now history has taken a different turn according to Marx which

Americans are too childish to understand. Americans still think you can buy justice and peace with money. Today in the world there is only power. In spite of yourselves your society is falling into leadership patterns pioneered by Communist Party. But you are too stupid and hypocritically childish boldly to make use of power to change the world. This is the age of power over men. The men of intelligence and sensibility out of working class and petit bourgeoisie must organize for power like Chinese Communist Party. In China Americans all the time talk talk democracy while they help reactionary warlords who steal from people. In spite of them China will march on forward with help of Soviets. All this democratic talk talk has become very silly and causes among Chinese people only hatred and scorn. Language of today is untrammelled power to make new China. If anybody objects and starts talk talk like Americans we strike him down. I cannot stand to hear all this nonsense fit only for trash heap. History has passed you by. Your childish hypocritical false civilization is on brink of disaster ... When you fall to ruin ... like the ruin of London and Berlin ... under the assaults of the Red armies ... from the disciplined people of China will only come happy laughter. *(His voice has risen to a shriek. He's taken with a hysterical fit of falsetto giggles. The girl in the raincoat pulls him to his feet and hurries him out the door.)*

MRS. EDWARDS: Well, it is real nice to know what our guests really think of us.

MISS SMITHERS *(with a nervous laugh)*: Where were we before Attila the Hun broke in? What our Chinese friend ... I mean enemy ... is saying is very much to the point, but he unfortunately has got it all backwards.

MRS. EDWARDS: It's as if our Rockefeller Foundation people who are fighting malaria should start breeding the anopheles mosquito instead of exterminating it.

MR. LECTURER: Politics becomes much easier if you rely on

the evil in human nature instead of on the good — terror and envy and hatred are powerful explosives — but the result, as the theologians taught, is wailing and a gnashing of teeth. We have no need to look for the theologians' hell beyond this world. In our time we have seen it on earth . . . That hell is behind all these things we have been discussing, the brute reality of war and slavery and the suffering that men delight in inflicting on each other . . . Our present industrial society has entered a phase where it can't do without the waste of production for war to keep its machines from clogging with their own productivity. It's interesting to note that, for a very different set of reasons, neither have the leaders of the Soviet apparatus found any way of keeping their Juggernaut going than by constant preparation for war. There is no occasion to believe that communism in China will follow any different course. We can only hope that the Chinese won't be too good at it.

MISS SMITHERS *(with tears streaming down her face)*: If there's no future for the world but constant war that just means the end of everything any decent person desires . . . Oh I knew I shouldn't have come. I shan't sleep a wink all night again.

MR. LECTURER: Mr. Jones, has socialism any answer to that dilemma?

EDDY JONES: Eventually, yes.

MR. LECTURER: But the current towards war has got to be dealt with right now . . . this year . . . It is already too late . . . Mr. Rufus, has capitalism any answer?

FRED RUFUS: All I can say is that the more socialistic society gets the more warlike it gets. But I see no way of turning that particular clock back. I see nothing to do except to keep the country strong and prepare for the worst and pray that the next war will be the last.

MR. LECTURER: If that's true we must immediately throw everything we have into saving the Republic. Wage workers and managers alike must forget the class war and think only about saving the Republic. By the Republic I mean those trends and currents in our society that build up the habits of selfgovernment and strengthen civil liberties and open up for every man the opportunity to find the place in our society his deserts entitle him to. If we can't save the Republic from destruction at home we shall not be able to save it from foreign enemies. If we manage to save it at home we need have no fear of the atomic bomb. Even if half our cities were destroyed the habits of a life of freedom and dignity would live on. If the White House and the Capitol at Washington were reduced to heaps like Berlin the Republic would live on in the behavior of the American communities that survived.

JAKE JEFFRIES (*with a whoop*): We'll hold them on the Mississippi.

THE JANITOR (*a stately, whitehaired man who has been standing in the door*): For the Lord's sake mister, be explicit. This ain't the Fourth of July . . . You must excuse me but I hear so many ends of lectures. I always come in for the final flourish and its all very exciting but nothing ever seems to come of it.

MR. LECTURER: Well, I'll try to be explicit but first maybe you'll tell the ladies and gentlemen something about your own political habits. What's the name of your Congressman?

JANITOR: I don't rightly know.

MR. LECTURER: What is your Congressional District?

JANITOR (*belligerently*): We're all good Democrats in my district and we vote the straight Democratic ticket or we know the reason why. I'll have you know, sir, that I'm a member in good standing of the Mulvaney Democratic Club.

MISS SMITHERS: Oh dear, oh dear. We'll go the way of the poor Athenians in the Peloponnesian War, but we haven't built our Parthenon yet . . . I do wish I could get people to read Thucydides.

FRED RUFUS: I guess we'll be more like the Carthaginians. They didn't leave anything behind.

EDDY JONES: Democratic socialism could save us.

FRED RUFUS: Free enterprise properly applied will go on making us, as it has in the past, the greatest nation the world has ever known.

MRS. EDWARDS: The American way of life . . .

MR. LECTURER: Please allow me to point out that the phrases we have just been using are merely magical formulae. They are not the tools that can be used in a reasonable investigation of national behavior. We have got to find exact terms if we are to learn enough about human behavior to be able to influence it. In the first place we have to go back to a description of what we've got. What we have been trying to describe is a society based on mass production and organized in a great number of administrative hierarchies. Our political life is based on an obsolete geographical arrangement that filled the needs of the mercantile and agrarian society of a century ago pretty well . . .

MRS. EDWARDS: But I thought you believed in our form of government.

MR. LECTURER: I do. The principles of representative government by checks and balances based on law and not on administrative whim are as sound as they ever were. What has happened is that the political structure no longer conforms to the economic and social structure. Paralleling the political setup we have a host of new forms of government set up by the needs of industrial management and of labor and of all the various classes of men that make up our society. Pressure groups are organs that have appeared because they were really needed, as links and channels between the corporate organizations that make up the community and the national and state and municipal governments. Some of these new organs are socially good and some of them are bad. We must start weeding out the bad and saving the good. The nation must be like a battleship stripping for action. We can no longer keep on board any apparatus that doesn't contribute directly to our safety.

If we are to save the Republic we must continually be aware of the aims of the Republic. Our safety lies in the fulfillment of these aims. You remember Lincoln's statement that the United States differed from other nations in that it was dedicated to a proposition. That proposition has remained basically unchanged through our history, though the means of putting it into effect change as the shape of society changes. That proposition implies that the cohesive force which holds our nation together is not religious creed or common ancestry but the daily effort to give to every man as much opportunity as is possible to fulfill himself in his own way, protected by law from the arbitrary measures of those in authority. The men who founded this nation tried the unheard of experiment of founding a state which would be the servant instead of the master of its citizens, of all its citizens. Our safety in each crisis in our history has been measured by how near we came to achieving that aim. Our crimes and failures as a nation, and there have been plenty of them, have always occurred in situations that found the electorate and its leaders hazily forgetful of the basic reason for the existence of the United States. In the old days our isolation gave us a vast margin for error. We are now entering a period when the margin for error is narrowing with breathtaking rapidity. The time is coming when every citizen worthy of the name will have to ask himself at every hour of the day: is what I am doing helping save the Republic or is it not?

MRS. EDWARDS: But how are you to tell? I find myself voting on all sorts of things I don't understand. I usually try to follow the lead of some reliable civic organization.

MR. LECTURER: We've got to learn how to tell . . . If we put half the energy into a drive to save our liberties, that the

Communists, for an example, managed even in this country to harness to their drive to destroy them, we will have done well. We've got to invent new methods for the participation of more citizens in the apparatus of industrial society.

MISS SMITHERS: But how can we? I'd love to be helpful, but I'm not as young as I was. I wouldn't know what to do.

A MAN IN ARMY UNIFORM (*who has been silently chewing gum in a corner*): Don't forget our amphibious landings. During the war we carried out the first successful amphibious landings since Julius Caesar landed in Britain. It took ingenuity, but we did it.

THE MAN WITH THE FOREIGN ACCENT: My dear sir, how about Napoleon in Egypt?

THE MAN IN ARMY UNIFORM: Napoleon never crossed the Channel. We did.

MR. LECTURER: That's the kind of discussion that never ends. I think everyone will admit that as a people we don't lack inventiveness. We must apply inventiveness to our problem of reorganization . . . Along with the complications and frustrations forced upon us by this growth to giantism of the corporate organizations we've been talking about have come all sorts of inventions that make humane control easier; new methods of handling paperwork that can eliminate the drag of bureaucracy on efficiency, calculating machinery, sorting and sampling machinery, the teletype . . . One example is the famous checkwriting machines in the Department of Agriculture.

FRED RUFUS (*laughing*): One of the great technical advances of the Roosevelt régime.

MISS SMITHERS (*very much the schoolteacher*): The fact is that the first ones were introduced under President Hoover . . . but calculating machines reduce man to a cipher.

MR. LECTURER: We must harness our technical knowledge more directly than we have in the past to the task of increasing liberty and opportunity day by day. Instead of asking is this measure or this turn of affairs tending toward the security of this or that class of citizens we must ask: is it tending to increase personal liberty for all and that opportunity for the pursuit of happiness which is the American heritage? Testing organizations by that standard we will find that some services can be performed most efficiently by the federal government, some by the states and cities, some by licensed monopolies, or cooperatives, some by private enterprise. Our nation is an immensely complicated edifice built on a series of constantly changing adjustments brought about by the stresses and strains of the struggle for survival among the multitude of organizations that make up our corporate life. We must never forget that giving a thing a name doesn't change it. Whether we call this peculiar arrangement of society that is growing up in America capitalism or socialism doesn't matter. What we must watch is how it affects every man and woman and child. The only gauge we have of its worth as a method of organizing society is how it affects each separate individual citizen.

A VERY YOUNG MAN (*standing in the doorway beside the janitor*): Good old American pragmatism . . . Take up each problem as it comes and try to bring to bear on it all the knowledge and enthusiasm you've got. Hurray!

MR. LECTURER: Every society has to be born again from time to time. Even in our short history as a nation we have had a series of rebirths; the various openings of the West, the inception of the railroad age, the invention of assembly line production, the renewed search for community planning and improvement and the renewal of the sense of responsibility of one for all and all for one that accompanied the first enthusiasms of the New Deal, have all been national rebirths. Since the aims of the New Deal were forgotten and degraded in lowest-common-denominator politics political inventiveness has been stalled in the doldrums. The time has come for a fresh surge of invention that will mould this soggy structure into the shape of the Republic. We have to remember, before it is too late, that this nation was founded not to furnish glamorous offices for politicians, or to produce goods and services, or handouts of easy money, but to produce free men.

The prospect before us is one of mighty effort against great odds but it is not all black. It is impossible to travel back and forth across this continent without seeing here and there the beginnings of a better balanced society. As that little Viennese doctor said in Akron, it is possible to see the beginnings of a beginning. There is no visible limit to the productivity of agriculture or of manufacturing. In spite of all the prophecies of the Marxist wiseacres our society has not yet solidified into rigid classes. Not even the struggle between the management of industry and the leadership of labor has produced a proletariat. We are still a mass of vague and rambling individuals who have barely begun to build ourselves a civilization. We lack standards, we lack ethics, we lack art, we lack that instinctive sense of direction that is the sign of an achieved civilization. But our faults may very well turn out to be our virtues. We have not yet let ourselves be rammed into the mould of a stratified society.

There are only rare moments in history when a community of men finds itself in the position to choose alternatives. We are in that position. For a very few short years we will be able to make the choice between a stratified autocratic sociey more or less on the Russian model and the self-governing Republic which is our heritage. The Republic must find its origins in the shop, in the union local, in the management conference room, in the school district meeting, in the county seat and the small town and the city ward. The Republic can be only attained by intelligence and courage and the selfsacrifice of the individuals who must dedicate their lives to leavening the lumpish mass. They must find the brains and the will. If enough of us want a selfgoverning society in which every man can participate to the fullest of his ability we can attain it.

It is dizzying to contemplate what the results for good might be of the release of energy that would come through the even partial achievement of a society in which most men could participate. Through all the cruelty and ignominy of history something has survived in men that responds to the touch of greatness. There was a certain greatness of spirit, and amplitude of life about the generations of men who founded in successive stages this Republic, which Americans today can respond to as the pioneers responded.

The prospect before us, ladies and gentlemen, is not all black. There is no security. The life of a nation, like the life of a man, is a gamble against odds. It takes courage and persistence and skill to swim against the current that runs so fast towards destruction. Once we have chosen our aim we must expend ourselves recklessly upon it. With all its faults and weaknesses our society has the best chance any society ever had to mitigate the domination of man by men, but only by the expenditure of all our brains and all our work in the service of the underlying proposition upon which the Republic was founded.

The exigencies of defense in modern war, if nothing else, may force us to decentralize industry. Decentralization would make easier the cooperation between the managements of industry, organized for production and profits, and of labor, organized for protection of wages and working conditions. At the same time decentralization would make necessary a revival of selfgovernment in the mediumsized towns and rural districts. Modern methods of communication have made huge concentrations of industry not only unnecessary but impractical. In war they will become prime targets and will have to be evacuated anyway. We have a continent to remake, a thousand cities to rebuild. New enterprises and new careers for thousands and thousands of Americans whose energies are now frustrated by the pressure of the abject multitude would be opened up by such a reorganization of national life. It would result in the greatest resurgence of opportunity since the opening of the west.

Our civilization is still raw and jerrybuilt. Nothing in it is permanent. Few of our cities are even worth saving. In the course of our short history we have started out on several different patterns of society and given up each one before it was completed. The time has come when we must find the definitive pattern. Today we have more experience of the pitfalls a selfgoverning society has to avoid, than we ever had before. We have a certain amount of painfully acquired knowledge about the nature of man, his limitations and his possibilities, which will put future political planning on a soberer plane than that of the past. We have in our crude and shaky social structure, endangered by the corruptions of lowest-common-denominator politics within and by the enemy without, the materials with which to build a society that will offer more justice and more freedom and more opportunity than any human society ever offered before. Our task is to shape the Republic to fit corporate industry and to shape productive institutions to fit the aims of the Republic.

To get a notion of the penalty for failure, all we have to do is to visit the ruins of Berlin or to imagine the lives men live in Prague or Bucharest or Moscow.

No nation can stand still. The theory and practice of selfgovernment in the United States must take a great spurt of renewal or else our nation and all its hopes will indeed, as the Marxists threaten, go down to ruin.

(One by one the Janitor has been switching off the lights in the conference room. The listeners have gradually filed out leaving no one but the Janitor with his hand on the last switch and the Very Young Man who stands before the

lecturer scratching his head through his closecropped sandy hair.)

THE VERY YOUNG MAN: Tell me, Mr. Lecturer, is this on the level?

MR. LECTURER (*looks at him unseeingly through moist eyes*): I believe so.

THE VERY YOUNG MAN: Okay. (*They shake hands briskly and he hurries out. While* MR. LECTURER *gropes for his hat and coat the Janitor switches out the last light.*)

— THE END —

"Now I'm just a country boy . . . Excuse me, my name's Jake Jeffries and I'm an Iowa farmer."

"I'm a manufacturer, retired because I refused to let other people tell me how to run my own business. My name is Fred Rufus."

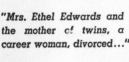

"Mrs. Ethel Edwards and the mother of twins, a career woman, divorced..."

A Man in Army Uniform: "Napoleon never crossed the Channel. We did."

"Miss Smithers, a retired schoolteacher

"My name is Jones, Eddy Jones. I'm educational director for a retail workers' union, a labor skate in other words."